MARGINALITIES

Diamela Eltit in her home during the author's visit in 1995.

MARGINALITIES

Diamela Eltit
and the Subversion
of Mainstream Literature in Chile

PQ 8098.15 .L78 Z77 2002
Norat, Gisela.
Marginalities

Gisela Norat

DELAWARE

Newark: University of Delaware Press
London: Associated University Presses

RITTER LIBRARY
BALDWIN-WALLACE COLLEGE
WITHDRAWN

© 2002 by Rosemont Publishing & Printing Corp.

All rights reserved. Authorization to photocopy items for internal or personal use, or the internal or personal use of specific clients, is granted by the copyright owner, provided that a base fee of $10.00, plus eight cents per page, per copy is paid directly to the Copyright Clearance Center, 222 Rosewood Drive, Danvers, Massachusetts 01923. [0-87413-761-6/02 $10.00 + 8¢ pp, pc.]

Other than as indicated in the foregoing, this book may not be reproduced, in whole or in part, in any form (except as permitted by Sections 107 and 108 of the U.S. Copyright Law, and except for brief quotes appearing in reviews in the public press).

Associated University Presses
440 Forsgate Drive
Cranbury, NJ 08512

Associated University Presses
16 Barter Street
London WC1A 2AH, England

Associated University Presses
P.O. Box 338, Port Credit
Mississauga, Ontario
Canada L5G 4L8

The paper used in this publication meets the requirements of the American National Standard for Permanence of Paper for Printed Library Materials Z39.48-1984.

Library of Congress Cataloging-in-Publication Data

Norat, Gisela
    Marginalities : Diamela Eltit and the subversion of mainstream literature in Chile / Gisela Norat.
        p.   cm.
    Includes bibliographical references and index.
    ISBN 0-87413-761-6 (alk. paper)
    1. Eltit, Diamela, 1949—Criticism and interpretation.   2. Postmodernism (Literature)—Latin America.   I. Title.
PQ 8098.15.L78 Z77   2002
863'.64—dc21   2001036784

PRINTED IN THE UNITED STATES OF AMERICA

For Albert and Katrina, now and always.

And for all peoples who have suffered the tyranny of an oppressor.

He has sent me to bring the good news to the poor,
to proclaim liberty to captives
and to the blind new sight,
to set the downtrodden free . . . Luke 4:18

Contents

Acknowledgments

Books are rarely written without the insights gathered from many authors and other predecessors recorded in print. Mine is no exception. When sources were available to me, I took special care to relate and credit accurately the ideas of those cited within these pages. Regardless of intent, I realize the flawed nature of human undertakings and thus state here my sole responsibility for any scholarly faux pas.

Though in the manuscript review process readers often remain anonymous, I nevertheless thank them, whoever they may be, for their contributions to the profession and hope they will recognize their useful comments in this book. There are many others, however, who I can explicitly name in acknowledging their part in this publication.

I am indebted to Silvia Nagy-Zekmi, Elzbieta Sklodowska, and Jonathan Tittler, scholar-friends whose reading of various essays and encouragement during their writing made an immeasurable difference in the outcome of this book. Also within and beyond this realm, a special thanks to Linda Gould Levine, a remarkable undergraduate professor at Montclair State University whose enthusiastic classroom teaching and commitment to scholarship continue to serve as models that I strive for in my career. She merits credit for catapulting me toward the study of literature in Spain, where experiences that will last a lifetime have led me to the world of academe. Her support, advice, and motivational "*No te rindas*" message glued to my computer still today have many a time carried me through the angst of writing.

Recognition is due María Inés Lagos for introducing me to Eltit's first published novel and infusing a graduate program with the study of Latin American women writers and feminist theories, which are at the core of this book. Sincere appreciation is also due to another esteemed Chilean, the author Diamela Eltit, whose very gracious hospitality and organized meetings with women writers and intellectuals in Santiago made me privy to national, social, and cultural circumstances that inform these essays. The extent of her genersotiy

9

in permitting me to quote from her books will be apparent to the reader.

A professional development award granted by the Agnes Scott College Committee on Professional Development funded my 1995 trip to Chile to interview Eltit. I also sincerely thank subsequent members of that committee, as well as President Mary Brown Bullock and Edmund J. Sheehey, Dean of the College and Vice President of Academic Affairs. Their support of my sabbatical leave during the academic year 2000–2001 allowed me time for immersion in scholarly pursuits and intellectual rejuvenation, vital to the completion of this book. For their contribution to making the Spanish Program a most pleasant working environment, a place where support in teaching and scholarship is genuine, I wish to thank my colleagues, Rafael Ocasio, Leticia Lemus-Fortoul Seymour, and Michael Schlig. I am also indebted to Juan Allende, political scientist at Agnes Scott, for his generosity in sharing materials, valuable insights and stories of his personal experience with the coup d'état in Chile.

Without the aid rendered by the dedicated library staff at Agnes Scott—Sala Rhodes, Resa K. Harney, Stacy Schmitt, and surely many more who over the gestation of this book have endeavored on my behalf—my writing, in many instances, would have been delayed and even crippled. Likewise operating behind the scenes but invaluable are technical support angels such as Neta Counts, Doug Talbot, Jackie Klock, and Laura Bishop as well as others that have moved on, but nevertheless are not forgotten by a computer-anxious damsel in distress.

Indeed, I am grateful to my sister Hildelisa Norat as well as to my friends Virginia Braxs, Polly Burtelow, Gail Bulman, and Magdalena Maíz-Peña who, perhaps unaware of their influence, have each in particular ways and at different stages of my writing provided words of encouragement that propelled me onward.

My earliest intellectual debt is of course to my parents, whose belief in the value of education and their example in achievement through sacrifice, self-discipline, and hard work constitute a legacy I hope to pass on to my daughter.

I owe my greatest debt to my husband, Albert L. Schweitzer III, for persevering through the entire project from inception to publication with relentless support. This book would remain unpublished were it not for his role as caregiver, confidant, adviser, reader, editor and spiritual beacon in my life.

Finally, my sincere thanks to all those who have played a part in the publication of this book, including Donald C. Mell, chair and board of editors at University of Delaware Press and Julien Yoseloff, director at Associated University Presses, whose detailed instructions, guidance and prompt responses to my questions reveal the inner workings of a top class operation at AUP. Christine A. Retz, managing editor, too is a genuine reflection of a professional at work. She has contributed to making this publication experience a pleasure. I trust that Dean Curtis, copyeditor, and Brian Haskell, senior production editor, know how grateful I am for their scrutinous reading of my manuscript. Although my last mention of appreciation goes to art director Maryann Hostetler, her creative work on the book's cover will be first in impressing readers.

MARGINALITIES

Introduction

Dɪᴀᴍᴇʟᴀ ᴇʟᴛɪᴛ (1949), ᴀᴜᴛʜᴏʀ ᴏꜰ ꜱɪx ɴᴏᴠᴇʟꜱ ᴀɴᴅ ᴛᴡᴏ ᴇxᴛʀᴀʟɪᴛᴇʀᴀʀʏ projects, has managed to carve out a place for herself within Chile's predominantly male literary establishment while challenging its mainstream culture with a female-centered, postmodern writing that subverts the traditional concept of the novel.

Her first publication, *Lumpérica* (1983) (English translation, *E. Luminata*, 1997) is abundant in technical ploys including mixed genres, neologisms, wordplay, multimedia codes, distorted syntax, fragmented narrative, and lack of a conventional plot. Despite the sparse reviews this novel received when it appeared, Eltit plunged ahead with her writing. In essence she dug in her heels, stood her ground—and eventually won critical attention in Chile. This recognition led to her receiving in 1985 a coveted Guggenheim Award, which supported the writing of her second novel, *Por la patria* [*For the Homeland*] (1986). While never courting the best seller crowd, Eltit has drawn interest among Latin Americanists in the United States. Her several trips to North America have included lecture positions at Berkeley and Columbia and conference tours at numerous other universities, among them Brown, Yale, Johns Hopkins, Georgetown, and Emory.

Eltit is not surprised when her books are described as "difficult," "experimental," "cryptic," or "unintelligible," yet she strongly disagrees with the accusation that her writing cannot be understood. In self-defense she points out that in principle anyone lexically equipped to read the newspaper can read a literary work; it's just that people are trained in certain kinds of readings more than in others.[1] Eltit has hinted that her reader cannot be a passive consumer, the spectator-type which the age of television has fostered.[2]

Nonetheless, she recognizes that the fragmented, unstable, open-ended, highly symbolic, sometimes contradictory, and, yes, even occasionally incoherent narrative, which has come to characterize her writing, is not reader-friendly. And precisely because it is not, her Joycean quality will—almost guaranteed—impress readers with a narrative that not only poses a challenge but invites manifold meanings, throwing wide open the door of literary interpretation.

15

Eltit's writing accommodates well the literary criticism theory of post-structuralist French critic Roland Barthes, as explained by Terry Eagleton:

> The most intriguing texts for criticism are not those which can be "read," but those which are "writable" (scriptible)—texts which encourage the critic to carve them up. . . . The reader or critic shifts from the role of consumer to that of producer. It is not exactly as though "anything goes" in interpretation, for Barthes is careful to remark that the work cannot be got to mean anything at all; but literature is now less an object to which criticism must conform than a free space in which it can sport.[3]

Not surprisingly, while affording the reader/critic many liberties, the very characteristics of the critically "writable" text, one which has "no determinate meaning, no settled signifieds, but is plural and diffuse, an inexhaustible tissue or galaxy of signifiers," as Eagleton describes, contributes to the interpretative difficulty (138). In the case of Eltit's writing, such features have estranged readers and critics alike.

Given the narrative complexities of Eltit's body of work, this study strives for a clear critical discourse with the hope of inserting her writing into mainstream academe where scholars interested in Latin American narrative, Latin American women's writing, comparative literature, and feminism in general will further study and compare her work with fiction being written by women in other countries and continents, not only in the Spanish-speaking world, but also in other cultures across the world. The feasibility of her work entering into dialogue with literatures far removed from Latin America is increasingly possible as more of Eltit's novels are translated into English and hence become accessible to intellectuals around the globe.

The essays presented here focus on individual works, rather than on themes, because the study is conceived as a practical tool for first-time or hesitant Eltit readers who seek discussion of a particular book or books and are not familiar with the author's entire production. Although each chapter was written to stand on its own, readers may find many points of intersection in terms of themes and literary construction. In fact, Eltit herself has observed that she has come to realize how her books often develop from loose ends and remnants left over from previous novels, all of which she regards as one singular textual body.[4] In this study I propose "marginality" (be it social, political, sexual, ethnic, gender, or literary) as the salient feature of the author's literary corpus.

Although Eltit is by no means a card-carrying feminist, nor am I convinced that literary postmodernist theories consciously have shaped her writing, I would describe her overall creative work as a feminist/postmodernist one. The author's predominantly female-centered narrative and her transgressive textual mechanics accommodate a feminist/postmodern reading which I use as a general theoretical frame in the essays presented here and more markedly so in the exegesis of *Vaca sagrada* (1991) / *Sacred Cow* (1995). To accent the interpretative richness which Eltit's texts offer the literary critic, I have varied the theoretical approach in individual chapters.

For instance, I have found theories connected to the Latin American "testimonio"—a literary mode fashioned to voice urgent victimization—and psychoanalysis—a means of accessing the human subconscious—helpful in elucidating the verbal harangue of the homeless and mentally disturbed protagonist of *El Padre Mío* [*My Father*] (1989). On the other hand, I employ cultural theory to draw parallels with the reality of the marginalized Mapuche Indians of Chile and the world of Coya, the female protagonist, in [*For the Homeland*]. Nevertheless, in general I turn to feminism as a lens through which to analyze the heavily gendered issues present in Eltit's narrative and to postmodernism as a way of understanding her writing style. I therefore now turn to a discussion of the strained relationship that has existed between feminism and postmodernism in order to frame the application of these respective theories with regard to Eltit's Latin American texts.

For more than a decade North American and Western European scholars have published volumes on "postmodernity" and the debate concerning the conflicting points of view on what constitutes the postmodern.[5] Some literary critics regard postmodernism as a critical shift from rationality, reason, order, and truth associated with Enlightenment thought and empiricist knowledge (Waugh, 4–5).[6] Others consider the postmodern an extension[7] of modernism while there are also those who see more rupture[8] than succession between modernism and postmodernism—for example, postmodern culture as a reaction against the elitism of classical modernism.[9] In a Euro-American context, Joseph Natoli and Linda Hutcheon assure us that "whether we see the postmodern as a moment, a movement, a project, a condition, or a period, *something* important is happening."[10]

In his introduction to *The Postmodern Condition*, Jean-François Lyotard uses "the word 'postmodern' to describe. . . . the condition of knowledge in the most highly developed societies."[11] No wonder that Latin American critics have questioned the validity of speaking of postmodernity in a region where premodern conditions still exist.[12] Nelly Richard remarks that "it would be inappropriate to speak of postmodernity" in a Latin America that cannot recognize itself in the image of a highly developed capitalistic North driven by consumerism and communications technologies, a sharp contrast to the underdeveloped economies of a South whose majority of the population struggles with critical shortages and poverty.[13] Given the history of foreign interventions in Latin America, it is not surprising that Latin American critics and theorists' dismissal of postmodernity mostly resides with a resistance towards cultural imports,[14] what Neil Larsen sympathetically calls "yet another neo-colonial attempt to impose alien cultural models."[15]

Others like Cynthia M. Tompkins see the question of postmodernity in Latin America differently. "Personally," says Tompkins, "being born and raised during Argentina's 'hyperinflation,' devaluations, state of siege, military juntas, 'Dirty War,' 'Proceso,' 'Malvinas War,' foreign debt, I would argue for a 'postmodern' lived experience. . . ."[16] Supporting Tompkins's argument, Sergio Zermeño observes a Latin America wholly postmodern in its (political, class, ethnic) divisions, a society marked by such incongruities as, on the one hand, the stress on individualism (probably exacerbated by the explosion of consumer goods and the desire to be one of those who owns a television set, personal computer, wireless phone, satellite dish, or car) and on the other the implementation of survival tactics that call for banding together (in squatter coalitions, neighborhood watch groups, supply pantries, communal kitchens, stitching circles, and the like).[17] From Zermeño's writing one not only gleans a polarized society where the have-nots resort to the indigenous notion of community in times of crisis, but also a schism between the practice of individualism and respect for the individual in a Latin America historically plagued by human rights violations. As the title of his book *(Con)Fusing Signs and Postmodern Positions* indicates, Robert Neustadt employs "the word 'confusion' to describe the generalized dis-orientation associated with Latin America in the age of postmodernity."[18] The readings of Eltit's creative works will show how the author combines linguistic instability and character marginality to symbolically portray a Latin America in crisis.

Unquestionably, "pre" and "post" modernist enclaves coexist in Latin America, as they do today in the United States where "different economic modes of being commonly jostle against one another," when, for example, a jet zooms overhead as cars pass the horse-drawn carts of the Amish in Pennsylvania.[19] Borrowing Raymond Williams's terms, this scenario of simultaneous "residual" and "emergent" elements is very ordinary in Latin America[20]—a region composed of the so-called "emerging" Third World countries. Consider that at this moment, somewhere in Chile the Mapuche shaman discussed in the essay on [*For the Homeland*] may be beating the *kultrun* (drum) for divine revelation just as a fellow Chilean accesses information globally via the World Wide Web. Following García Canclini's notion of a Latin America composed of "hybrid" cultures, Sylvia Tafra points out "the coexistence of Indian, African, Hispanic, colonial and Catholic traditions which influence social, cultural and political spheres." Not only do different races and heterogeneous cultures merge, but also different historical temporalities."[21]

Applicable to other Latin American countries as well, Jesús Martín-Barbero comments how in Colombia "the mass media, new technology and information networks give impetus to a powerful movement toward surpassing barriers and dissolving borders," thus accelerating the integration of the Colombian people and their cultures into a global market.[22] Indeed, the technological revolution has reached Latin America, generating modernization, albeit not on the same scale as in industrialized countries. Time and again, Eltit inhabits her books with those at odds with the world around them, those left behind on the fringes of a modern society.

In the Latin American literary arena, the "surpassing of barriers and dissolving of borders" occurred in the 1960s and 1970s when writers of the so-called "boom," such as Julio Cortázar, Carlos Fuentes, Gabriel García Márquez and Mario Vargas Llosa, attained recognition and commercial success outside their respective countries. As Doris Sommer and George Yúdice point out, for "boom" writers familiar with international literature, Euro-American modernist models (Joyce, Kafka, Faulkner) served as springboards for narrative innovations which exemplified the thrust of later postmodern aesthetics.[23] Reader appeal for the renowned "four" and other writers of the "boom" period—José Lezama Lima, Guillermo Cabrera Infante, José Donoso, Manuel Puig, Alfredo Bryce Echenique—can, in part, be explained by the fact that, internationally, readers recognized a ludic approach which both crowned and dethroned established world authors. Whether interpreted as gestures of deference or disguised irreverence, Latin American writers often parodied foreign texts by plagiarizing, deforming, borrowing, and duplicating them.[24] As the reading of *E. Luminata* notes, the protagonist's eroticized rubbing with the likes of a Lezama Lima, James Joyce, Pablo Neruda, Juan Rulfo, Ezra Pound, and Robbe-Grillet implies her sexual as well as literary autonomy,[25] in essence it constitutes Eltit's parodic sacrilege of canonical modern patriarchs.[26]

The stage for the Latin American "new narrative," as James Higgins terms it, had been set in the 1940s and 1950s by pre-boom writers—among them Jorge Luis Borges, Alejo Carpentier, and Juan Rulfo—who had broken away from the regional novel of the 1920s, a literature that largely attempted to present, in the tradition of nineteenth-century realism, the geography, peoples, and conditions of life in remote areas of Latin America.[27] This was a didactic as well as a political literature in so far as it attempted to raise public awareness, influence public policy, and bring about social change (Higgins, 92).[28] With respect to its sociopolitical agenda, the Latin American "testimonio" of the 1980s, discussed in the second chapter of this study, acts as a medium for recording the outcry of victims of dictatorship, war, and ethnic persecution and has revived the realist, instructive, and political aspects of the regional novel.

That women writers were left out of the "new narrative" circle is no secret. Moreover, such exclusion was not limited to the area of fiction or Hispanic literary establishments. In 1983, Craig Owens wrote "The Discourse of Others: Feminists and Postmodernism" specifically to address postmodernism's oversight of sexual difference. At the time Owens remarked that given the significant development of a feminist practice in almost every aspect of cultural production, the neglect or repression of feminist voices in postmodern theories suggested that "postmodernism may be another masculine invention engineered to exclude women."[29]

Until recently debates on postmodernism remained predominantly phallocentric. The names of Jacques Derrida, Michel Foucault, Jean-François Lyotard, Jean Baudrillard, Jürgen Habermas, Andreas Huyssen, Ihab Hassan, Fredric Jameson, and Roland Barthes feature on the "list of men, speaking to men" who Kate Fullbrook further notes "have claimed the right to speak for and of the condition of the whole of the culture" (73).[30] As groups, including feminists, have claimed the right to speak for themselves, they have been marginalized or left out altogether from the intellectual, white, male conversation. The stronghold of male predominance in the prestigious realms of Latin American academe is all the more reason to marvel at how Eltit's unorthodox writing has achieved recognition within intellectual communities in Santiago, Chile, and abroad.

For in addition to the gender inequities which the books of most women writers still face in the publishing world—a topic discussed in the chapter on *El cuarto mundo* (1988) / *The Fourth World* (1995)—within academic literary programs, and the generally depressed reading market in Chile, Eltit's strong inclination for transgression also has played a role in her obscurity. Indifferent to the seduction of the mass market which catapulted such writers as Isabel Allende, Angeles Mastretta, and Laura Esquivel into international stardom,[31] Eltit has stated: "I don't care about fame because I know what I'm writing. I'm quite aware that I'm not going to sell much. I'm not saying this is an heroic or even a complacent attitude on my part because I invest a lot of time writing and I don't profit anything, but I chose this [writing] and it's what I want to do."[32]

When Jean Franco points out that Latin American women's best-sellers "all belong to the category of art romance," she identifies a basic characteristic lacking in Eltit's production. Franco further explains the gulf between two categories of writers:

> There is, however, a growing divergence between the international best-selling writer (and a feminism of equality), on the one hand, and the neo-avant-garde for whom the seduction of romance merely reproduces the seduction of commodity culture under neo-liberalism. For this neo-avant-garde it is a new aesthetic which is also "political" in the broadest sense of the term that is now urgently needed.[33]

Hence, attaining success is more likely for those women writers who do not stray too far from the family romance, a literary category designated to them by traditional notions of gender appropriation. Eltit's predilection for the "new narrative," the "neo-avant-garde," or the postmodern, whichever label one prefers, combined with feminist leanings have delayed her insertion into the Chilean mainstream literary community.

In the preface to *Postmodernism and Its Critics* (1991), John McGowan states that feminism is one of the four most prominent variants of postmodern theory, yet he presents reasons for not including it in his study of the other three—post-structuralism, the new Marxism, and neopragmatism. It may be argued, however, that it is a matter of mutual exclusion, for feminism too has ignored postmodern theories, choosing to engage in a female-centered conversation. But feminist critics, among them Jane Flax, Barbara Creed, Patricia Waugh, Magali Cornier Michael, Nancy Fraser, and Linda Nicholson, have pondered the dearth of dialogue as well as the intersections and relations between feminism and postmodernism.

According to Nancy Fraser and Linda Nicholson, one of the main reasons for the rift is postmodernism's drawing from traditional philosophical discourse to address broad issues of Western culture while feminism, more pragmatic, deals heavily in social criticism of a local nature. In keeping with this observation, Magali Cornier Michael remarks on the incompatibility of the two dialectics given postmodernism's apolitical and ahistorical tendency in contrast to feminism's concern with addressing (and redressing) the historical oppression of women.[34] Another "major obstacle seems to be postmodernism's questioning of the humanist notion of subject," notes Cornier Michael; "[F]eminist critics reject the idea that, just when women have finally attained the position of being able to define themselves as subjects, the subject is in their view being eradicated" (24).[35]

In Latin America, early feminist writings through the 1960s and 1970s generally varied on the theme of search for self and a rejection of patriarchal oppression. Specific issues of protest included the barring of women from the public sphere and their entrapment in the home.[36] Mercedes Valdivieso published Chile's first outright feminist novel, *La brecha*, in 1961/*Breakthrough* (1986). Although the novel lacks literary sophistication, as the title suggests, a wife's "break" with tradition by leaving home to seek personal autonomy was thematically bold for the country's ultraconservative society of the time.

In the 1970s the consequences of military takeovers in countries like Chile, Argentina, and Uruguay shifted the focus of women's writing away from oppression in the home. Government repression became a foremost concern for a large segment of the population of the Southern Cone. Where once feminists had targeted the home as the prisonhouse of women, under military rule writers also turned their attention to state persecution. Hence women produced a literature of domestic politics, that is, their fiction illustrated how traditional domesticity and political reality had become inextricable in female existence.

Evidence of national politics as a literary theme continued to prevail in literature published in the 1980s as paramilitary police routinely kicked down the doors of the traditional female bastion and those suspected of subversive activity disappeared. In a culture where tradition designates the home as the protective, albeit oftentimes oppressive, space for females, intrusions by police transgress cultural tenets. Thus, especially in Southern Cone women's writing, the figure of the dictator noticeably superseded the tyrannical patriarch of old.

Eltit's ability to reconcile the sort of pragmatic women's issues espoused by feminism and the apolitical/ahistorical devices of postmodernism while at the same time exposing state repression is apparent from her first book, *E. Luminata*. Her next three novels—

[*For the Homeland*], *The Fourth World,* and *Sacred Cow,* reinforce the author's unorthodox cultural production, a creative body of work that continues to be characterized by a feminist orientation, a strong leaning for postmodern aesthetics, and a wholehearted investment in Chile's sociopolitical reality. Although Eltit bridges the feminist/postmodernist gap in several of her novels, in this study I have chosen *Sacred Cow* to expressly illustrate the text as undeniably female-centered while at the same time wholly postmodern.

Deconstructionist tenets that inform postmodernism and even modernism are especially problematic for feminism because they maintain that the text and its linguistic apparatus are all that count.[37] Let us recall Roland Barthes's 1968 essay where he ushers in the age of the reader and "the death of the Author" as a way of stamping out the author's life from textual interpretation of his/her work.[38] Following the disappearance of the author as subject who informed the text came the 1970s displacement of the character as subject who sustained the plot. After all, traditional plots were on the decline.

But whereas postmodernist male authors could afford to eradicate the subject in plain sight of the dominant literary and political institutions which traditionally espoused their work, for women writers, achieving recognition for themselves as writing subjects or for their writing about female subjecthood was "the" struggle vis-à-vis the establishment. "Postmodernism," Waugh explains, "expresses nostalgia for but loss of belief in the concept of the human subject as an agent effectively intervening in history, through its fragmentation of discourse, language games, and decentering of subjectivity. Feminism seeks a subjective identity, a sense of effective agency and history for women which has hitherto been denied them by the dominant culture."[39]

Furthermore, pursuant to the issue of subjectivity, Waugh reflects on the incongruity between the aspect of postmodernism which is informed by modernity's Enlightenment thought such as the ideal of autonomy and the belief in absolute self-determination, and that of feminism rooted in women's experience of conflicting demands of home, work, and the larger community.[40] Let us not forget that for most women in Latin America female autonomy is an oxymoron.

One must also bear in mind that while feminism focuses on a social agenda, postmodernism's main concern is an aesthetic one. Simply put, by its very nature a feminist text is heavily invested in theme (content), while a postmodern text is mainly defined by style (narrative device). Also true for Latin American feminist writers, Dina Sherzer suggests that many North American feminists shy away

from postmodernism because its focus on linguistic and textual acrobatics detracts attention from their feminist message.[41] As the essays on *E. Luminata*, [*For the Homeland*], and *Sacred Cow* present, these
three novels are heavily invested in "textual acrobatics" yet effectively put forth a political as well as a feminist agenda.

Incompatibilities surely exist between postmodernism and feminism, but so too do points of intersection. In literary terms, both
practices disrupt the dominant culture, undermine the canon, question authority, work from the margins, address subjectivity and representation, embrace the popular, engage in practice as well as
theory, and ultimately emphasize difference and pluralism—which
fosters "sensitivity to racial, ethnic, gender, and class difference."[42]

In the literary tug-of-war to differentiate modernism from postmodernism, Vincent B. Leitch suggests that "the marginalized subaltern figure—for example, the nonwhite, the non-European, the
nonmale, the nonheterosexual, and/or the non-middle-class" (the
sum of which could portray a woman) plays a key role in defining
postmodernism.[43] Leitch points to the " 'eruption of difference' or
the 'flowering of the eccentric' as the predominant cultural fact or
force of the times," one in which "the new centrality of oddity not
only renders postmodernism different from modernism but constitutes the essence of postmodernism."[44]

"Odd" certainly describes every single one of Eltit's protagonists.
To borrow Sue Golding's phrase, Eltit concentrates on "pariah bodies"—among others, the politically persecuted, incarcerated, mentally ill, homeless, sexually deviant, and the impoverished. In my
view, the author transforms a marginal cast of characters into literary
symbols and inserts them in a broader literature of the voiceless and
dispossessed. In this respect, Eltit's writing transcends national borders just as the "culture of poverty" described by anthropologist
Oscar Lewis in his study of poor families in Mexico some three decades ago still applies today to marginal sectors in Chile as well as
across Latin America.[45]

With a feminist perspective and a postmodern style, Eltit's books
create a space for "difference." As I further explain in the chapter
on [*My Father*], Eltit herself is a literary "misfit" whose writings reflect her decision to question mainstream institutions. Following
Ihab Hassan, Sherzer notes that postmodernism like feminism essentially deconstructs, displaces, demystifies Western culture's logocentric, ethnocentric, and phallocentric master codes in order to
challenge conventions, institutions, and authorities.[46] Patriarchy is
one such institution that Eltit routinely undermines in her writing.

While the majority of women in Latin America resist the "feminist" label, most will admit to significant gender bias in both the public and domestic spheres. For this reason, female-centered concerns continue to proliferate as themes in fiction written by women. A survey of contemporary novels substantiates Sherzer's point that advocacy for change in women's status demands communicative writing which differs from the experimental leanings of postmodern aesthetics.

Latin American women novelists who have incorporated in their texts aesthetic elements associated with postmodernist writing (metafiction, fragmented structure, multiplicity of voices, of genres, or plots, nonlinear or nonchronological narrative, etc.) prove too many to name here. But for the most part traditional literature reigns. In the case of Chile, most women publishing today, among them Marcela Serrano, Ana María del Río, Pía Barros, Alejandra Basualto, Sonia González Valdenegro, and Guadalupe Santa Cruz, have not ventured far from recognizable narrative modes. By contrast, Eltit and a handful of others, among them Cuban Julieta Campos in *The Fear of Losing Eurydice*, Brazilian Clarice Lispector in *Agua viva*, Argentine Luisa Valenzuela's *El gato eficaz*, and Colombian Albalucía Angel's *Las andariegas*, can be credited with producing unconditionally postmodern texts. Of these writers, Eltit has consistently combined a feminist/postmodern agenda that has become her literary trademark.

Besides acting as manifesto for subversion in literary construction and liberating female eroticism, *E. Luminata* sets the course for what has been the sociopolitical aspect of Eltit's writing—concern for the dispossessed of Latin America.[47] "What troubles me is not just Chilean destiny, but Latin America's," the author has stated, while confessing as well her "obsession" with matters that specifically affect Chile.[48] Despite Eltit's solidarity with the socioeconomically marginalized, those exploited and culturally excluded, the author has made it clear that she does not set out to write with a social agenda in mind.[49] By the same token, her writing consistently reflects how important "social" issues and the "Latin American condition" are to her.[50] As it relates to writing, Eltit explains: "I work on two fronts. A social one, that could be cultural, and one which deals with literary creation."[51] In recognition of these two concerns, this study overall pays equal attention to the sociopolitical and aesthetic modalities present in Eltit's writing, although certain readings may favor one over the other.

Literature has been part of Eltit's life ever since as a student attending the Saint Rose School in Santiago she was introduced to Spanish literary classics written in a baroque language that intrigued her while alienating most of her peers. What fascinated her about those books, she recalls, was not so much the themes, but recognizing how the Castilian of Spain had developed into the Spanish that Chileans speak.[52]

This early attention to language is reflected in [*For the Homeland*] where language itself is a protagonist, one steeped in colloquialisms, able to function in the argot of marginalized sectors and to articulate indigenous elements at the very root of Chilean identity. Eltit's propensity for the vernacular in her novels serves as a vehicle for transgression since, as she observes, the Chilean literary establishment tends to idolize "cultured" language.

Resisting bourgeois convention, Eltit's writing turns society's undesirables into cultural subjects worthy of literary inscription—hence, her celebration in [*For the Homeland*] of *lo indio*, the indigenous dimension which many Chileans would rather deny. Further, in her two extraliterary projects, which are studied here together, she records and publishes the discourse of the mentally ill and homeless protagonist of [*My Father*] and cooperates with photographer Paz Errázuriz in *El infarto del alma* [*The Soul's Infarct*] (1994) capturing a slice of life of the patients interned in a psychiatric hospital outside of Santiago.

To some extent Eltit's attraction to that which is marginal can be attributed to growing up in lower-middle-class neighborhoods of Santiago, a space she was to abandon physically but that left an indelible mark in her psyche. The daughter of separated parents, Eltit remarks that her mother was an ambitious woman, "in the good sense of the word," who saw to it that she obtained a college degree and had a profession.[53]

After completing undergraduate studies in education at the Universidad Católica de Chile (1967–72), Eltit was admitted to the Universidad de Chile in 1973 where she spent the next three years pursuing a graduate degree in literature in the Department of Humanistic Studies. The author recalls that the years 1972–85 were especially trying times because of her obligations to full-time teaching, raising a family, completing her graduate degree, and writing, tasks made all the more difficult by the military coup d'etat headed by Gen. Augusto Pinochet which in 1973 ousted the democratically-elected government of Salvador Allende. Life under the long dictatorship (1973–89) that followed would also leave its mark on Eltit.

Fear ran rampant throughout Chile in the years following the coup. People were afraid to talk, and even more to be talked about; they measured their words and analyzed everyone else's. During that period (accusatory) words could literally kill. Under such circumstances speech became a lethal weapon. Eltit points out that no other situation could have prompted her to reflect so profoundly on the subject of language as living through those years in Chile.[54] While Eltit claims that writing about life during the military regime always poses the risk of trivializing what was an unfathomable, often unbearable situation, reference to the dictatorship is a common denominator—a subtext—in every one of her novels, a theme that affects literary construction and hence contributes to her divergence from both the largely apolitical postmodernist texts and the feminist romance novels of traditional female writers.

The topic of fear, for instance, remains at the core of *Sacred Cow* even though the novel was written after the restoration of democracy in Chile and during Eltit's tenure in Mexico as cultural attaché for the Chilean government of Patricio Aylwin. The author points out in an interview with Ana María Larraín that writing this book was made more difficult by the climate of change—a change in geography, the psychic change that comes with being over forty, and personal changes that could have led to a crisis if she had not decided to concentrate on writing.[55]

Given the mention of aging and crisis in the interview, the onset of menopause may well be at the root of the unorthodox depiction of menstrual blood in *Sacred Cow*. However, in the chapter I explore the link between this bodily emission and dictatorship. As we will discuss, Eltit's focus on menstruation challenges a male-centered literary canon which has upheld (and led women writers to internalize) taboos surrounding the physiological and sexual realities of female existence. Taking Chilean circumstance into consideration, menstruation simultaneously evokes other more encompassing national realities such as bloodshed from political persecution and AIDS as another potential form of genocide.

In keeping with the "emergent" and "residual" elements in Latin American society mentioned earlier, the postmodern qualities of *Sacred Cow* suggest the highly modern technological notion of the "hypertext" as a strategy for reading Eltit's writing, one which uses a female physiological function to depict the horror of disappearance and torture as realities of citizens of Third World countries.

Several chapters in this study draw out Eltit's indictment of systems of oppression, be they patriarchy, dictatorship, imperialism, or the literary establishment vis-à-vis women writers. As interpreted here, *The Fourth World* presents the theme of literary vocation from a feminist perspective. The novel proposes a dialogue between the sexes as a vehicle for surmounting the gender differences that alienate the twin protagonists and interfere with true kinship. Hence, symbolically Eltit calls for establishing a fraternity among the extended family of Latin American writers because despite individual renown, outside their respective countries ultimately they are grouped as Third World inhabitants. Like in other of Eltit's books, textual construction in *The Fourth World* reflects the crisis of Chilean life under dictatorship. In connection with the theme of political oppression Eltit too suggests the need for Latin American fraternity, a regional brotherhood capable of uniting to curb North American foreign intervention and imperialistic control.

Similarly, in the multilayered reading of *Los vigilantes* [*Vigilant*] (1994) a woman—wife, mother, citizen, and writer—struggles to free herself from the controlling gaze of her estranged husband, a patriarch whose power over her allegorically parallels the dictator's vigilance over the citizenry, as well as the paternalistic watchful eye of the United States over Latin American affairs, and the literary establishment's position with respect to women writers.

The last in-depth chapter focuses on [*Vigilant*], in my opinion a more accessible text for readers, critics, and translators which may mark a turning point in Eltit's writing -perhaps the beginning of a new body of literature that can draw wider readership. By contrast to her previous work, in [*Vigilant*] and in her subsequent novel, *Los trabajadores de la muerte* [*Workers of Death*] (1998), the author has shed the radically avant-garde style of her earliest books. In these novels, whose other parallels I note in the epilogue, Eltit adopts a more linear narrative and the semblance of a straightforward plot that attenuates the complexities characteristic of her writing. The readability factor, which consequently eases the job of translation, serves as a litmus test for the integration of this literature into both the national canon and the international market. However, Eltit's focus on Chilean margins and her invitation to look beyond its borders is one aspect of her writing that has not changed.

Despite the author's resistance to categories, Eltit can be associated with feminism as a female-centered novelist who not only liberates female bodies but women's writing potential as well. She also qualifies as a postmodernist for her manipulation of literary artifice, obscuring genres, and innovative liberties, just to name a few. Eltit's creative work demonstrates a solidarity with the dispossessed, also part of the postmodern endeavor which allows for multiple and heterogeneous voices from the margins. I trust that this examination of Eltit's narrative will serve as springboard for further scholarly attention to this unique Chilean voice in contemporary Latin American literature.

1

Lumpérica: Liberating Body/Language

UNQUESTIONABLY SUBVERSIVE IN BOTH CONTENT AND FORM, THE NOVEL *Lumpérica* (1983)/*E. Luminata* (1997) is a daring multimedia graphic re-presentation of sexual and literary female expression within a subtext of political repression.[1] Almost seven years in the making, this first novel of Diamela Eltit was produced in an environment hostile to creativity. As the mother of three, Eltit worked full-time as a teacher in a Chile swept by disappearances, fear, and serious shortages. During the years under authoritarian rule, language became a precious as well as dangerous commodity, often coded, camouflaged in double entendres to communicate what could not be said directly. "This led to a collective aphasia," Chilean critic Guillermo García Corales reminds us, "that, in intellectual circles, was called the Cultural Blackout."[2]

The political situation triggered a need for expression not only among the literati—all Chileans felt the loss of a long-standing democracy, which was tantamount to losing their voice. For some, turning to the written word salvaged a sense of dispossession. Eltit denies such a catalyst, pointing out instead how she had already completed graduate work in literature and was very involved in writing workshops at the time of the military coup in 1973. Somewhat contradictory, Eltit maintains that *E. Luminata* would have been written the same way with or without a dictatorship, yet she admits that the censor's bureau, which controlled publications at the time, kept creeping up in her mind while writing the novel. Today Eltit distinguishes herself as one of the few writers of her generation who published during the dictatorship, and she can joke that the manuscript slipped through because the official at the censor's office did not understand her writing.

From a perusal of its pages a reader can quickly determine the book's marginal status within mainstream literature. The text varies greatly as to the amount of print on each page. Some pages feature a few sentences, or merely a phrase or fragment of a sentence. Others

29

consist of clusters of paragraphs identified with roman numerals or capitalized headings. Variations in margins, font size, and page layout as well as distorted syntax and lack of punctuation contribute to the unconventional nature of Eltit's text.

"I join various literary genres: from the novel, poetry, theater, essay, the language of visual media and cinematography," Eltit explained in an interview with Ana María Foxley. "It is a way of shattering the novel as a monolithic form of chronological storytelling" (41).[3] Conscious or not, it was also a way of depicting a shattered Chile, a country in crisis. In essence Eltit launched her own coup with a complex novel that denounced both literary and political repressive institutions, an agenda she continued to pursue in subsequent fiction, but most explicitly in *Por la patria* [*For the Homeland*] (1986).

Although textual marginality certainly constitutes an important feature of the book, I will concentrate here on the less obvious mechanisms of sexual subversion with respect to a female's autonomy. In *E. Luminata* the female body is erotically inscribed by and within an erratic, predominantly nonlinear, postmodern narrative that defies conventional notions of literature and hence resists categorization.[4] In "This Sex Which Is Not One," French theorist Luce Irigaray writes of the multitudinousness of female sexual pleasure. After describing the wanderings of a masturbatory female hand, Irigaray proclaims:

> But *woman has sex organs just about everywhere.* She experiences pleasure almost everywhere. . . . [O]ne can say that the geography of her pleasure is much more diversified, more multiple in its differences, more complex, more subtle than is imagined. . . .[5]

Irigaray's bold focus on female sexuality as a matter worthy of theoretical inscription serves as analogue for Diamela Eltit's erotic explorations in *E. Luminata*. Irigaray associates woman's dispersed sensuality with her use of language, a "language in which 'she' goes off in all directions and in which 'he' is unable to discern the coherence of any meaning."[6] Considering the uniqueness of female sexuality, Irigaray urges that "One must listen to her differently in order to hear an *'other meaning' which is constantly in the process of weaving itself, at the same time ceaselessly embracing words and yet casting them off to avoid becoming fixed, immobilized.*"[7]

Although I agree with Irigaray about the more subtle nature of female sexuality, in her enthusiasm to formulate a theory of female pleasure she comes dangerously close to presenting women as ruled by their libido, and unable to communicate since their language is incoherent to men. Men do not fare well either in that they are the ones "unable to discern the coherence of any meaning" in women's language. Were it strictly a matter of anatomy, women do not have "sex organs just about everywhere." Nonetheless, Irigaray's basic premise that women's bodily experiences play a vital role in the wide spectrum of female existence certainly holds true for the female subject in *E. Luminata.* Eltit purposely contrives an ambiguous language to inscribe both a female consciousness and to subvert conventional patriarchal language. This Chilean author must be read "differently" if one is to extract meaning from a text that constantly constructs and dismantles itself.

The link between femaleness, multiplicity, and vagueness suggested by Irigaray is to some extent exemplified by Eltit's employment of narrative, poetic, photographic, cinematic, and theatrical techniques to assemble a fragmented narrative—a written collage—which allows the reader/viewer/spectator a loose interpretive rein. In fact, the text itself admits manifold meaning: "[T]he writings open to more than one interpretation occurred there."[8] Moreover, literary ambiguity and gender intersect in the novel—"Every one of these signs is decipherable for her" (101)—not only in so far as it is a female subject who can decipher the text, but among the "decipherable signs" in *E. Luminata* are those that signal female sexuality. Bodily self-exploration and sexual expression have, culturally, been grounds of transgression for women. *E. Luminata* invariably sets out to re-appropriate and re-present a female subject's sexuality through the usurpation of patriarchal conventions.

Eltit's "novel" production—the adjective being more appropriate than the noun—is set in a public square in Santiago, Chile with a woman, E. Luminata, as its protagonist. The derelicts that inhabit the square at night keep to the periphery while E. Luminata takes up the center of the plaza. Coincidentally, just as Eltit published this novel she met a true-to-life derelict that she makes the protagonist of her next book. The fact that in this novel a woman freely occupies a traditionally male-dominated forum is from the outset a significant gesture, one turned subversive when she displays herself in erotically explicit poses. Furthermore, on the subject of defiance the feminist slogan "the personal is political" holds true for *E. Luminata*—and all of Eltit's other novels—since textual indicators suggest that the protagonist's nocturnal escapade disobeys curfew in a Chile under military rule.

This chapter explores how *E. Luminata* defies taboos regarding female sexuality, eroticism, and desire—a central focus in *Sacred Cow* as well. Although other Chilean contemporaries—among them Pía Barros, Ana María del Río, Marcela Serrano, and Isabel Allende— also address female sexuality in their writings, the topic is commonly depicted within a context of traditional, heterosexual relationships. Eltit's novel, however, presents a "performance" devoid of love interest. Furthermore, in this study of *E. Luminata* I show how, paradoxically, Eltit adopts the conventions of pornography and religion—the former a patriarchal mechanism of female sexual objectification and exploitation and the latter a locus of female sexual repression—to liberate and return sexuality to the female subject.

Throughout women's history, female sexuality has been exploited, enslaved, repressed, controlled, and/or condemned under the auspices of patriarchal institutions. While the double standard allows men to escape the stigma of sex outside of marriage, traditionally for women, sex was—and for many, in many places, remains—synonymous with sin. Especially as it pertains to women, the concept of sin is the mainstay of both pornography and religion. Pornography capitalizes on the notion of the female body as forbidden territory, an attitude fostered by religious conventions that thrive on the body's sacredness.

A first reading of the Spanish version of the novel suggests that the protagonist's original name—L. Iluminada—appropriately hints at the character's show of: (L)asciviousness, (L)ewdness, (L)ibido, and (L)ust. Ultimately, Eltit's multilayered writing reveals that this female's subversive public display of perversion encompasses a call for sexual, literary, and political (L)iberation.

APPROPRIATING THE DISCOURSE OF RELIGION AND PORNOGRAPHY

E. Luminata begins with the protagonist, who bears the same name, lying in a provocative manner on the grounds of a public square: "Anyone can testify to her half-open lips and her legs stretched out on the grass—crossing or opening—rhythmic against the backlight" (14). Clearly a taboo act, E. Luminata transgresses the Law of the Father, which symbolically denounces her by way of a giant neon sign flashing its intermittent lights onto the square from atop an adjacent building. Once darkness befalls the city, its powerfully luminous presence rules over the plaza from on high. Evocative of the biblical account of Creation: "God said, 'Let there be light,' "[9] the square's territory, described as "a ghostly set in its desolation, its emptiness" (192), is miraculously transformed by the light from the giant sign.

The biblical passage further notes: "He called the light day, and the darkness night. So evening came, and morning came, the first day."[10] Similarly, the first chapter of *E. Luminata* begins at night and the last chapter ends at dawn. Hence, theoretically the novel takes place during one night but, as Agata Gligo points out, the time could as well correspond to months, years, a lifetime.[11] This sense of timelessness would also support the concept of God. Given the political situation in Chile at the time, the neon light also suggests the godlike eye of the dictator, ever vigilant over the population under curfew.

To continue with the biblical motif, the letters projected onto her body by the neon advertisement fascinate E. Luminata: "She saw the sign projecting itself onto her gray dress. . . . She tried to figure out which sign was falling on her. . . . She remained absorbed in that a long time, calculating in the distance which letter most likely corresponded to her position" (198–99). Not only does the sign provide the dark square with light but it also emanates words. In the Gospel according to John, "When all things began, the Word already was. The Word dwelt with God. . . ."[12] Thus language within the symbolic order has, from the beginning, been attributed to the patriarch's domain. A challenge Eltit proposes in *E. Luminata* is the subversion of patriarchal space and discourse.

A series of narrative indicators also suggests the apparatus of pornography operating in the text. For example, when the vagrants, described as "The ragged people of Santiago . . . pale and stinking" (14), saunter into the square as they do nightly, E. Luminata continues her provocative gesticulations, which although tiring, become more erotic with each flash of light that falls on her body: [H]er own fleeting poses which derive her as far as exhaustion, turned on by the advertisement that falls in light upon the center of the square. . . . She waits anxiously for the illuminated sign and that's why when she feels touched she stirs all over, with her breast heaving and her eye moist" (14). The scene unquestionably turns pornographic when the woman reaches orgasm under the light of the sign and the male gaze of the vagrants.

Likewise indicative of pornography is the flashing neon sign that commercially advertises the body: "Though that's nothing new: the sign announces bodies for sale. That's right, bodies are sold in the square. Not at a fixed price" (18). In this context, a phrase such as: "The deal's done already" (20) hints of a deal struck with a prostitute. Consequently, a porno flick is implied by the disclosure that E.

RITTER LIBRARY
BALDWIN-WALLACE COLLEGE

Luminata's orgasmic scene has been filmed: "That's how she does her first film shot" (20). Furthermore, the sign's neon lights flooding the area are specifically red—"The predominant color of its legend was red filtered through neon tubes" (195)—a detail that metaphorically transforms the square into Santiago's red light district.[13]

In a patriarchal society, pornography—that is, any medium of representation depicting erotic behavior with the purpose of causing sexual arousal—is heavily invested in catering to male desire.[14] The setting in the opening chapter of E. Luminata evidently conforms to the traditional convention of pornography: the availability of an eroticized female body for visual or corporal male consumption. For the vagrants-turned-spectators in the square, this consumption is basically voyeuristic in nature. In Pornography: The Other Side, F. M. Christensen includes among peep-show clientele "men who are painfully shy or sexually inhibited, men whom women regard as unattractive or as losers, . . . men cut off from other sources of female companionship, men who are physically or psychologically impaired. . . ."[15] Socially, "The ragged people of Santiago . . . pale and stinking" are certainly a group of losers embodying male undesirability (14).[16] As such, the female body—E. Luminata—is not wholly available to them except in their role as voyeurs. Eltit's attraction to marginal characters transcends fiction, as will become especially clear in the chapter on El Padre Mío [Our Father] and El infarto del alma [Soul's Infarct], books dedicated to true-to-life vagrants and mentally disturbed Chileans.

Insofar as E. Luminata uses cinematic techniques in its literary address, film theory may enlighten the text—however, such fundamentals as who films and why remain a mystery. The filmed sequences in the novel share "the act of looking" so important to pornography.[17] Theoretically, E. Luminata, as erotic spectacle, draws the look of the reader along with that of the vagrants. Laura Mulvey points out that women filmed in exhibitionist roles traditionally function on two levels: as object of desire for the characters within the movie (for example, the vagrants in E. Luminata), and also as object of desire for the spectator within the auditorium (in this case the reader).[18] In films where the focus is on the female as erotic object, "The man controls the film phantasy and also emerges as . . . the bearer of the look of the spectator."[19] Mulvey's article was published in 1975. "It is by now accepted," Maggie Humm writes more than a decade later, "that women are the objects of a male gaze in mainstream cinema."[20] Where does this leave a female spectator? Let us consider the theories provided by Mulvey and Teresa de Lauretis.

Mulvey identified two basic "structures of looking" in a conventional cinematic production.[21] While the male spectator adopts a scopophilic look, voyeuristic in that looking at the other as erotic object in itself produces pleasure, the female spectator adopts a narcissistic look in order to identify with the image of the woman on the screen as object of male desire.[22] These two "structures of looking" would explain the position of the film viewer (or the reader in *E. Luminata*) relative to the woman as erotic object assuming that (1) the spectator (reader) is heterosexual, and (2) the female image presented is attractive enough to incite male desire and/or female identification.

De Lauretis, on the other hand, proposes a theory that suggests the possibility for a female spectator to alternate "feminine" and "masculine" viewing positions. De Lauretis notes that according to Freud, femininity is based on the suppression of the libido; that is, little girls strive to be masculine. Since the girl's phallic phase is never totally repressed and, in fact, often reemerges throughout a woman's life, "feminine" identification with the object of the gaze alternates with "masculine" identification with the gazing subject, depending on whether "femininity" or "masculinity" takes the upper hand.[23]

In this respect, E. Luminata similarly alternates "feminine" and "masculine" roles. If on the one hand she appears in erotic poses suggesting a pornographic representation of the female as desired object of the male gaze (los pálidos/the pale ones), on the other, Eltit subverts the female subject's aesthetic image by disdaining patriarchal codes of femininity to the point where E. Luminata looks mannish. In a desexualizing gesture she crops her hair.[24] Likewise, her attire is far from stylish: "She is wearing a gray dress rather longer than what is in fashion. An almost shapeless dress cinched at the waist by a cord, also gray. She does not manage to strike a brilliant figure, though certainly one somewhat jaded or scarcely noticeable" (190).[25] Clearly, this description does not present the dress-to-attract look inherent in the tradition of female fashion. On the contrary, her long, loose-fitting outfit with a cord around the waist is reminiscent of the habit and cincture of monastic garb and, by extension, celibate life.[26] E. Luminata does not conform to an image that would arouse male desire because Eltit's agenda is the exploration of female desire stripped of patriarchal constructs of femininity. Seemingly departing from the notion that "women are objects of desire rather than desiring subjects," Eltit eliminates outer signs that eroticize femininity in order to focus on the female's erotic subjectivity.[27]

In patriarchal societies—Chile's included—where only heterosexuality is accepted as normal, representations of female sexual desire are overwhelmingly phallocentric. Notably, despite the eroticism contained in the first chapter of *E. Luminata*, there is no heterosexual contact to produce the orgasmic pleasure so uninhibitedly manifested by the female protagonist:

> E. Luminata in the center of the square starts to convulse again. The pale people rotate their heads to get a better angle. . . . Attentive, they rivet their gaze on the baptism, while the illuminated sign directly strikes her who, frenetic, moves her hips under the light: her thighs rise from the ground and her drooping head pounds from so much striking against the pavement. . . . [T]hat lighted sign spread across her body writes E. Luminata. . . . (15)

The sign undoubtedly has a polymorphous character: profane in the apparent phallic power of its light, and religious in that it performs "el bautizo" [the baptism]. Sex and religion seem at odds in the erotically charged passage, yet the two aspects can be reconciled by turning the symbolic baptism into a marriage union wherein the patriarch traditionally has provided the female with phallus and (family) name. "[T]hat lighted sign spread across her body writes E. Luminata" (15).[28] Besides the godlike qualities of the giant sign emanating light as well as words onto the square and E. Luminata's body, further "sign" of male supremacy is its apparent orgasm-producing power and its capacity to baptize with a name. In this regard, female sexuality and identity are not simply connected to the patriarch but dependent on him. After all, the patriarch's phallus and name are the instruments that mark the female as male possession. Even in Eltit's subversive representation the female subject is shaped by and within the phallogocentrism of Western culture.[29] Moreover, patriarchal ideology rooted in religious tradition undermines and controls sexuality through the concept of "sin," inscribed in the text and supported by related terms such as: baptismal, redeemed, obscenity, wantonness, purification, the sacrament (20–21). "I've been raised in a Catholic tradition and that is not of little consequence," remarks Eltit in an interview with Ana María Larraín. "On the contrary, I would say that it is a defining aspect for those of us who have experienced it, to a great extent because its practice integrates the concepts of guilt and sin."[30]

Insofar as there is no primary male protagonist as object of E. Luminata's desire, theoretically her orgasmic experience could be attributed to her conscious fantasy life.[31] For example, let us consider section 1.3 of chapter 1 a portrayal of E. Luminata's fantasy at work. While not losing total touch with the surroundings—the plaza and its inhabitants—each thought sequence in this section ends with a focus on a female body. Extracting these concluding sentences from the text would produce an exploratory progression of lesbian sexual pleasure as follows:

> . . . and my madonna face looking into her madonna face. . . . and my madonna face seeks her madonna mouth and inside touches her pro-fane tongue. . . . and my madonna tongue moistens her tremulous ma-donna tongue. . . . and my madonna tongue touches her madonna breast and moistens it. . . . and my madonna lips suck her madonna breast longingly. . . . and my madonna mind entreats her madonna mind and touches it. . . . and my madonna furrow seeks her infertile madonna furrow. . . . and my madonna hand touches her hot madonna knees. . . . and my madonna knees clamp her madonna knees tightly. . . . and my madonna hands spread her madonna knees and they lick her. (34–36)

Peter Michelson notes how "women's sexual fantasies seem con-nected to their autonomy."[32] Fantasy life is a safe place to exercise female autonomy, thus in the passage E. Luminata, as a desiring les-bian subject, transgresses societal heterosexuality. In light of this, the constant repetition of the word "madonna" underscores the subversion of sexual and religious patriarchal ideology.[33] As an act of transgression, it shares pornography's disdain for what Susan Griffin calls " 'holy' prudery."[34]

Although sedate by today's standards, depiction of female erotic fantasy can be found in *House of Mist* (*La última niebla*, 1947), an as-pect that earned María Luisa Bombal the position of precursor of Chilean women inscribing female sexuality in their books today. Among these is Ana María del Río whose *Siete días de la señora K.* (1993) became instantly popular among university students and the reading public alike. With the husband on a business trip and the children at camp, the protagonist, an ordinary housewife and mother, discovers her sensuality (and her body) during the seven days she spends home alone. Another writer, Pía Barros, runs the gamut from orthodox portrayal of female sexuality in conflict with repressive patriarchal dictates—*El tono menor del deseo* (1991)—to a narrative poetics verging on pornography—"Foreshadowing of a Trace" in *Astride* (1992). The short narratives "Scents of Wood and Silence" and "Desolate Before the Window" found in *Astride* spe-cifically focus on fantasy life, a topic Barros continues to explore in "Amigas en Bach," *Signos bajo la piel* (1994), but unconventionally since in the story female heterosexual fantasy turns out to liberate lesbian desire. Publishing in Santiago, which retains many provincial attitudes towards sexual mores, Barros has consistently exhibited a transgressive nature in regard to female eroticism.

In *E. Luminata* female sexuality is animalized in a series of thirty-one canto-like[35] compositions with a mare as thematic unity.[36] Michelson points out that "As [women] continue to discover their [sexual] terms . . . they have also begun to put them pornographically. Women, too, have been obliged to assert their own myth of animality in order to explore it" (135)[37] In E. Luminata's metamorphosis, however, the female unleashes her sexual passion in a heterosexual context: "A filly in heat needs a stud" (63). Erotic imagery abounds, as in the female's genital preparation to be "ridden": "[H]er haunches tremble to transport them; she becomes stained, broadens, fattens, grows stronger to really support this mounted pack . . ." (64). The mare provokes her onlookers, "the lumpen," by acting in a sexually solicitous manner: "[A]pproaching neighs at them, moos at them, scraping the concrete with those hoofs/trots/gallops to fire them up, tempting them with such business" (64). Her "terms," however, include autonomy: "[S]he would stop following orders . . . always disobey the command of other legs, so that her feet would mark a path different from the mounted's" (65)[38]. Resolute on autonomy, the mare ultimately rejects her rider, which by extension implies the phallus: "Bucking, shaking, throwing that rider off her haunch" (71).

Allusion is made to pornography not only in the filming of the mare's copulatory revelry, but in a lens focus that fragments the body: "Two mountings: the rider himself and the other who aims at her with the camera, but not at the whole beast, just at the flank" (72). In its close association with pornography as a medium of female sexual exploitation, prostitution is also suggested: "[T]hey line up to mount her, the lumpen itself is roaring/is about to jump the fence" (72). A simplistic moral of the representation might be to say that autonomous female sexual behavior when unbridled by patriarchy is labeled promiscuous and, therefore, becomes susceptible to exploitation.

In *E. Luminata* female sexual autonomy without exploitation is ultimately vindicated through masturbation. Feminist literary and clinical studies have been largely responsible for dispelling the myth that mature female sexuality rests solely on heterosexual intercourse and vaginal orgasm.[39] Validation and celebration of the clitoris is no doubt implied in E. Luminata's autoeroticism:

> She didn't achieve displeasure because her legs gave out. She didn't achieve displeasure because entirely beautiful she rubbed her breast.

She didn't achieve displeasure in the interweaving of her hairs, on the inner sides of those same legs there remained mobile particles. These same particles at her gaping lips. Along with the coquetry of her open legs: the eyelids and the awareness of *a solid body*—her own—which suited to different situations was *able to acquire a special autonomy. . . .* (emphasis mine, 102)

Masturbation as an autonomous means of attaining sexual pleasure is further highlighted in the original text by the recurring neologism "refrote" (94–95), evidently from "frote," that is rubbing or friction.

This repetitive action associated with masturbation connects the body to the text: "gaze and text, body and mind are rubbed together" (105). The disjunctive narrative style of *E. Luminata* requires reading and rereading, a constant (masturbatory?) going back and forth over the pages in a search for meaning, for the pleasure of deciphering the elusive text. As noted in the introduction, Elzbieta Sklodowska has observed a parodic sacrilege of canonical modern patriarchs. E. Luminata's eroticized "rubbing" with the likes of a Lezama Lima, James Joyce, Pablo Neruda, Juan Rulfo, Ezra Pound, and Robbe-Grillet—"With any Tom, Dick or Harry rubs antennae" (77)—implies her sexual as well as literary autonomy, albeit the influence that the very inclusion of these names suggests.[40]

Body and text are also linked insofar as the fragmented narrative mirrors the female image within society. "Woman in patriarchal society exists in fragments," declares Gary Day, "which, interestingly enough, is the idiom of hardcore pornography, where the parts are greater than the whole."[41]

Socialized to be aware of their body, women learn not only to take self-inventory but also to compare themselves with other females. Section 4.4 records a self-splitting gaze that inspects its own body as if mirrored in someone else. Toenails, toes, soles, eyes, hands, fingers, palms, arms, wrists, waistline are all scrutinized. Evidently avoiding particularly erogenous zones, the gaze focuses mainly on the extremities, concluding with the non-carnal soul: "Her soul is being E. Luminata and offering herself as another. Her soul is not being called diamela eltit/ white sheets/ cadaver. Her soul is to mine the twin" (90). This piecemeal focus responds to the traditional pornographic articulation of the body as pointed out by Day. Nonetheless, spotlighting nonerotic areas effectively neutralizes the sexualizing gaze, and including the soul as spiritual component lends a sense of wholeness to the fragmented female image. Hence, although in varying degree, both pornography and religion—body and soul—inform the text.

The reader should keep in mind that the emphasis on corporal fragmentation mirrors Chilean society torn apart by the military coup. The recurrent references to a camera and filming as well as the preoccupation with the "gaze," be it the voyeuristic gaze of the vagrants, the self-inspecting gaze of the protagonist herself, or the godlike neon light that seems to watch over the square at night, reflect a Chile under state vigil. People who live under oppressive regimes will tell you that they feel watched all the time. Individuals under constant surveillance often develop an overwhelming fear of being denounced to officials. Undoubtedly, as someone who lived in Chile during the entire period of the dictatorship, Eltit cannot help but capture her own experience. As we will see in the last chapter on *Los vigilantes* [*Vigilant*], the book's very title foreshadows the protagonist's obsession with her neighbors' gaze.

The starring role of the body in Eltit's first book and the deliberate piecemeal focus on every part of E. Luminata's body thus parallel the watchfulness under which Chileans lived at the time. Significantly, the female body is repeatedly presented as injured —this too points to the political subtext alluded to by torture (as specific as electrical charges to genitalia) and general physical disfigurement.[42] "She remained unrecognizable in her terror of electricity. . . ," we read, "scarcely blinked in the room when they were getting ready to make her comfortable. She forgot everything. Even the woman who closed her legs and back to the light shaft again, where a sunbeam fell on the big table. . . . " (81).[43]

Stagings of sexual pleasure share the narrative repertoire with those of physical pain.[44] As discussed earlier in chapter 1/scene 1, E. Luminata poses for a camera that captures her orgasmic exhibition. Immediately afterwards, in scene 2 the lens zooms in as she wounds herself: "Her hands reach out, she grasps the nearest tree and brings her face toward it. . . . She smashes her head against the tree again and again until the blood overflows the skin, it bathes her face that blood . . ." (24). The alluded script for scene 2—also or alternatively—calls for "Production of the cry" (28), a scream produced after E. Luminata bashes her forehead against the pavement. From a feminist perspective, this kind of self-punishment can suggest how women internalize society's indictment of female orgasmic pleasure outside of heterosexual bonds. The section following the head wound(s) consists of the "madonna" lesbian fantasy identified previously. After that erotic scene, self-inflicted harm is again depicted: "[F]acing the fire she brings her hand near, stretches her hand out over the flames and lets it fall upon them. . . . And her hand open over the flames changes color, her face turns red. She looks at her hand, the blisters that are rising, the contractions of the fingers" (41–42).[45] Hence, the sequence of events sets a pattern of sexual activity followed by intentional physical injury. Symbolically, then, the pleasure-seeking female ultimately punishes herself for expressing and satisfying her desire. But also consistent with the motifs of pornography and religion, this violence against the body evokes both hard-core pornography and self-mortification or martyrdom.[46]

In *E. Luminata* the profane and the religious are found simultaneously woven into the text. It is worth noting that the only time E. Luminata speaks in erotically-charged chapter 1 is after each incident of violence: the head wound(s), the burned hand. The two words she exclusively articulates in chapter 1, and throughout the entire book, are: "—I'm thirsty—" (25, 29, 42, 48, 100). Insofar as the Spanish phrase "tengo sed" [I'm thirsty] in an erotic context communicates sexual desire, the following passage implies the prospect of satisfaction: "If she's to repeat in the story—I'm thirsty—anybody, even the most ragged of them, [would anoint her lips] in order to leave her satisfied" (34).[47] These same two words, however, are uttered by Christ on the cross, and his lips are also moistened: "Jesus, aware that all had now come to its appointed end, said in fulfillment of Scripture, 'I thirst'. A jar stood there of sour wine; so they soaked a sponge with the wine, fixed it on a javelin, and held it up to his lips."[48] Evidently, the words "tengo sed" [I'm thirsty] coalesce the erotic and religious elements of textual construction.

E. Luminata emerges as both whorish and Christ-like. She is a "public" woman, a woman who expresses her sexuality in a public square. Written into her script is the punishment for the sins of the body, for lust and carnal pleasure. Christ's script had also been written for him, his suffering for the sins of humanity came to pass "in fulfillment of Scripture." E. Luminata, like Christ, delivers her message in public; similarly the poor, the homeless, the sick, "los desarrapados"/"the ragged people" make up her audience. Meaningfully, the underlying implication in this dual female image is the shattering of the traditional stereotypes of woman as either whore or virgin. From a feminist perspective, Eltit's symbolic rendition depicts a female who embodies both qualities.

SUBVERTING FICTION: THE AUTHOR'S BODY/WRITING

The violence, bodily harm, and self-punishment incorporated in E. Luminata's script spills into reality in chapter 8. Titled "Dress Rehearsal," it is introduced with a shadowy picture of a woman exhibiting cuts on her arms. Although only the left side of her face is distinguishable, a distinctive mole on the upper lip matches the picture of Eltit featured on the inside jacket of the book. As Lagos points out, these two pictures as well as the one appearing on the book cover which depicts the author's face twice projected onto a wall, and her name inserted in the text all suggest that Eltit's writing does not pretend to be solely fictive.[49]

"Dress Rehearsal," studied by Robert Neustadt as "performance" art, describes and meditates on the six cuts the right hand inflicts on the left arm.[50] Given the nature of the introductory picture and the topic of the "rehearsal," Eltit has evidently subverted her own fiction by writing herself into the text. Significantly, the sacrificial act as such is not introduced until the last page of the chapter: "She keeps her sight fixed with quick blinks. The fingers of her right hand hold up the small sharp blade. Without looking she brings it toward her hide. The Dress Rehearsal is going to begin" (165). Using the same technique, and contrary to convention, the dedication—"A Zurita"—of the Spanish *Lumpérica* appears on the very last page of the book.[51] Clearly, this gesture connects the "Ensayo"/ "Rehearsal" to Zurita, and by extension, to reality in his role as dedicatee.

Nelly Richard provides proof of this link in *Margins and Institutions: Art in Chile Since 1973.* Regarding the use of the body for artistic purposes, Richard identifies Raúl Zurita and Diamela Eltit as two Chilean writers who have engaged in painful "acts of resignation . . . modeled on *sacrifice* or *martyrdom.*"[52] For example, Richard records that in 1980, Eltit cut and burned her arms and then read part of her work in a brothel.[53] A significant act in keeping with pornography as motif in her work, Eltit apparently uses her body as an artistic slate onto which she symbolically inscribes the pain and suffering that comes with sexual exploitation. Likewise, in a religious vein, the self-mortification is also a ritual exorcism, a purification.

Although a brothel is almost exclusively associated with female exploitation and misery, Richard notes that Eltit also worked in other socially marginal areas such as psychiatric hospitals, flophouses, and jails, which she calls "zones of pain." "My concern is to expose these places," Eltit is quoted as saying, "to become one with them by my physical presence. My wish is not to morally change them, but only to show that they actually exist. . . . It is a form of individual pain confronting the collective pain."[54] Again, let us not forget that at the time of military rule, widespread fear and violence literally had turned the whole of Chile into a "zone of pain."

In the next two chapters the focus on [*For the Homeland*], [*My*

Father], and [*Soul's Infarct*] demonstrates Eltit's diligent effort to include marginal Chileans in the literary patrimony—a task that one particular group, the Mapuche Indians, has begun to undertake themselves by publishing in their traditional language. My reading of [*For the Homeland*] brings to the foreground indicators that strongly point to Eltit's concern for the indigenous peoples of Chile, a group that has its own story of collective pain to tell.

Women in the visual and plastic arts have used the body as instrument for artistic expression. In *From the Center: Feminist Essays on Women's Art,* Lucy R. Lippard discusses European and American women's "body art." This kind of art "focuses upon the body or body parts—usually the artist's own body, but at times . . . other bodies, envisioned as extensions of the artist him/herself."[55] Lippard records the various ways women have used themselves in attempts to de-censor the female body. For example, she cites the words of Carolee Schneemann, an artist whose work is concerned with sexual and personal freedom: "I use my nude body . . . as a stripped-down, undecorated human object. . . . In some sense I made a gift of my body to other women: giving our bodies back to ourselves."[56] Like Eltit, French artist Gina Pane "has cut herself with razor blades, [she has also] eaten until she was sick, and subjected herself to other tortures."[57] These women are exceptional; nonetheless, Lippard notes that if most women artists do not go to this extreme, "the fear of pain, of cruelty and violence, surfaces frequently in their work."[58]

Eltit's artistic rendering in "Dress Rehearsal" proves that she does not fear but rather embraces pain. In the "rehearsal" turned ceremony the knife replaces the pen, cutting substitutes writing, the body becomes the page: "[T]his third cut . . . is scarcely graffiti on the skin of the arm . . ." (150). Evidently, in *E. Luminata* the body and writing are linked. Moreover, disfiguring the body reflects the mutilation of language in the text. In fact, "Dress Rehearsal" does not begin with corporal, but with linguistic deformation: "She moo/ s/hears and her hand feeds mind-fully the green disentangles and maya she erects herself sha/m-an and vac/a-nal her shape. She analizes the plot = thickens the skin: the hand catches = fire and the phobia d is/members" (150–51). Worth noting, the term "shaman" embedded in this text serves as a kernel that will sprout into a major theme in Eltit's next novel, [*For the Homeland*], a postmodern text in which language itself will continue to play a central role.

This relationship between physical and linguistic violence had already been suggested in the episode where E. Luminata burns her hand over the bonfire:

[W]ith her mouth stuck to her hand she broaches the opposite meaning of her phrase. She deconstructs the phrase word by word, syllable by syllable, letter by letter, by sounds. Twisting its phonetics. Altering the modulation she converts it into a foreign tongue. It is no longer recognizable. . . . She has disorganized language. (43)

Neither burned hand nor language are "recognizable." Symbolic disfigurement of the hand (that writes?) reflects the de(con)struction of conventional discourse: "burn and word as one" (45).

Significantly, discourse in the text is monopolized by males as their patriarchal domain. For example, the only dialogue in *E. Luminata* revolves around an interrogation of one man by another—further allusion to Chilean national reality at the time. Whether in a superior or subordinate capacity, the male voice dominates the text as does the written word. Hence, it follows that a female's attempt to speak or write constitutes a disruption of logocentrism and therefore a blatant transgression.

In chapter 5—entitled "Quo Vadis?"—section 5.3 particularly can be read as a representation of the difficulty a woman writer confronts when she undertakes a new (dis)course, breaks away, deviates from the literary canon. The role E. Luminata plays as a writer struggling for personal expression is important as a counterpart to her manifestations of sexual autonomy. For a woman, both goals entail challenging patriarchy. The square as initial stage for female eroticism now turns into a page: "[S]he was no decoration for the square but just the reverse: the square was her page, only that" (100). Consequently, the focus is redirected from body to intellect: "Passed along from image to word . . ." (101).

In "Quo Vadis?" E. Luminata simulates writing with her finger the words "where you going" on a lamppost and on the center surface of the square (113). The pretense becomes reality when a patriarchal figure symbolically grants his permission to write by supplying her with a writing instrument, albeit of an erasable medium: "[O]ne of the pale people reaches out a piece of chalk to her. Almost dragging herself over the ground, she begins to construct large letters that take up the entire center of the square. Gone across and the—where you going—allows her a new arrangement" (113). By virtue of writing in a public place her words—not entries in a journal, private correspondence, or recipe notations— are of patriarchal concern. Given the self-reflexive nature of the scene, "Quo Vadis?" marks female writing as questionable. E. Luminata literally inscribes a question that can be interpreted as: Where do you think you're going (with that type of writing)?

In the plaza, once finished, E. Luminata stands back to await the reception of her writing, fully cognizant that it is questionable: "[A]ttentive as she is to the approving movement of the lumpen . . . she knows she has introduced a break in her attitudes and that's exactly why she hopes . . . others may really begin to read and then catalogue the action" (113–14). The male group hesitantly approaches her writing and after pondering her written words—where you going—they trample them in a hostile act of rejection: "Finally they cover them completely with their feet. . . . [S]lowly their feet rub against the ground. As in an improvised dance, their rhythms rub out the chalk, destroy her title. They move off. A gray stain spreads over the center of the square, gone are the letters" (114).

The portrayal of the woman writer in a patriarchal literary circle continues with the female putting up a fight. Unyielding, E. Luminata rewrites her words even larger, and this time stands right by them: "She remains there, stopped alongside a letter. . . . before turning her eyes to the pale people who watch her from the darkness" (114). But finally grown tired of waiting for a sign of recognition, she symbolically acknowledges her defeat and literally down on her knees she rubs out her own writing: "She patiently goes back down on her knees on the ground and with the hem of her dress begins to rub out the writing, calmly, methodically, meek" (115). Immediately "the pale people" emerge to confirm the erasure.

In reaction to the disparagement, E. Luminata defies them to write by handing each a piece of chalk. But writing proves a difficult task, as is apparent from their gestures: "Head between hands, shoulders drooped . . ." (115). After much laboring they fail to write. Finally, they acknowledge her presence and she literally abandons the margins to take up the center with her writing. "They detect her and fling the remains of the chalk into the grass. They go toward the benches and leave her the site of the reading and at last the 'where you going' is she herself in the center of the square . . ." (116). Her literary endeavor was a challenge and a gamble, but patriarchy finally acceded to her words, thus she triumphed: "For the first time her smile convulses her/she has seen the complete phrase. . . . [A]s a gambler she has won. . . ." (116). Met with initial disapproval, E. Luminata's writing is eventually accepted, albeit reluctantly, and granted a space for expression.

Given Eltit's unorthodox style, finding acceptance—yet alone inserting herself into mainstream literary circles—is still a struggle. In *E. Luminata* and as we will see consequently in the books to follow, the topic of writing recurs frequently, although never in an overt way. I suspect that because Latin American women are socialized to believe that females accomplish more with subtle manipulation rather than with confrontation, most do not feel comfortable with forceful tactics. Hence, the myriad of indictments in Eltit's texts is symbolically represented and must be unearthed by the critic. As the reader will note in my multilayered reading of her novels, regarding the topic of writing I find that *The Fourth World* and [*Vigilant*] most explicitly contain Eltit's views on her craft as it is hampered by gender and undermined by a patriarchal literary establishment.

E. Luminata's nonconformity and marginality vis-à-vis mainstream literary discourse stands as an exemplar of a postmodern text, a novelistic style that Eltit continues to develop until its culmination in *Sacred Cow*. I say this because while in *E. Luminata* narrative and linguistic distortions are obvious to the point that the page format bears the stamp of experimental literature, *Sacred Cow* achieves the illusion of conventional narrative. That text's sophistication compared to *E. Luminata* attests to Eltit's literary evolution. For this reason, in the discussion of *Sacred Cow* I specifically focus on Eltit's manipulation of feminist content and postmodernist style, thus highlighting how the author bridges the gap between feminism and postmodernism. [*Vigilant*], the next published novel, is written in a straightforward fashion that marks a sharp shift from the strong postmodernist leanings that Eltit had cultivated until then. Surprisingly, the novel not only has a plot, but one that unfolds with the female protagonist's letter-writing activity, a traditionally gender-specific mode of writing. However, writing style aside, one must not lose sight of the fact that "marginality" remains at the root of all of Eltit's work.

In *E. Luminata* the chapter that follows the protagonist's struggle to have her writing accepted, appropriately includes a section titled "The Graffiti in the Square." Graffiti, from the Italian "graffiare," to scratch, conveys the concept of a socially marginal writing. According to John Bushnell's research on the subject, historically there is a direct link between the adoption of Christianity and graffiti as scratchings made by the faithful on ancient church walls.[59] Predominantly illiterate, worshipers would most often simply scratch in crosses; those who could would elaborate with various religious inscriptions.[60]

Graffiti, as a rudimentary written sign of Christianity, logically contains the notion of persecution, a notion that can be linked to the very words E. Luminata authors. "Quo Vadis," taken from "Domine, quo vadis?," meaning "Lord, where are you going?," appears in the Apocryphal *Acts of Peter* composed circa A.D. 190. An anecdote based on that text relates that Peter in flight from Rome during the persecutions of Nero "meets Jesus on the Appian Way:

And when he saw him, he said, 'Lord, whither goest thou?' And the Lord said unto him, 'I go into Rome to be crucified.' "[61] Is it coincidental that E. Luminata—bleeding, burned, scarred, embodiment of a martyr—writes during a period when a Nero-like Pinochet rules the land?[62]

Like the words—Quo vadis—that E. Luminata inscribes in the plaza, modern-day graffiti appears in open public areas, usually consists of a few words, a short message or design, and is often a tool used by members of a subculture to express their marginality.[63] Graffiti ultimately represents transgression against and persecution by the official culture. The mere presence of graffiti in public places also indicates the dominant culture's lack of control, its inability to stifle minority expression. Paradoxically, graffiti is for and by the masses, something Eltit's writing is not—albeit her concern for and inscription of Chilean marginalities. Ultimately, the paradox can be reconciled given the political subtext of a novel written in a repressive state where graffiti was surely a popular vehicle for venting public dissatisfaction.

E. Luminata does not conform to literary conventions and, as such, shares with graffiti the concept of transgressive, and hence marginal, writing. Graffiti, which is often signed in some manner, does not necessarily intend anonymity, but autonomy. The theme of autonomy as it pertains to writing is well reflected in section 6.2, "The Graffiti in the Square." For example, each page announces a different possibility for literary address: "Writing as proclamation," "as folly," "as fiction," "as seduction," "as meshing gears," "as sentencing," "as rubbing," "as evasion," "as objective," "as illumination," "as mocking," "as abandon," "as erosion (121–133).[64] The short writings that follow each heading, however, do not proceed to develop the topic announced. Writing misleads and thus manifests autonomy within the text itself.

Literary autonomy is implied throughout the section. For example, there is the hint of a subconscious writing unfettered by conventional language rules and therefore seemingly incomprehensible: "[T]hose people discourse on other foundations, something impossible to understand fully, because the places wherein they are proposed derive from the most primal, from the disintelligence . . ." (121). Reference is also made to women's quest for creative autonomy despite a borrowed patriarchal discourse: "[T]heir immutable expressions inhibited us . . ." (122). Not so very long ago, writing by women was virtually ignored and considered trite simply because it was not produced by the pen of a patriarch: "They weren't contemplating us since this limited thought did not illumine the glistening dust jacket of the divine" (122). Straying from the family romance signifies refusing the prototype of women's literature.[65] The disorderly text inscribes another kind of writing, one that becomes capable of filling in the gaps in women's writing as it develops literary autonomy: "[T]his disorder . . . implicates work completed by the one who receives honors which he gets on loan for holes that others have left. . . . [T]hese edifices . . . gleam in full autonomy" (123). Thus the call for autonomous, unrestricted writing is ideally conveyed through the concept of graffiti which, lawless, responds only to the creativity of the writer.

"The Graffiti in the Square" also connects writing and female sexuality. At the bottom of each page, as if simulating a subliminal message, graffiti-like footnotes inscribe largely sexual innuendoes. For example, the "footnotes" appearing on the first four pages of the section connote lesbian eroticism:

> She wrote: like the most cracked of madonnas I lent [her] my body stretched out in the square so [she'd] lick it.[66] She wrote: stretched out on the lawn I told you all the beautiful words, madonna, so you wouldn't stop, madonna I told you beaming. She wrote: I get wet in pure torment, yes madonna, I get drenched. She wrote: crack me with branches madonna, inflame me with leaves. (121–24)

The next set of footnotes alludes to a heterosexual theme evocative of prostitution:

> She wrote: [that one in rags madonna soils me, stains me].[67] She wrote: send me to that other man madonna, oh yes send me at once to all the others. She wrote: drag me to the water madonna, find me that spout. She wrote: I'm peeling madonna, I'm opening up. She wrote: maybe they're not coming madonna, maybe tonight they're not coming back. (125–29)

Whereas the topic of lesbianism portrays a solicitous female who willingly surrenders her body to sexual pleasure, the passage involving heterosexuality expresses repulsion—"soils me," "stains me"— and the need to be cleansed—"drag me to the water."

After highlighting sexuality, the footnotes then touch on the other major theme in *E. Luminata,* language itself:

> She wrote: they're humbug all these words. She wrote: they imprison me, they bring me down those words. She wrote: they're fleeting words madonna, hardly even stammering. (130–32)

The grievance voiced here against censorship extends to both literary and sexual expression.[68] Coming full circle, the last footnote suggests a unity of female mind and body as the site of textual/sexual inscription: "She wrote: illuminated entirely, turned on" (134).

Clearly implying E. Luminata under the neon sign, she is "turned on," that is, intellectually illuminated but also sexually aroused.

E. Luminata, as central figure in the square, represents a new female image. Her looks and demeanor subvert the conventions of femininity. Significantly, this includes exercising the traditionally male prerogative of sexual autonomy. In *E. Luminata* the protagonist transgresses taboos of female sexual expression. Desire and eroticism are abundantly and uninhibitedly displayed. Disassociated from any form of family structure, which typically acts as the censoring agent of female sexuality, E. Luminata engages in a spectrum of sexual experiences. Heterosexuality, however, is not depicted in a favorable light. Yet the female has, and exploits, other viable options for sexual expression and satisfaction: lesbianism, autoerotism, sexual fantasizing.

Despite presenting an innovative portrayal of a new female archetype, *E. Luminata* cannot liberate the female subject without inscribing the source of oppression. In other words, as Eltit textually inscribes her new model, she has no choice but to refer to the cultural phallogocentrism within which women develop and exist. This she does, paradoxically, by appropriating the conventions of pornography and religion as respective loci of female sexual exploitation and repression.

Pornography and religion as phallogocentric constructs have mutilated female bodies and minds. In the text, the violence culturally perpetrated against women is reflected through corporal as well as linguistic disfigurement. The radical displacement of traditional gender role and femininity requires an equally subversive inscription. Hence, narrative, linguistic, and thematic transgressions combine to represent E. Luminata's expressions of literary and sexual autonomy.

Ultimately, however, no reading of Eltit's work can escape reference to Chile's political reality at the time she was initiated as a writer. This holds true for many of Eltit's contemporaries, including such women as Pía Barros, Ana María del Río, Marcela Serrano, and Isabel Allende, whose books, regardless of theme or style, overtly or surreptitiously inscribe Chilean political circumstance and thus comprise the literary legacy left by a long, brutal dictatorship.

Eltit believes that a writer produces but one work with the various books composing different parts or moments of the one big book.[69] In keeping with this philosophy, all of Eltit's novels inscribe a preoccupation with power—be it sexual, literary, or political—within an economy of marginality where attaining, exercising, maintaining, or losing power is what distinguishes the oppressor from the oppressed.

2

El Padre Mío and *El infarto del alma:* "Testimonio" on Homelessness as Metaphor for the Chilean Homeland

Given the derelicts that inhabit *E. LUMINATA* and Eltit's concern for humanity's dispossessed as worthy of cultural inscription, it is not surprising that the author took a special interest in a homeless man that she discovered living on some isolated lot of Santiago. In fact, she came upon him in 1983, the same year she published her first novel. According to the book's introduction, starting in 1980, Eltit and video artist Lotty Rosenfeld wandered through shelters, prostitution areas, and impoverished districts of Santiago, driven by a keen interest in the social and cultural realities of the population's marginal sectors.[1] Eltit aimed to capture the world of the urban vagabond and develop an aesthetics of the outcast.

El Padre Mío[2] [*My Father*] (1989), a seventy-page book of transcriptions, gathers the homeless man's speech as recorded by Eltit in 1983, 1984, and 1985, after which time she lost track of his whereabouts. During those years all appearances indicated that the subject had permanently settled on the isolated lot with no protection from the elements. Surrounded by discarded items and old newspapers, his story about surviving government repression may well have been a tale fabricated from what he read and distorted by his disturbed mind. However, though mentally ill, the subject of [*My Father*] did not abandon language. In fact, Eltit observed that when he saw her approach he would immediately begin talking. Let us keep in mind that the appellative "My Father" identifies both Eltit's protagonist and his antagonist, a high-level, corrupt government official who supposedly uses that alias for his fraudulent dealings.

The protagonist of [*My Father*] is not the only nonfictional outcast in Eltit's writings. Years after publishing the recordings, insanity became the focus of an extraliterary project, *El infarto del alma* [*Soul's Infarct*] (1994), in which Eltit teamed up with photographer Paz Errázuriz to portray the patients of the psychiatric hospital in the town of Putaendo, outside of Santiago.[3] Although interned and removed from public view, these mostly indigent individuals, like My Father, are homeless.

However, unlike [*My Father*] in which the protagonist's voice is heard avidly narrating his own ordeal, silence predominates [*Soul's Infarct*] since it is above all a book of photography. The black-and-white photographs of couples attest to the human need for companionship, perhaps an indicator that My Father's copious speech in Eltit's presence offsets his lone existence. To Errázuriz's images Eltit contributes a text that conveys insights on the asylum and its inhabitants as well as her creative rendition of the possible mental ruminations of patients. Eltit acts as the conscious of the interned, communicating for them what the disturbed man of [*My Father*] does for himself.

In this respect, one recalls that in his work on asylum and prison confinement Michel Foucault derided the power of the intellectual for "the indignity of speaking for others."[4] But the text in [*Soul's Infarct*] becomes secondary in so far as Errázuriz's lens overpowers Eltit's pen. Words pale in allure next to the pictures of the demented subjects. The reader of [*Soul's Infarct*] is foremost a viewer for whom, I suspect, Eltit's text may ultimately be superfluous since each individual tends to create her/his own story for the anonymous pictures. Also pertinent to Errázuriz's photographs of the insane, Elsa Dorfman points out that we can stare at the mentally retarded in Diane Arbus's portraits "in a way that we couldn't stare . . . if we met them on the street. We can be fearful and curious and safe all at once. They are Other."[5]

Given the visual "testimony" on insanity presented in [*Soul's Infarct*] and Eltit's input on the topic, commentary here will refer to the book's points of comparison with [*My Father*] in a study that principally argues for the legitimacy of the homeless man's story as a "testimonio" of Latin American literature. Is it (in)credible to the reader? Due to the informant's mental state and fragmented discourse, this reading draws from reader-response theory the concept of "filling in the gaps" for interpretation.[6] Given also the particularities of this account, a reader's awareness of the process of producing (or questioning) meaning while reading [*My Father*] becomes as important as "understanding" the text itself. Therefore, this study integrates a phenomenological approach that considers the reader's mental processes during reading rather than striving solely for an exegesis as the critic's optimum product.

Eltit's choice of subject and her aesthetic vision reflect her class consciousness, for she has stated (and her texts prove) that the Latin American condition matters to her deeply.

> A great theme remains current in Latin America, a great problem: the chronic poverty of these countries, the alarming social inequality. . . . There continues to be, and more so each day, a great divide between the groups with money and the popular segments. . . . Not everyone has the same abilities, the same history or a favorable background. But a person should not be destined and forgotten for not having these. I believe that the topic of attaining a certain social equilibrium remains fundamental. They can pronounce all the speeches that they want, but chronic poverty still exists. One definition associated with that which is Latin American is to be poor.[7]

As I will highlight in the next chapter, the author's intellectual commitment to the underprivileged continues in *Por la Patria* [*For the Homeland*] (1986) where, as I read it, Eltit creates a literary space for representing the indigenous peoples of Chile. In an observation that applies wholly to Eltit's production, Djelal Kadir notes that "The fate of the dispossessed commands an urgency in the conscience of *Lumpérica*'s protagonist and in the art of its author."[8]

Given Eltit's social concerns, the homeless certainly fall among those worthy of textual representation. She observes that vagrants transgress social institutions—which act as the keepers of private domain. Home, work, schools, clubs—and psychiatric hospitals as the one in Putaendo—will literally keep people off the streets. By contrast, street dwellers refuse refuge and impose themselves on society's gaze, which makes them subversives who defy societal structures.[9] Their insubordination extends to every aspect of family and civic life. Disenfranchisement from the economy means that they do not work to support themselves, pay rent, pay taxes, participate in a consumer market, or obey community restrictions. Who do vagrants answer to? No one, and obviously there is inherent freedom in undermining the established system—a liberty that the patients of Putaendo depicted in [*Soul's Infarct*] do not enjoy given the regulations that come with internment.

Subversion is also characteristic of Eltit, the writer, one whose break from conventional prose structure, syntax, and lexicon, especially in *E. Luminata* and, as we will see, in [*For the Homeland*], exemplifies radical experimentation in Chilean literature. Eltit has commented that in her circle she is considered an eccentric writer; indeed her work remains displaced from the mainstream Chilean literary establishment.[10] She recalls that *Cobra* by Cuban novelist Severo Sarduy paved the way for her finding a distinct style, one that she describes as "the freedom from all styles." "I allowed my own voices to speak," Eltit assures us, "I also allowed the traditions that inhabited me to speak, and I permitted a disorder and a disregard of that tradition."[11]

But tradition is alive and well, baroque tradition, that is, one that has been revived by Latin American writers like Sarduy under the label of neo-baroque.[12] Language as literary exploit is of utmost importance in the baroque. Obscurity of meaning achieved through such elements as neologisms, hyperboles, hyperbatons, wordplay, distorted syntax, and discordant images contribute to the hermetism and eccentricity characteristic of baroque writing.[13] That Eltit can be called a participant in neo-baroque aesthetics is especially clear upon examining her first novel, *E. Luminata.*[14]

Like Eltit's "eccentric" label within the writing circles of Santiago, the vagrants she sought out and the insane captured by Errázuriz's camera are among the country's marginal inhabitants who live on the fringes of mainstream society (notably, the psychiatric hospital in Putaendo as the most notorious in Chile exists far removed from the country's capital or center).

With respect to the protagonist of [*My Father*], parallels can be drawn here between writer and subject. For example, disorder and nonmainstream narrative, that is, a disregard for what most Chileans consider traditional literature, illustrate Eltit's writing style as well as the precarious existence of the vagabond in a highly rule-oriented, structured, and regulated community. In fact, the vagrant is an appropriate metaphor for Eltit's writing of the 1980s, one that embodies resistance as a conscious dereliction of Chilean (literary) tradition. As Kadir notes, "Eltit's art of urgency violates with impunity the sanctioned norms of the novelistic genre as the masculinist tradition has willed it to posterity."[15]

Surely, in [*My Father*] the protagonist's incoherence is, for many readers, analogous to Eltit's early novels (especially her first two). The "No se entiende" [incomprehensible] label that many critics then conferred on Eltit can describe her fiction as well as the rambling of this particular protagonist, My Father.[16] But labels aside, as a writer Eltit is already "cast as alterity" since geographic birthplace, political circumstance, and gender situate her in the "predicament of otherness."[17]

Omar Calabrese associates the concept "vague" with a neo-baroque literary discourse that takes on "a vagabond-like wandering . . . , a roving around its own content."[18] If mainstream literature is equated to classical art, then Eltit's first works can best be labeled baroque for their experimental qualities. Calabrese points out that authoritarian states like the Nazi and Stalin regimes labeled the avant-garde "degenerate art," a morphologically accurate designation since "all 'baroque' phenomena are produced by a process of 'degeneration' (or rather, 'destabilization') in an ordered system."[19] Thus, in literature as in art, the baroque defies the canonical genres produced by the classical or mainstream value systems.[20] In this respect, [*Soul's Infarct*], as visual and textual portrayal of the insane, certainly qualifies as both "degenerate art" and "baroque."

When Eltit published *E. Luminata* she was indeed the waif of the Santiago writing establishment. Repudiation of conventional style coupled with her gender meant bearing a double (marketing) handicap. The accusatory tone of Eltit's early novels, also detected in My Father's soliloquy, can be deciphered by most readers, yet difficulties abound in their unorthodox delivery. Both writer and subject are deviants, one in literary style, the other in lifestyle. It is not surprising therefore that the author would meander through the city's peripheries in search of marginal dwellers, which is—by Latin American standards—subversive behavior for a woman.[21] In order to inscribe life at the fringe of society, the author, albeit temporarily, becomes marginal herself (in a literal sense Eltit leaves home and walks the streets).

Chilean city streets surged as a literary theme notably in the seventies because of state-instituted restrictions.[22] Curfew suddenly made getting around the city unlawful and dangerous for the populace. "In my opinion, the military coup erased the city," points out Eltit, "moving through it was conflict-ridden and all that was public was suspect."[23] In Eltit's writing, public space as metaphor for repression first appeared in *E. Luminata*,[24] where, as seen in that chapter, the anonymous female protagonist defies curfew and spends the night in a plaza. Significantly, it is a woman who symbolically takes back the night by appropriating a prohibited space.

Given the culture of surveillance that predominated Chile during those years (especially in poor sectors registering high discontent), Eltit's wandering through city streets as well as recording a subject in public view shows a degree of defiance that parallels the author's protagonists. In *E. Luminata* and [*My Father*], vagrancy, whether fictional or real, temporary or permanent, serves as a platform for resistance. Nearly two decades after the original publication of *E. Luminata* and a few years after the plebiscite that returned democratic elections to Chile, Guadalupe Santa Cruz uses the streets of Santiago as setting to portray in *Cita capital* (1992) the effect of military rule.[25]

In considering an aesthetics of the urban vagabond, Eltit evokes the exorbitance of baroque art in general and sculpture in particular. Indigents normally carry all their possessions with them. Such an accumulation of objects extends to the multilayered assortment of clothing they wear.[26] Paradoxically, excess exudes from their penury. Moreover, a three-dimensional sculpture is among the few art forms that can be designated outdoors, exposed to the gaze of the citizenry. The vagabond's physical existence is exposed to public view, much like the human subject that prevailed in classical sculpture. However, far from the statuary "models" of antiquity, vagrants, as human spectacle, represent what society least wants to contemplate or admire.[27] As such they become the visibly invisible, especially in large urban areas.

Eltit's literary attempt to record an aesthetics of human destitution conjures up the outcasts depicted by Spanish court painter Francisco de Goya y Lucientes, whose art was influenced by the grotesqueness of seventeenth-century baroque and the ideas of eighteenth-century Enlightenment. Like the philosophers of the Spanish Enlightenment, Goya was preoccupied with reason and superstition, authority and emancipation, society and the individual. Let us note that reason and its abandonment, authority and its abuse, freedom and its suppression, and the individual's oppression in society are key topics in Eltit's production, which is typically marked by political consequence.

Goya's self-appointed role as witness to a nation was captured on canvases depicting penetrating observations of Spanish society. Water carriers, knife grinders, beggars, the insane, the poor, the prosecuted were as much subjects of the artist's palette as were royalty, military heroes, and important officials. The photographs of [*Soul's Infarct*] provide an immediate link to Goya's sketches as they cut across time and national difference. Moreover, Goya's illustrations of the wretched existence of Spanish subjects can be compared to Eltit's literary representations of the sordid aspects of Chilean life under the, now historical, dictatorship. The much-feared Spanish Inquisition of Goya's time is mirrored by the Chilean secret police, Dirección de Inteligencia Nacional, popularly known as simply D.I.N.A. Both, as institutionalized, repressive systems, carried out trials, incarcerations, tortures, and executions of nonconformists in the population. Whether the ideology at hand was religious or political in nature, these organizations relied heavily on reports and accusations filed by regular citizens. The other's gaze could brand someone an outcast and even levy an ill-fated death.

The homeless and the insane—as pivotal subjects of [*My Father*] and [*Soul's Infarct*]—denote society's misfits, a lot for which the baroque reserved a place. As González Echevarría points out, the monster as commonplace figure of baroque literature, the dwarfs of Diego Velázquez' paintings, and the indigenous deities that native artisans included in the friezes of Latin American church architecture are all representations of marginal elements.[28] Góngora's monstrous giant, Polifemo—in *Fábula de Polifemo y Galatea* (1613)—is symbolically as much a pariah as the homeless and demented represented in Eltit's work. The baroque provided a break with Greco-Latin tradition, a trait that Eltit certainly manifests in both narrative content and the style of its inscription.

Mental illness and vagrancy—although not essentially associated—beset the protagonist of [*My Father*] and many of the patients of Putaendo before their institutionalization. A vagrant scarcely has use for verbal communication, detached as s/he is from the community's social, cultural, and economic orders (much like a stone sculpture, present and visible but not interacting with its surroundings). Eltit observes that language often seems lost to a homeless individual, utterances are reduced to sounds and isolated words.[29] In a study of homelessness, one man explains the lack of communication with others in this way:

> People become self-absorbed in their own minds when they're homeless. . . . I call it "mental inwardness" . . . If you don't have decent clothing, or you're dirty and have no money, you're looked down upon. People turn their heads. . . . So you don't fit in. Society rejects you, doesn't care for you, and you begin to lose hope. When that happens you just sit alone, thinking about your problems. Dejected. And with no human contact you just totally block everything out. The outer world gets canceled out.[30]

In [*Soul's Infarct*], Eltit narrates her impression of one patient, Juana la loca, who may not be insane, but who, as a child, arrived at the hospital with her ill father and remained after his death. Consequently, she has no possibility of functioning in the outside world. "Perhaps she and her father together turned mad from homelessness," comments Eltit.[31]

As noted previously, Eltit noticed that the subject of [*My Father*] would begin his litany as soon as she approached his area. In effect, involuntarily Eltit became his witness; having a listener prompted him to verbalize his "mental inwardness" to the extent that he then rarely stopped talking. Although his monologue was not altogether coherent, he was not only expressing an inner world normally inaccessible to others, but also showed the need to share it with the Other, in this case Eltit.

Reaching out to the other is precisely the theme of [*Soul's Infarct*]. The text that Eltit provides to accompany the photographs emphasizes the patients' urge to engage the other as love object, conceivably to help cope with the traumas associated with abandonment, forced sterilization, indigence, illness, and internment. Through Errázuriz's portraits and Eltit's text we become witnesses to the residents' ability to communicate and form intimate bonds despite "mental inwardness" and other limitations.

Dori Laub identifies three levels of witnessing in relation to his work with Holocaust survivors that may be useful here considering My Father's traumatic experience as a victim of state oppression. The first level involves memories of a lived experience, being a witness oneself as survivor of an event.[32] On a second level, usually an interviewer is a witness "as the immediate receiver" of testimony; as sympathetic listener, the interviewer may or may not have had a similar experience as the one being recounted and/or recorded.[33] The third level entails both the narrator's and the interviewer's awareness of the process of witnessing itself; both are conscious of their respective roles as well as the reactions of the Other, and both share "the sense that there is a truth that we are both trying to reach."[34]

Although not apparent from a cursory reading, [*My Father*] includes the three levels of witnessing described by Laub because recording this account requires a relationship, silent perhaps yet viable, between the homeless man who gives witness of his lived trauma and Eltit as "immediate receiver" of his story. Furthermore, "truth" is an aspect of witnessing for both Eltit's informant who is interested in accusing those that have done him wrong and for his listener, desirous of having this Chilean, symbol of the dispossessed, voice his truth, albeit, if it is his "loca verdad" [demented truth] as termed by Jean-Michel Ribettes.[35] But how is a participatory relationship possible, the reader may ask, if the informant's discourse reveals that he is crazy?

Work with the mentally disturbed in her practice of psychiatry led Silla Consolli to conclude that analyzing their discourse—the semantic, narrative, stylistic, syntactic, and phonological aspects of speech—is insufficient because all speech-act links the speaker to the addressee; since the exchange does not take place in a void, it involves the participation of the listener, and thus the circumstances surrounding the interlocutors must also be taken into account when evaluating the actual production of speech.[36] According to Consolli, all speech-act involves a risk. "One never emerges untouched by a speech-act," she notes, "a word can, depending on the circumstances, render service, please or make time pass; can articulate a demand or a desire, advise or command. But it can also hurt, submit, unmask, ridicule and even drive mad. Moreover, one can feel secure, understood or misunderstood, recognized or unacknowledged, authenticated or invalidated. . . ."[37]

In [*My Father*] the protagonist assumes a risk when he relates his story to Eltit; his insistence on speaking and the topic of his account attest to his capacity to recognize the power of speech described above. What were the circumstances surrounding this exchange? On the most observable level the homeless man commands speech in order to tell his truth while Eltit listens and records his tale. But since I contend that [*My Father*] constitutes a plausible testimony, the informant (speaker) and Eltit (addressee) have established what Algirdas Julien Greimas terms a veridiction contract, a tacit agreement between sender and receiver.[38] Yet the participants' exchange involves a more subtle relationship.

First of all, according to Consolli's observations of patients, an account involves a trade: fondness for a story. Fondness provoked in the addressee is communicated—through a word, a gesture, or behavior—to the narrator who feels at ease to relate his account.[39] Secondly, the narrator's account entails a demand of the addressee's interest, a request for love, an enterprise of seduction, the hope of teaching the Other something that s/he does not already know.[40]

In this regard, Eltit's "words, gestures, or behavior" must have communicated her desire to listen and serve as depository of the vagrant's account. The mere proximity necessary to record him and the recorder itself conveys a solicitousness conducive to an exchange. Moreover, by later transcribing his discourse Eltit acted as instrument for the subject, albeit unknowingly, to author himself. The publication of his soliloquy is now public record and, symbolically, his words count (much the same as Errázuriz's photographs evidence the existence of those interned in Putaendo). Given the effort involved in any transcription, the informant fulfilled his request for love, his desire to interest his addressee, his quest to tell her something she did not know. Arguably a mutual seduction between speaker and addressee has taken place, but more so this homeless man seduced Eltit into a book project and the reader/critic into probing his account for meaning.

Much the same dynamics holds true between the patients of Putaendo's psychiatric hospital and Errázuriz—however, the exchange for fondness results in photographs instead of an oral account. In [*Soul's Infarct*], Eltit comments on the patients' emotional manifestation when she and Errázuriz, who had visited the asylum many times, enter the hospital grounds: "[T]he happiness that engulfs them disconcerts me when they shout: 'Aunt Paz. Aunt Paz is here.' Over and over as if they could not believe it and they kiss and embrace her more and more and they kiss and embrace me also, men and women before whom I must disguise the profound shock that the precariousness of their destiny provokes in me."[41] Akin to My Father's chatter as a plea for attention, one particular resident attaches herself to Eltit's waist and walks along with her murmuring "Mamita" [Mommy].

In the prologue to [*My Father*], Eltit observes that this man's destitution, madness, and inconceivable accusations seemed representative of Chilean society during the dictatorship (1973–89). "He is Chile, I thought. The whole of Chile in pieces in this man's illness; shreds of newspaper, fragments of extermination, syllables of death, commercial slogans, names of deceased. Here is a profound crisis of language, an infected memory. . . . It is a shame, I thought."[42]

Indeed My Father represents the entire country, both the persecuted and persecutor. Notably while Eltit uses the denomination to name the homeless man, he in turn uses "My Father" to name the powerful government official responsible for his ruin and the demise of many others like him. Hence, "My Father" also embodies the almighty dictator, General Pinochet, whose pivotal figure conjures the religious image of God previously discussed in *E. Luminata* with respect to patriarchal control. Borrowing Fredric Jameson's term, My Father can be interpreted as a "national allegory," a description really applicable to all of Eltit's books.[43]

Eltit notes her informant's "profound crisis of language," his "infected memory," and refers to "shreds," "fragments," "syllables" that call to mind Jean-François Lyotard's notion of "the differend," which was coined in connection with witnessing in the post-Holocaust era. Lyotard describes "the differend" as a state wherein "something 'asks' to be put into phrases, and suffers from the wrong of not being able to be put into phrases right away."[44] This difficulty with the tellability of a life experience, the crisis of language that Eltit identifies in the homeless man, hinders the expression of his truth. Precisely both informant and therefore the text that records his discourse suffer from "the differend," . . . "an unstable state and instant of language wherein something which must be able to be put into phrases cannot yet be."[45] Characterized "by what one ordinarily calls a feeling" and an inability to put it into words, this state also includes "silence, a negative phrase" that must be overcome if the possibility of witnessing is not to be smothered.[46] As such, are the recordings that Eltit transcribes to generate [*My Father*] valid as source of this compatriot's "testimonio"? Ultimately each reader negotiates the text for meaning, but in what follows, this reading argues that the informant's story contains enough "truth effect" to legitimize it among the order of Latin American "testimonio."

KEEPING COMPANY WITH THE (IN)SANE: (IN)CREDIBLE TESTIMONIO?

An individual's command of language along with the ability to remember undermines an authoritarian regime's quest to erase a nation's memory. In the next chapter we will see how memory acts as a powerful weapon of survival for the protagonist, Coya, as prisoner and as embodiment of the struggle of the indigenous peoples of Chile to safeguard their history. Notably, in My Father's case, his reality seems anchored in the memory of state oppression, a memory that may be truly his, fabricated or borrowed (from newspaper stories), but one that he recounts endlessly.

Laub's work with Holocaust survivors reveals that there are many cases of mental inwardness, that is, silence, or what Lyotard designates "negative phrases." These people have hardly spoken about their trauma, "but even those who have talked incessantly feel that they managed to say very little that was heard."[47] No doubt that My Father wants to be heard, through the one civilizing factor of language he manifests the desire to serve as living testimony of his ordeal.

Given Chile's decade-long dictatorship at the time of the first transcription (1983), this indigent and disturbed man embodied a living metaphor for the homeland in that his mental illness symbolically depicts several aspects of Chilean reality in the aftermath of the coup d'etat of 1973. Madness, for example, seemed palpable in the severity of the reprisals unleashed against political adversaries. Furthermore, the informant's indictment of government officials and his testimony of surviving persecution, even death, must have reminded readers of their years under military rule, especially since his testimony contrasted with the public image General Pinochet attempted to portray from the outset of his government. As wards of the state, the patients in Putaendo, too, metaphorically elicit memory of forced incarceration by a military regime that stripped detainees of all rights and through abusive practices catapulted many into madness.

In their analysis of the dictator's speeches pronounced during 1973–76, Giselle Munizaga and Carlos Ochsenius have summarized the characteristics Pinochet transmitted to Chileans about his government, one that was supposedly for law-abiding citizens, impartial, strong, righteous, conscious of its duties. Pinochet portrayed a regime that had nationalistic objectives, a spirit of public service, practiced just authority, worked for the moral recuperation of the country, and considered hard, honest work the only effective means for progress and as the source of human dignity.[48] The dictator's discourse further claimed that unlike the previous (Allende) government, his administration was not Marxist, self-worshiping, tyrannical, totalitarian, corrupt, or self-centered, and it was not one to abandon its duties to its citizens, nor did it harbor immoral intentions or murderous ideas.

Some of these distinctions, however, were realities that many Chileans were subjected to under military rule and that, moreover, are in tune with the homeless man's description of his maddening experience with government authorities. Indeed, as Eltit proposes, this informant embodies a metaphor for a homeland where today mental disorders are common even among the rank and file of the armed forces. And of course, one can learn of the kinds of psychological trauma suffered by civilian survivors of detention and their families from autobiographical writings of Chileans like Luz Arce, who relates her ordeal in *El infierno* [*The Inferno*].[49]

Madness, more than a stigmatizing label stamped on citizens, became a combat weapon for Latin American state officials anxious to elude explaining human rights violations committed by paramilitary units. We need only recall that in the 1970s the mothers of Plaza de Mayo in Argentina were branded madwomen for accusing the government of making people disappear. Unlike the "collapse of witnessing" which Laub attributes to the silence surrounding the Holocaust while it occurred,[50] Latin America produced both inside witnesses who had been victimized themselves and outside witnesses, which included family, neighbors, colleagues, passersby, and even prison guards.

Hernán Valdés's book *Tejas Verdes: Diario de un campo de concentración en Chile* [*Green Tiles: Diary of a Concentration Camp*] (1974), published a year after the military coup, and *The Little School: Tales of Disappearance & Survival in Argentina* (1986) by Alicia Partnoy are examples of inside witnesses who write about their personal experience of surviving detention. Acting as outside witness, in her novel *Conversación al sur* (1981) / *Mothers and Shadows* (1986) Argentine author Marta Traba portrays the invisibility of the mothers who rallied weekly to induce the regime to release information on the missing. In the novel, street and pedestrian traffic avoid the plaza altogether during the protest, and businesses in the immediate area close their

doors. The official stamp of "insanity" renders the protestors virtually silent as well as invisible since they literally are deprived of eye-
witnesses.

Judging the vagrant of [*My Father*] as a madman would also turn
him invisible even though he lives outdoors in sight of the community. Notably, photography books like [*Soul's Infarct*] and Diane Arbus's *Untitled* make public figures out of those typically kept out of
society's gaze.

Traba and Eltit inscribe a state where individuals—whether fictional or real—are discarded as rambling lunatics for voicing government wrongdoing. Much like the homeless souls whose plight
many passersby see but none succor, the sight of individuals detained in broad daylight by paramilitary personnel conjure up feelings of sympathy in onlookers as well as relief that they themselves
are not the victims of such terrible misfortune. Whether a homeless
person or a detainee, both are exposed to society's gaze and public
opinion. The homeless protagonist of [*My Father*] conjures a metaphor that extends beyond Chilean borders, not only because he is
persecuted, but also because he is destitute. Let us keep in mind
Eltit's voiced concern that poverty afflicts a majority of the population of developing countries.

Today's shelters in the United States associated with the homeless
are reminiscent of the soup kitchens of the Great Depression and
its devastating economic crisis. However, in Latin America the soup
kitchen ("la olla común" [literally, community pot])[51]—overwhelmingly run by women—brings to mind periods of political repression
that left numerous households without male breadwinners. The
homeless man of [*My Father*] does capture a slice of Latin American
life; and his image, featured on the book jacket as proof of his existence, triggers an association with the "testimonio."

The 1980s saw the surge of publications of testimonial-like accounts or "testimonios"—as designated in Spanish[52]—as well as critical studies on this type of literary production. "By 'testimonio' I
mean a novel or novella-length narrative in book or pamphlet (that
is, printed as opposed to acoustic) form," specifies John Beverley;
moreover, it is "told in the first person by a narrator who is also the
real protagonist or witness of the events he or she recounts, and
whose unit of narration is usually a 'life' or significant life experience."[53] Also, "[t]he situation of narration in *testimonio* has to involve an urgency to communicate, a problem of repression, poverty,
subalternity, imprisonment, struggle for survival, implicated in the
act of narration itself."[54]

In light of Beverley's definition, let us consider to what extent [*My*

Father] fulfills these and other characteristics of "testimonio" as proposed by critics of the genre. The intention here is not to theorize about "testimonio" (nor question if it is a genre) but rather to postulate the inclusion of Eltit's text in this literary category. Of course, the premise here is that the informant's account musters enough "truth effect" to render the story credible to the reader, for "Unlike the novel, 'testimonio' promises by definition to be primarily concerned with sincerity rather than literariness."[55] As a noteworthy point (although not evidence of "truth"), the informant of [*My Father*] maintains the same story in the three consecutive years of Eltit's recordings.

No doubt that My Father's novella-length story, told in a first-person narrative, deals with a significant personal life experience which involves an urgency; past persecution, present dire poverty, and mental instability attest to it. As to sincerity (what George Yúdice calls "authentic narrative"), the informant repeatedly assures his interlocutor that what he is saying is true, that it happened as he describes. This aspect of the informant's plea is in keeping with Yúdice's observation that in testimonio "[t]ruth is summoned in the cause of denouncing a present situation of exploitation and oppression or in exorcising and setting aright official history."[56]

Another important aspect of "testimonio" is that the very word "translates literally as 'testimony,' as in the act of testifying or bearing witness in a legal or religious sense."[57] In [*My Father*] the informant intends to bear legal testimony of his ordeal. In fact, the discourse itself hinges on his indictment of Chilean government officials. The vagrant's discourse clearly seeks to secure media coverage in order to testify publicly and disseminate his accusations. Albeit the mental illness that distorts the informant's reality, such a campaign plan contains, in Greimas' words, "marks of veridiction" since it suggests a certain degree of lucidity.[58]

Let us keep in mind, however, that distortion per se should not disqualify [*My Father*] as a "testimonio" since following Elzbieta Sklodowska's lead, scrutiny of *The Autobiography of a Runaway Slave*—a book based on the failing memory and jumbled discourse of a 105-year-old former Cuban slave and that ushered the way for Cuba's Casas de las Américas Contest to establish a prize category in "testimonio" as genre—reveals that the editor himself complains about the "incoherence of his interlocutor's story."[59] "If I had transcribed his story word for word," comments Miguel Barnet, "it would have been confusing and repetitive."[60] He further admits that "in many cases my informant was unable to remember precisely. . . . Esteban's life in the forest is a remote and confused period in his memory."[61] The final text's extensive paraphrasing, reordering, and intervention by the supposedly nonobtrusive and self-effacing Barnet led Sklodowska to observe the "palimpsest-like structure" of *Autobiography* and mediated testimonial writing in general.

Ultimately, the Latin American "testimonio" hinges on "truth." This important aspect became a point of contention in the case of the Guatemalan indigenous human rights activist and 1992 Nobel Prize laureate, Rigoberta Menchú, accused of distorting or outright lying about the account of the deaths of family members and key details of her life presented in the "testimonio," *Me llamo Rigoberta Menchú y así me nació la conciencia* (1983)/*I, Rigoberta Menchú: An Indian Woman in Guatemala* (1984). "Nobel Winner Accused of Stretching Truth," read a *New York Times* headline.[62] While Ms. Menchú has suggested that Venezuelan anthropologist Elisabeth Burgos-Debray is the person responsible for any problems with the text, Ms. Burgos-Debray claims "every phrase in the book comes from what Rigoberta Menchú said on the tapes."[63] Hence, getting to the "truth" can be a problematic matter in "testimonios."

In attributing the "testimonio" label to [*My Father*] the reader should then consider the state of memory, oral ramblings, distortions, and even lies of informants like Esteban Montejo and Rigoberta Menchú, as well as the amount of intervention by the interviewer, compiler, transcriber, and/or editor of the text. Certainly the question of "authorship" can be controversial since the first stage of bearing witness in a "testimonio" generally involves a recording of the subject's story by a professional (often a social scientist, journalist, or writer) for later transcription because in many cases the informant lacks the skills to write the personal account.[64]

Gaby Brimmer, compiled by Mexican journalist and novelist Elena Poniatowska, is one example where the informant lacks the physical ability rather than the intellectual skill to write her own account. Although mentally sharp and educated, the cerebral palsy Gaby Brimmer suffered at birth caused severe paralysis. With her left foot—the only body part she could control—and the use of an electric typewriter, Brimmer managed to communicate with others and compose poetry. Obviously, the extremely disabling nature of the condition rendered the subject physically silent and socially marginalized. For Brimmer oppression is rooted in a physical handicap.

A connection can be drawn between the subjects of [*My Father*] and *Gaby Brimmer*, for both are first judged—reader included—from the perspective of an able-bodied/minded world. For the observer, appearances are deceiving. Brimmer, confined to a wheelchair, is trapped in a convulsive but otherwise paralyzed body that looks mentally retarded but conceals a highly intelligent being. Likewise, the homelessness and jabbering of Eltit's informant suggest lack of reason. Yet within the scope of his distorted reality, this man actually tells a story.

As informants, both My Father and Gaby Brimmer also fall within the marginalized sector which in Latin America often serves as witness in "testimonios." It is not uncommon that the criminal, the insane, the native, the poor, or the oppressed are among those who may offer insiders' accounts and thus become the "autobiolocutors"—to use Rosemary Geisdorfer Feal's term—of their own stories.[65] As is also common with "testimonios," the professional compiler's credentials—in this case a novelist—lend credibility to the account given the informants' precarious civic position.

The basic features of "testimonios" shift when the informant's position in society is neither precarious nor in need of another's validating credentials. In Chile, for example, the advent of prosecuting military officials accused of crimes against civilians during the dictatorship has altered a principal characteristic (that of informant marginality) associated with "testimonios." The officers who related their testimony to journalist/writer Patricia Verdugo in *Caso Arellano: Los zarpagos del Puma* [*The Arellano Case: The Puma Lashes Out*] (1989) do not belong to a marginalized sector, but rather to Chile's powerful military. One of its power elite, Gen. Carlos Prats González, former commander in chief of the army under Presidents Eduardo Frei and his successor, Salvador Allende, wrote *Memorias: Testimonio de un soldado* [*Memoir: A Soldier's Testimony*] (1985), a book published posthumously by his daughters.[66]

Among the stories of civilian survivors of political persecution, Mili Rodríguez Villouta also records in *Ya nunca me verás como me vieras: Doce testimonios vivos del exilio* [*You'll Never See Me the Same Again: Twelve Live Testimonies of Exile*] the account of ex-commander Efraín Jaña who was forced into exile after being charged with treason by the military. Not only the issue of marginality but also that of legitimacy becomes apparent for readers especially in such a book that includes the voices of both civilian and military constituencies. Where a compiler records the testimony of ranking officials— whether active or dismissed—the professional's task shifts from inscribing the stories of the voiceless—as in conventional "testimonios"—to presenting the perspective of authorities or those once in authority. Paradoxically, the literary mode typically representing the victims of persecution can also promote the adversary's account. Although the "testimonio" has prevailed in Latin America as the vehicle of voicing oppression, this does not mean that "testimonio" is defined by the "victim."[67]

In a "testimonio" the production process—including identification of the subject, the recording, transcribing, and editing—generally forms part of the book's preface. Eltit's introductory statement conforms to this aspect of a "testimonio." The degree and type of editing that the professional executes has become a controversial matter within the genre.[68] This issue, however, does not affect [My Father] since Eltit maintains that the text at hand is the verbatim transcription of three separate recordings. In other words, since the text is not mediated, Eltit has avoided editorial intervention, the kind of complete self-effacement that Miguel Barnet was not able to accomplish in Autobiography of a Runaway Slave. With nonmediation too, Eltit leaves the risk of arbitrary interpretations to the reader/critic and with it avoids the moral and ideological pitfalls that many an editor/author has inadvertently ventured into.[69] Moreover, Eltit cannot be accused of ideological opportunism or commercial aggrandizement from the misfortunes of the oppressed since the book had a very limited run; she did not expect it to sell well (which it did not) and the scarce attention it received from a handful of critics was to be expected from the Chilean literary mainstream.

But [My Father] does not steer entirely clear of the testimonial controversy. Sklodowska raises the issue of protean critical opinions when it comes to the degree of "literariness" required to entitle or disqualify a book as a "testimonio." Some critics complain that in the desire to consecrate the "testimonio" as exemplary genre of a genuine and revolutionary Latin American literature, many books with hardly aesthetic value have been given the label; on the other hand, one critic goes so far as to list the shortcomings that constitute lack of "literariness," thus endangering a book's claim to the "testimonio" label.[70] Apropos, Eltit commits several of the sins listed such as transcribing the recordings verbatim, not organizing the information into a coherent structure, and ordering the book according to each interview as it was recorded. In other words, for that particular critic Eltit's lack of intervention engenders lack of literariness, a total disregard for poetics for which [My Father] would fail this particular testimonial litmus test.[71]

Art, however, was not what Eltit had in mind when transcribing the vagrant's account, but a slice of life at margin's edge. In any case, "in an age of the blurring of the canon," Sklodowska warns, "a demarcation based on aesthetic criteria is, for certain, problematic."[72] In the same vein, Greimas comments that "the concept of literariness often appears to be just a useful label attached to a ragbag full of troublesome questions."[73] I agree, especially given the circumstances of the informant in [*My Father*], that lack of "literariness" should not weigh solely in contesting whether it is a "testimonio."

Continuing on the topic of controversy in "testimonios," the fact that Eltit's name appears on the cover of [*My Father*] as well as on the title page featuring "Francisco Zegers, editor" raises the question of authorship. To what extent is Eltit author of this book whose every word is that of the informant? Yet without Eltit's recording and transcription, the subject's discourse would have been lost forever and the text would not exist. In an introductory note to the book Eltit mentions the inclusions of pictures by Lotty Rosenfeld, which do not appear in the book. When asked, Eltit explains that the remark was inadvertently left in the text after the editorial decision was made to exclude the pictures. Thus the reader experiences Francisco Zegers's authority with respect to the book's lack of visual component originally intended by Eltit. Each of the three chapters ends with ellipsis, indicating a continuation in the original discourse that is not reproduced in the text. Who determined what would not be transcribed? Consequently, [*My Father*] also shares in a controversial aspect of "testimonio."

Geisdorfer Feal proposes the term "ethnobiography" to describe texts where an individual provides an oral biography while an ethnographer writes the particulars of that self-representation. A trained professional's reliance on the subject as direct source of this type of nonfiction work does not, however, preclude questionable issues. "If we suspect autobiographers of exaggeration or distortion," points out Geisdorfer Feal, "why should we accord higher credence to the second party who writes of another's life?"[74] The point here is that in an ethnographic or testimonial-type text, distortions are admittedly committed by both parties (informant and compiler). If such is the case in the dealings of supposedly lucid individuals, then how weighty or disqualifying are distortions to the credibility of a mentally ill individual? This is an important question because, traditionally, a key characteristic of a "testimonio" is the existence of a direct and reliable informant.

But the issue of reliability can be controversial. For instance, let us consider the case of military officials who have gone public with their testimony about national incidents while still serving a dictatorial regime. Is it not probable that the "testimonios" of those bound in allegiance to the armed forces contain "distorted truth?" What is the difference between distortions produced by the mental disorder of Eltit's informant and those of a survivor of torture or of military

personnel with a grievance to air or a secret to hide? Should testimonios be admitted or dismissed based on the informant's mental
state? Hardly, since testimonios overwhelmingly feature persecuted
individuals who have experienced traumatic incidents and therefore
are to a greater or lesser degree "disturbed."

Laub's work with Holocaust survivors attests to the varying degrees
of traumas. Some have internalized victimization as their fault or
they are disturbed in the sense that they have assumed responsibility
for the atrocities they witnessed;[75] others who have kept silent for
decades have become victims of a distorted memory and suffer from
delusions which invade their daily existence. For some, memory, especially for those survivors "not telling," has become so distorted
that they themselves question the reality of the actual events.[76] When
such individuals begin to give testimony, is it discarded as the discourse of "disturbed" individuals? Certainly not.

In [The Inferno], Luz Arce, a detainee turned informant for
D.I.N.A., writes about her borderline insanity during periods of intense depression. Oftentimes torturers aim to debilitate the victim's
psychic and physical being in order to achieve compliance. However, as Arce recounts, if the torturer goes too far, insanity or death
may result. Referring to the case of Arce and Marcia Alejandra Merino, another political dissident who writes Mi verdad: más allá del
horror, yo acuso [My Truth: Beyond the Horror, I acuse] to recount how
she turns informant for the military, Eltit asks: "How are we to deal
with discourse provoked under those conditions [of torture]?"[77]

Given the circumstances surrounding the stories of Arce and Merino, Eltit posits that "autobiography cannot be read literally as the
truth. Instead, it should be taken as the theatricalization of the ego,
as a biographical mise-en-scène where the 'I' activated in the text is,
ultimately, a fiction."[78] Furthermore, she observes: "Torture, a fas-
cist tool of power, the body, a limited space, confession, a theater
where truth and lies, life and death confront each other: these elements forced me into a reading I would define as exploded or
smashed. How could anyone emerge unscathed from the memory
of abuses of such proportions?"[79]

My Father's account, therefore, should not be discarded based on
his mental illness since the "testimonios" of others—like Arce, Merino, and ousted military personnel—who experienced persecution
are prone to as much distortion. Ultimately, each reader of testimonios must negotiate the text for "truth effect" since credibility is
subjective. Therefore, borrowing Sklodowska's phrase, the reader
must be willing to approach [My Father] with "testimonio-seeing
eyes."[80]

Perhaps the uppermost reason for procuring a credible informant in "testimonios" is linked to the individual's role as a representative of others with similar life experience. "Testimonio represents an affirmation of the individual subject," points out Beverley, "but in connection with a group or class situation marked by marginalization, oppression, and struggle."[81] Clearly, in Eltit's text the informant's "I" predominates since his focus is on individual circumstances. His account, however, is "not just a personal story"[82] because as distinct from autobiography the informant also manifests concern for other public servant who, like him, will be targeted for extermination.[83] Making public his individual adversities is a way of seeking personal exoneration and serves to warn others in the hope of preventing further injustice.

A key question that arises then is how to validate this informant's testimony given the obvious signs of mental illness, a condition that may be precisely what facilitated the protagonist/informant to speak out uncensored since only a madman would dare to speak his mind about a dictatorial state. In order to rank the text as a "testimonio," the task of the reader/critic calls for legitimizing the speech of a subject whose mental condition and fragmented discourse threaten to invalidate his story. The incipient concerns are: (1) making sense of the subject's chatter and (2) validating the subject as a credible informant. To tackle the endeavor, reader response theory can provide one avenue for approaching a book that offers multiple meanings. Along with nonsense the transcription contains enough "truth effect" and "truthsaying" indicators to tempt the reader to pursue a credible tale, an "authentic narrative."[84]

In any event, the informant perceives himself as giving "testimonio," or testifies to the ordeal leading to his becoming homeless and disturbed. From all appearances the traumatic ordeal caused the mental illness that interferes with his recounting. Too often homelessness is equated with mental illness when in fact, as noted earlier, destitute individuals have pointed out that living in utter indigence is what drives one insane.[85] By attributing the protagonist's mental state to social rather than biological factors (as psychiatry generally views insanity), a reader can overcome the temptation of discarding My Father's soliloquy as nonsense.[86] There is no doubt, however, that in regard to this text the individual reader's sensibilities play a key role in interpretation.

Questioning whether the text involves a "testimonio" is colored by the fact that Eltit has revealed the subject's true-life situation. For example, given Eltit's postmodern literary antecedents, had the text been presented as a work of fiction, most readers would have assumed the protagonist's discourse was the author's deliberate technique, and therefore the question of legitimacy would never arise. However, Eltit presents him as a schizophrenic, and the reader's natural reaction is to consider the informant's validity. As Sklodowska points out, the recounting of truth and the depiction of reality constitute key factors in testimonial literature, but it all comes down to the reader's perception of the informant.[87] In regard to [My Father], the opinion the reader forms of the subject (as a legitimate informant) ultimately determines whether the individual confers the "testimonio" label on this text. But let us also take into account Sklodowska's warning about the elusiveness of the "testimonio" as genre, one in which the reader must often contend with its interplay between fact and fiction, between truth and falsity, history and fiction, science and literature.[88]

What follows illustrates my steps in validating [My Father] as "testimonio," albeit the testimony of a disturbed man whose reality is certainly no less real to him and probably not much more distorted than accounts made by other persecuted Chileans.

A READER'S PERSPECTIVE: "FILLING IN THE GAPS" TO DECIPHER (NON)SENSE

The reader of [My Father] will quickly determine that interpreting the text is difficult because the speaker excludes as much information as he includes. To some extent this occurs because in the informant's disturbed mind he speaks to an interlocutor who is in a more knowledgeable position than the reader. Therefore, making sense of the text forces the reader to actively participate in piecing together information that produces meaning.

Reader-oriented theorist Wolfgang Iser points to "the gaps left by the text itself" that the reader must fill in.[89] Considering the source of [My Father], "filling in" the interstices of the subject's discourse is an essential exercise in understanding the text. How differently this is done by readers depends on the premises with which they launch a critique of the book. By way of example, Ivette Malverde Disselkoen approaches the book as the discourse of a schizophrenic whose rambling represent the imaginings of a disturbed mind.[90] This perspective produces an interpretation quite different than the reading proposed here.

Despite—or because of—My Father's obsessive babble, the reader will detect certain recurrent statements. Scrutiny of the text reveals, in fact, that basic information remains unchanged in the individual recordings Eltit conducted in a three-year period (1983–85). The redundancy in speech points to a particular life experience that has literally caused the clock to stop for this man. His mind is trapped in episodes that he mulls over constantly; reality is reduced to certain incidents. Paradoxically, the annoying repetitions that the reader is tempted to skim ultimately contribute to the story's truth factor because redundancy is an inherent element of oral narrative.[91] Although lack of connection between the informant's inner mental reality and his outer physical world suggests insanity, his discourse does give evidence of his acute awareness of his situation. Moreover, his accuracy regarding personal names and locations in Santiago also afford the subject another margin of credibility.

Arguably, from a Freudian perspective the mind often represses traumatic experience, but in My Father's case the high frequency of certain information suggests that his memory retains what is most significant to his story. In an attempt to gain some manageability over the chaotic soliloquy, I organized the information that appeared most often according to broad topics. For example, the following issues recur in the informant's speech: government corruption, criminal activity, aliases, persecution, testimony of victimization, and a preoccupation with personal vindication. However, although the protagonist's assertions are many, the explicit links are few.

Once the jumbled declarations of the disturbed informant are sorted, how can the reader construct (or extract) a viable story? The shady nature of the disclosures which compose the account steers the reader into an investigative role. From the broad topics noted above one can determine that crime is the core element of the subject's story, its matrix.

Reducing the themes of discourse even further by merging them into manageable categories produces an ordering principle. I then classified the initial groupings under three rubrics (identity, scheme, and motive) which proved more practical in reconstructing the informant's story. The basic question that can be formulated from the three categories (identity, scheme, and motive) is **who** does **what** and **why**? This question will serve here as the ordering principle for navigating My Father's garbled testimony.

Identity: Who *does what and why?*

The primary identity issue that the reader must contend with is the appellation "el Padre Mío"/My Father, which designates both the protagonist and the antagonist. Significantly, this is also the title of the text whose underlying question Who is My Father? remains unanswered for the reader. In the introduction Eltit refers to the demented subject as My Father, however in the text itself the protagonist never mentions his own name even though he does identify himself with the Badilla-Padilla Figueroa family (44, 47, 57–58). For the most part his soliloquy concentrates on repeatedly accusing someone with the alias "My Father" of perpetrating his downfall.

In the context of the oppressive climate that prevailed in Chile during the military regime (1973–89), this confluence of identity—victim and victimizer—as well as the many aliases appearing in the book suggest that no one really knew who was who. The Chilean military claimed that they were fighting a war against dangerous armed communists. Dissidents claimed that no such armed struggle existed, only peaceful groups seeking economic and social reform. As far as Eltit identifies the homeless man as symbol for the homeland, he embodies the fabrications and distortions (including the aliases used in military operations as well as in the civilian underground) that each side conferred on the other.

Luz Arce, the detainee turned D.I.N.A. agent, belongs to both groups. Her double identity presents a point of contention for readers of [The Inferno]. According to her account, the only way to put an end to routine victimization at the hands of military police was to provide them with the names of comrades. Naming meant subjecting others to the same brutal repression she experienced, but from her perspective, bargaining for her life left no option other than to cooperate with the authorities. The realization that she had turned into an indirect vehicle for torturing others produced great inner conflict and psychological trauma in Arce, more painful, she claims, than the physical torment she had endured. But because Arce did not end up physically destitute, a reader is less likely to ponder the "truth" of her story or her confession of feeling insane.

Even before the dictatorship, Chile as a nation had been hurled into a state of turmoil that is symbolically represented in the disjointed soliloquy of the disturbed, homeless citizen. As noted in chapter 1, and as we will discuss in the next chapter on Por la patria [For the Homeland], Eltit's first two novels were characterized by fragmented syntax, neologisms, and experimental forms, which earned her the reputation of "not making sense." With the publication of [My Father], Eltit presented a true-to-life yet anonymous citizen whose discourse reflected the national crisis she had been rendering through the language of her fiction.

The first clues of identity in [My Father] are presented in the introduction Eltit prepares for the book. Emphasis is made on this homeless man's ability to meet basic bodily needs despite his constant state of delirium which divested him of everything, including his own name. Eltit also points to the subject's insistence on giving testimony even though his discourse lacks explicit biographical information. Similar to the introduction of Arce's [*The Inferno*], before reading Eltit's transcription of the soliloquy the reader deduces the relationship between surviving and talking.

Laub identifies in Holocaust survivors a common imperative to recount their experience that reminds the reader of My Father's accusatory and untiring harangue. "This imperative to tell and to be heard," notes Laub, "can become itself an all consuming like task. Yet no amount of telling seems ever to do justice to this inner compulsion."[92] The reader may judge Eltit's informant insane, but the fact remains that his discourse reveals a traumatic experience which has made him a "mad," that is, a very "angry," survivor, one who suggests: "debería servir de testimonio yo" (57) [I should serve as witness].

My Father's own discourse does provide some clues as to his identity. A key issue is his political partisanship. "[Y]o le di parte del sufragio al señor Allende por el Partido Socialista y Comunista" (41) [I gave part of the vote to Mr. Allende for the Socialist-Communist Party]. "[Y]o sí que soy comunista y socialista, claro que lo soy . . ." (46) [I'm a real communist and socialist, of course I am . . .]. Significantly, he also ranks himself among the "privileged," those who enjoy "preferences and guaranties" (25–26). He also reveals that the powerful "My Father" once lived with him, even though at the time the informant was unaware of his ties with the Chilean administration (25).[93] The informant also takes pride in owning or having access to a car before his misfortune: "Porque yo vengo en auto en esa fecha" (46–47) [Because at that time I got around in a car].

Based on his self-representation it appears that the informant was a public servant with either some clout or at least with access to an influential political circle. In fact, his discourse emphasizes a setup—some twenty years prior—linked to his knowledge of transactions of corrupt government officials. But his status had its drawbacks, for he was a man with a cash value on his life: "A mí me corre una póliza de seguro de vida de los hombres de privilegio y de preferencia, y a mis familiares también" (26) [I was covered by life insurance for privileged and preferential men, as was my family]. As Malverde Disselkoen observes, "it is precisely his superiority which has caused his marginalization."[94]

Given that Eltit's recordings took place in 1983, 1984, and 1985, the subject's downfall, some twenty years earlier, occurred between

1963–65, a decade before the start of Pinochet's dictatorship. Furthermore, he repeatedly admits to learning of the corruption when he was thirty-one years old, which means he is in his fifties at the time of Eltit's transcription. The subject's insistence that he never served as an accomplice to "My Father" is an important aspect of his identity. Significantly, despite the twenty years that have lapsed, and his absolute indigence, this man's obsession is to tell his story in order to clear his name.

Keeping silent or repressing a traumatic experience for long periods of time is not uncommon among survivors since, as Shoshana Felman notes in referring to Albert Camus's insight, "consciousness is always lagging behind reality."[95] Where has the homeless man been for twenty years? At least for a while the informant was taken out of the psychiatric hospital and was put to work: "[D]espués que salí de ahí, donde estuve dos años recluido para silenciarme, . . . El Pisa-Huevo que había en la Quinta Bella . . . me llevó a la propiedad de don Omar, que tiene una industria cerca de Pedro Donoso, me estuve ganando ocho, quince, dieciséis millones de pesos cuando salí de ahí" (49–50) [After I left there, where I was confined to shut me up, . . . The Bastard at Quinta Bella . . . took me to Mr. Omar's property that has a business near Pedro Donoso, where I was making eight, fifteen, sixteen million pesos when I left]. But his discourse suggests that the release was not permanent then.

He also remarks on his escapes from death: "me volví a escapar, una vez más, de la mortandad" (56) [I escaped again, one more time, from death]; "Yo volví a escapar de la mortandad dictada por el hombre" (60) [I escaped again from a death orchestrated by man]. Was it after regaining freedom that he began to talk or did he keep silent for years? Precisely because such questions go unanswered in a text dedicated to witnessing injustice, "The 'literature of testimony' is thus not an art of leisure but an art of urgency"; giving testimony jars memory and serves to "bring the 'backwardness' of consciousness to the level of precipitant events."[96]

By the time Eltit published this book in 1989 the case of this vagrant served to remind Chileans of current events in the homeland.[97] The persecution, madness, and destitution suffered by this one citizen implicitly aimed to jolt a nation's consciousness as to the consequences of dictatorship, a reality that had continued all around them for sixteen years.

Previously, we had alluded to the connection between surviving and talking. Especially in the case of political dissidents, survival during confinement may depend on "not talking" because very often after providing the information sought by authorities, prisoners become dispensable to the interrogator/torturer. Also, refusal to talk and name may spare others a similar fate. However, in the event of release—as is the case with Luz Arce and Marcia Alejandra Merino— talking about the experience may serve as an act of defiance and a survival mechanism. Paradoxically, for these women, talking about the close encounter with death reinforces the victim's survival; telling becomes a way of reminding themselves that they made it out alive.

In [*My Father*] the protagonist's homelessness and madness (the result of persecution and institutionalization) separate him from ordinary life. Language, his only precarious link to the past and present, provides My Father with the means to denounce and thus participate to some extent in society. Talking about his ordeal is as essential to his survival as meeting other subsistence needs. Moreover, since the informant is aware that he is blowing the whistle, his discourse constitutes a retaliatory act or at the very least "speaking bitterness,"[98] but bitter "truth," he insists.

Here let us consider that the difference between a transcription of a demented "individual" and a demented "informant" lies in establishing the person's intent to testify—"debería servir de testimonio yo" (57) [I should serve as witness]—and the reader's perceived credibility of the informant. Aware that in order to get help he must first be believed, the vagrant insists throughout the account that he is telling the truth: "Lo que le estoy conversando no es mentira" (27) [What I'm saying is not a lie]; "le converso todas estas cosas, porque son así" (42) [I say all these things because that's how they are]; "fíjense que yo les estoy hablando la verdad" (59) [look, I'm telling you the truth]; "Más franco no puedo hablarle" (65) [I can't speak to you more honestly].

Felman's point that "the term madness is borrowed from the language of others, in which it implies a judgment, a condemnation" plays a part in the opinion a reader forms of the informant.[99] For Malverde Disselkoen the subject is a schizophrenic who verbalizes his delirium. I argue here that he does more than simply talk, the text reveals an informant who articulates his purpose for speaking.

Before judging or condemning the homeless man as insane, the reader should consider signs that this man is somehow in touch with reality. In fact, there are several instances in the account that suggest that the subject is clearheaded about the changes he has undergone. The first transcription (1983), for example, indicates awareness of physical deterioration: "[A]hora estoy casi inutilizado yo" (24) [Now I'm almost useless]. This self-representation is again reiterated at the close of that account: "Antes de perder la firmeza de mi cuerpo, de una sola cachetada podía tumbar a un hombre yo, pero ya no soy el mismo . . ." (34) [Before losing my strength I could knock down a man with one blow, but I'm no longer the same guy . . .]. At one point he articulates looking forward to getting well (''cuando me reponga") [when I recuperate]), which again indicates awareness of his present state.

Body image thus filters through as an aspect of the informant's identity. While he suggests pride in his previous physical condition he also recognizes his present limitations. Thus as Felman observes, a madman can be a wise man because "Though outside of society, the narrator nonetheless considers himself 'in the know.' "[100] "Yo no soy ignorante" (65–66) [I'm not an idiot], remarks the vagrant. He also realizes the passage of time: "de esto que le estoy hablando han pasado unos cuantos años" (69) [I'm talking about things that go back some years]. In fact, it is an awareness of personal drawbacks that compels the informant to seek help in publicizing his ordeal. He is not blind about himself for he shows reason; he may manifest characteristics of madness, but after all, as Felman points out, reason and madness are inextricably linked for madness cannot occur where the phenomenon of thought is absent.[101]

In addressing his unidentified interlocutor(s)—most probably during Eltit's recording and Rosenfeld's videotaping[102]—the informant frequently switches between "usted" and "ustedes" (the singular and plural formal form of the "you" pronoun in Spanish). The following sequence illustrates this shift between one and more interlocutors: "[P]ero eso *ustedes* no lo saben. . . . Eso lo sé yo no más. . . . Lo que *le* estoy conversando no es mentira. . . . Así es que *ustedes* ya lo saben, por eso es que *les* doy esta explicación. . . . Me echaron la culpa a mí de lo que *le* estoy conversando" (emphasis mine, 25–31) [But you people don't know that. . . . Only I know that. . . . What I'm telling you is not a lie. . . . So now you people know, that's why I'm giving you this explanation. . . . They blamed me for what I'm telling you]. But just as he could be addressing Eltit and Rosenfeld or talking to imaginary interlocutors as a manifestation of his illness, the second person pronoun also draws you the reader(s) into the appeal for attention.[103] Although who it is exactly that he addresses remains unclear, this vagrant is aware that without complicity from others he cannot relate and remedy his situation.

The other important question of identity is masked by the alias of the official who the informant blames for his ruin. The principal perpetrator in the story is identified as "My Father," a mastermind at fraud and embezzlement. This influential bureaucrat supposedly controlled a circle of business partners, accomplices to his corruption. "El Padre Mío da las órdenes ilegales en el país" (23) ["My Father" gives the illegal orders in the country], assures the informant at the beginning of the account. In fact, his discourse becomes a one-man crusade to uncover a slew of illegal dealings and fraudulent identities within a very corrupt administration (most likely prior to Pinochet's regime since affiliation with the Communist Party then carried some recognition). Notably, the informant accuses many of being communist frauds, especially "My Father": "Ellos no son comunistas aquí, El Padre Mío es comunista con la cédula de identidad, pero lo hace por negocio (26). . . . el Padre Mío no es comunista, sino que es oportunista" (46) [They're not communists here, "My Father" is a card-carrying communist, but he does it for benefit. . . . "My Father" is not a communist, but an opportunist]. In contrast, let us recall his assurance of sincere partisanship: "Pero yo sí que soy comunista y socialista, claro que lo soy, y di el sufragio por él, por el señor Allende" (46) [But I'm a real communist/socialist, of course I am, and I voted for him, for Mr. Allende].

Time lapses into the next administration with frequent mention of Pinochet. Did his vocalness about his party affiliation play a part in his persecution? Chilean history tells us that it most probably did. Pinochet is not only named often, but is closely associated with "My Father." Are they one and the same? Did the vagrant read in discarded newspapers that Pinochet rules the country, thus confusing him with his powerful antagonist, a man who gives illegal orders in the administration, has occupied the ranks of the armed forces, and has usurped bank guarantees? Curiously, the informant insists on not knowing just how powerful "My Father" was in the administration, an assertion many Chileans could express about Pinochet before he took over the country.

Aliases abound in the story including easily recognizable names like Allende, Pinochet, Frei, Alessandri, and Perón (who the informant accurately associates with Argentina) as well as less known names that can be associated with senators and dignitaries (Luengo, Hiriarte, Hormazábal). Obviously, the use of aliases means that there was a need to hide individual identity. However, this type of knowledge also suggests that the informant must have been an insider in this network. As he states, "Yo soy uno de ellos" (67–68) [I'm one of them]. It makes sense that where stakes are high, falling in disfavor could mean silencing or extermination. In fact, the scheme against the informant included both.

Scheme: *Who does* **what** *and why?*

Principally, the informant discloses illegal activity, the nature of which eventually leads government officials to target for elimination those who know too much. Let us recall that crime is the matrix of [*My Father*]. The fragmented account reflects the broken man the informant has become. Aware of his downfall, the informant secretly voices his accusations to someone that he perceives as capable of helping him in his personal crusade for justice. Circumstances have prompted him to talk, to challenge, to accuse. However, the reader must keep in mind the paradox at hand. The informant is alone in a public place (a barren lot) and therefore there is neither a true confidant nor true confidentiality. Eltit becomes eavesdropper turned witness and through her transcriptions the reader appropriates this role as well.

What we learn from the first transcription is the overall scheme plotted by the informant's powerful antagonist and his cohorts. The following sequence of statements extracted from the 1983 recording presents a sketch of the informant's a tale and constitutes the crux of the two subsequent recordings as well:

El Padre Mío da las órdenes ilegales en el país. Hace muchos años que subsiste de ingresos bancarios ilegales, del dinero que le pertenece a la concesión del personal de la Administración. . . . [A] mí me planearon por asesinato y enfermo mental. . . . A mí me tienen planeado más de veinte años en esos asuntos. . . . [E]l Padre Mío vive de la usurpación permanentemente . . . Tiene hombres influyentes que le arreglan los papeles, los archivos que ocupan cargos en el Estado. Se deshizo de ellos ya que ninguna persona que vivió con él le conviene. . . . A mí me intentaron matar antes por él, cuando necesitó dinero él . . . [M]ataron a mis familiares. Se deshizo de ellos porque a él no le convenía. . . . A mí me corre una póliza de seguro de vida de los hombres de privilegio y de preferencia, y a mis familiares también. . . . A mí me quería tener en un recinto recluido para silenciarme, para que yo quedara silenciado en el personal de la Administración. . . . (23–28)

["My Father" gives the illegal orders in the country. For years he has lived from illegal bank deposits, from money that belongs to the Administration's personnel funds. . . . They set me up as an assassin and as mentally ill. . . . For twenty years I've been set up in connection with those matters. . . . "My Father" lives permanently from usurpations. . . . He has influential men that fix the paperwork, the records, they hold State positions. He got rid of them because it was not a good idea to have anyone around who had lived with him. . . . He tried to get me killed once before when he needed money. . . . My relatives were killed. He got rid of them because they were not desirable to have around. . . . I'm covered by a life insurance policy for privileged and preferential men, and my family is as well. . . . He wanted to have me confined to an institution in order to shut me up, so I would be silenced with respect to the Administration's personnel. . . .]

Despite the speaker's mental condition, the reader can extract meaning from his discourse. Supposedly, "My Father" and his associates regularly dealt in illegal banking transactions and insurance fraud. Since the informant seems well aware of the embezzlement and fraud, it makes sense that he and his family were targeted for their life insurance policy. "Se la cobró" [He cashed it in], says the informant, referring to "My Father" and the life insurance coverage (26).

In the last transcription (1985) he reiterates the link between "knowing" and the fate of his family: "[M]i familia . . . ahora no están en esta existencia, porque esta persona se deshizo de ellos. Porque toda persona que está relacionada con estos compromisos no conviene" (61) [My family . . . now doesn't exist because this person got rid of them. Because anyone connected to these dealings is undesirable]. The family becomes guilty by association; this automatically politicized enemy must be disposed of for security reasons. However, just as important, what the subject did not know about "My Father" also drastically affected their lives: "Yo vine a saberlo a la edad de treinta y un años que el Padre Mío ocupaba cargos en la Administración" (27) [At the age of thirty-one I found out that "My Father" held positions in the Administration]. We can glean from the following comments that "not knowing" was an important factor in the setup that cost the informant his sanity: "yo no lo sabía" (44) [I didn't know it]; "El Padre Mío me ocultó siempre esos asuntos" (46) [My Father always hid those matters from me]; "yo ignoraba quién era él" (49) [I didn't know who he was]; "Yo no lo supe" (55) [I didn't find out]; "Porque yo lo ignoraba" (59) [Because I wasn't aware of it]. The scheme against him had to be foolproof and well masterminded since the officials involved had to cover up illegal cashing of bank guarantees, counterfeit operations ("máquina para hacer billetes," 59, 63, 65, 66–67) [a machine to make money] and dealings involving "el medicamento" (24, 32, 44, 56, 61) [the medicine], possibly a drug-related venture.

The homeless man's story elicits sympathy because the gist of his tale is horrid enough to drive anyone crazy. As recorded in the first transcription, persecution takes the form of a frame-up and attempted murder. Another aspect of the ordeal included forced institutionalization. "[E]n el Hospital Siquiátrico estuve dos años para silenciarme, por lo que le estoy conversando. Allí fui llevado a la fuerza" (30) [In order to shut me up about what I'm telling you I was in the psychiatric hospital for two years. I was taken there against my will]. In the last recording there is more detail about this contrived scheme to eliminate him. "[F]ui planeado por asesinato y enfermo mental y depravado por el trago en la locución, en los periódicos, en la Comisaría, en el Juzgado . . ." (56) [I was accused of assassination and mental illness and alcohol depravity on the air, in the newspapers, at police headquarters, and in court], elaborates the informant. The conspiracy against him included serious charges (murder, insanity, and alcoholism) that were widely publicized to insure destroying both his reputation and sanity. There were other incidents of persecution although the order of events is unclear. "[Y]o fui atropellado y chocado en tres oportunidades, y escapé de morir triturado" (56) [I was run down and car-crashed on three occasions, and I escaped being crushed to death], the informant is also recorded as saying.

The text definitely contains a "scheme" directed against the informant, but the informant also reveals his own "scheme" or plot against the system that has destroyed him. "Yo puedo hacer mis diligencias" (61) [I can take the necessary steps], the informant remarks, "Pero me tienen que conseguir un locutor y un periodista para que el hecho se de a conocer" (58) [But you have to get ahold of an announcer and a journalist in order to get the word out]. Using the persecutor's strategy, the informant intends to use the media to air his grievance and denounce government corruption.

Here again we must make note of the informant's clearheadedness. Since he plans to serve as public witness, he realizes that a man's image affects his credibility. "¿Saben lo que me hace falta?" [Do you know what I need?] he comments to the illusory ally. "Una indumentaria en condiciones" (60) [Clothing in good condition]. Convinced that appropriate attire is essential for the success of his plot, he continues to insist on this detail: "[M]e hace falta buena indumentaria en condiciones, porque yo no puedo ir a despretigiar adonde tengo que asistir" (66) [I need clothing in good condition or I'll ruin my reputation where I need to go]. His prior statements about making a public appearance suggest that the plot consists of scandalously exposing top officials through a press conference. "Por eso le converso todas estas cosas, porque son así y está en ustedes que se reunan con numerosas personas para asistir yo" [That's why I'm telling you all these things, because that's how it is and it's in your power to get many people together and have me attend], the informant points out. Again, he reasons enough to recognize his powerlessness; it is in others' hands [está en ustedes] to help him get the word out.

In fact, his discourse indicates full awareness of his situation: "Yo llevo mi existencia en estas condiciones sabiendo lo que les estoy explicando yo" (69–70) [I exist in these conditions knowing full well what I'm explaining to you]. This man realizes the madness of attempting to act on his own, he is as impotent as his body; he lacks (physical potency, prestige, confidence, clothes, shelter) and therefore is symbolically castrated. But again, the informant is not altogether devoid of reason for he also anticipates the hideous plot's questionable feasibility by arguing for partisanship organization. "[P]ero ellos son dos hombres no más para unas cuantas personas organizadas al ponerse de acuerdo" (60) [But they are only two men once people organize themselves and come to an agreement], he claims, referring to the top in command.

An analogy can be drawn between his personal grievance and that of Chileans at the time of the recordings (1983–85). History proved this demented informant quite insightful. The 1989 plebiscite that voted Augusto Pinochet out of office as president of Chile and chief commander of the armed forces was due to organized partisanship effort. Enough citizens took up their cause to defeat the powerful dictator. Symbolically, the country's internal division during the years of military rule is reflected in the informant's very discourse, which suggests an uneasy division of self, a coexistence of health and illness, of reason and madness.[104]

The 1995 Chilean Supreme Court sentencing of the former chief of the secret police, retired army general Manuel Contreras Sepúlveda, and an army brigadier, Gen. Pedro Espinoza, for the 1976 assassination of Salvador Allende's chancellor Orlando Letelier in Washington D.C. during Gen. Augusto Pinochet's regime (1973–90) is an unprecedented case in Chile.[105] Popular unrest over Contreras's initial refusal to serve his jail sentence showed a population deeply scarred and clamoring for justice despite the almost two-decade wait. Eltit's informant too recounts a twenty-year ordeal and the appeal he makes to his (imagined) interlocutor is certainly an uncanny coincidence with the persecution of Letelier. Two powerful men were no longer above the law. Contreras was forced to serve a jail sentence and Pinochet could not muster enough clout to protect him. The words of Eltit's disturbed informant are worth repeating: "[P]ero ellos son dos hombres no más para unas cuantas personas organizadas al ponerse de acuerdo" [But they are only two men once people organize themselves and come to an agreement].

Motive: *Who does what and* **why?**

There is no need to linger on why "My Father" and his associates plotted to exterminate those who knew too much about their illegal schemes. Evidently greed, power, corruption, and irreverence for life all factor into their actions. Why they were able to do so with impunity would warrant an extensive study on the mechanisms of power and the exercise of authority. The operations of top officials depicted in [*My Father*] points to a common phenomenon in corrupt regimes.

In retrospect, the reasons that motivate both protagonist and antagonist(s) are intelligible to the reader. The setup is aimed to prevent precisely what the informant does—talk. "Yo fui planeado . . . por cómplices sin miramientos . . . para que yo terminara mal, para que esto no se confirmara" (60–61) [I was set up . . . by accomplices without scruples . . . so that I would end up badly, so that this would not leak out], he explains in the third transcription.

Reader hindsight also reveals why the informant's testimony apparently becomes clearer or easier to read as one progresses through the text. The syntactic fragments or phrases that compose the informant's assertions are repeated enough throughout the transcriptions that readers can become familiar with the informant's soliloquy and form a pattern of reading and deciphering. Connecting and contextualizing the informant's statements facilitate clues useful in "filling in the gaps." [*My Father*] forces the reader to extract information embedded in the informant's discourse and organize it into grammatical structures that contain meaning. As far as reader engagement is required, [*My Father*] is no different than the fiction—*E. Luminata* or [*For the Homeland*]—that Eltit published before the transcriptions made it into book form.

In the introduction to the book, Eltit mentions that street dwellers generally retreat from language, paradoxically positioning themselves in the public arena while thwarting civic interaction. This homeless man's incessant conversation was exceptional. Without the subject's motive to speak, Eltit would not have been able to record and transcribe his discourse turned text. Ultimately, therefore, the book's existence lies in "why" the informant speaks.

One of the most persistent assertions throughout the three transcriptions is the variant of the phrase: "yo no soy cómplice con él" [I'm not his accomplice]. Here lies the crux of the subject's motive. Such a statement explicitly denies personal wrongdoing while acknowledging others' impropriety. The informant's motive is twofold: 1) clearing his name while 2) naming the offenders responsible for his persecution. But although the emphasis is on the "I" who has experienced despotism firsthand, the subject recognizes other victims. "[S]abe usted por qué los matan?" [Do you know why they kill them?], the informant asks the confidant, "para quedarse con las propiedades de ellos . . ." (25) [In order to keep their properties]. Moreover, the informant includes a warning to others: "Si ustedes no se ponen de acuerdo, la mayoría, están todos planeados para el exterminio" (28) [If you people don't come to a majority agreement you are all set up for extermination].

The account remains focused on an individual, ill-fated story. Nevertheless, the discourse suggests that his persecution is not unique but rather representative of injustices committed regularly. The following excerpt illustrates that the informant's testimony is not strictly self-serving, but includes consciousness of a collective as well:

> Pero el Padre Mío subsiste de ingresos ilegales, porque les cobraba la póliza de seguro de vida a mis familiares y ellos no percibían ese dinero. Yo no soy cómplice de ellos, con el exterminio general. Por eso no se confíen ustedes, ustedes están planeados, y a mí me planearon porque a ellos no les convenía yo . . . No quería [el Padre Mío] ser descubierto, por lo que le estoy conversando yo, para que este hecho no se diera a conocer a la publicidad. (47–48)
>
> [But "My Father" lives from illegal deposits, because he would cash in on my relatives' life insurance policy and they didn't notice that money. I'm not their accomplice, with the general extermination. Don't trust them, you people are set up, and I was set up because I was undesirable. . . . ["My Father"] did not want to be uncovered, for the reason I've been telling you, so that this would not leak out to the media].

Denunciation, self-exoneration, and also admonition (to others) compel the informant to speak. In fact, given his harsh living conditions, it appears as if speech and survival are inextricable. In other words, the will to live is contingent on the need to testify.

The three main components of the ordering principle (**Who** does **what** and **why**?) presented here involve a personal negotiation with the text to produce meaning and narrative legitimacy. The sociohistoric context of the account helps to validate it as a nonfictional narrative, albeit its apparent distortion by memory and illness. In the case of [*my Father*], the informant, social marginality, and the quest to denounce unchecked civil rights violations by state officials positioned the subject's account within the literary classification of "testimonio" that predominantly inscribes those excluded from mainstream channels of representation. But ultimately each reader must determine whether this individual's story qualifies as a "testimonio."

From a literary standpoint, and putting aside the question of genre categorization of the informant's account, the poverty-stricken homeless man of [*My Father*] cuts across Chilean borders to

represent the dispossessed of Latin America, whose plight and persecution is seldom acknowledged and, least of all, recorded. His
marginality, so much more moving because he was once among the
privileged, evokes, for me, a fraternity with the indigenous population of America, who once ruled the continent and today are practically landless, driven mad with despair over the loss of their
homeland. My exploration in the next chapter of the indigenous
topic in Eltit's *Por la patria* [*For the Homeland*] notes that they, too,
have never stopped protesting ill-treatment and extermination, but
most have ended up inhabiting isolated Chilean territories like this
urban vagrant living on a barren lot in Santiago. Eltit's transcription,
a marginal publication for sure, allows one man to speak on his own
behalf and by so doing indirectly gives a voice to the homeless of
Latin America who live in silence, aphasic under the weight of poverty and oppression.

3
Claiming Indigenous Roots in *Por la patria*

To BE "INDIO" IN CHILE IS TO BELONG TO A MARGINALIZED GROUP. THE novel's protagonist, Coya, bears a name indicative of indigenous noble ancestry.[1] Yet, like the homeless man in [*My Father*], she experiences persecution and imprisonment. Her life too is a struggle to survive. Understanding an indigenous theme in *Por la patria*/[*For the Homeland*] (1986) hinges on recognizing a palimpsest of a modern Chile where nationhood was formed at the expense of erasing native peoples' cultures from national identity.

The study of this novel continues the exploration of marginality as principal theme initiated in *E. Luminata* and further pursued in the extraliterary projects examined in the previous chapter. However, attention here focuses on Eltit's tentative incursions into the realm of native Chilean culture, a fitting topic for her nonmainstream literary agenda since she clearly departs from the Eurocentric tradition that exalts Spanish over indigenous ancestry.

I contend that in [*For the Homeland*] the author attempts to narrate a nation of multi lingual/cultural/social realities, thus demythologizing a false homogeneity that inculcates in Chileans the myth that they are the English of South America. This study looks at Coya as a symbolic figure that incarnates marginalized Chileans, including the mestiza, the Indian, the witch, the poor, and the persecuted. From a nationalistic perspective and through the language of the unconscious, Eltit articulates marginality as grounds for inscribing the country's other faces. Out of the Chilean kaleidoscope of social outcasts the Indian population has persevered centuries of injustices.

A number of indigenous groups make Chile their home, but for the purpose of analyzing [*For the Homeland*] I concentrate on the Mapuche who, notorious for their resistance, represent native peoples' struggle against European infringement upon their way of life.[2] Also known as "araucanos" (a term thought to stem from the Quechua *auka*, meaning savage), this Indian nation had a long history of fighting against Spanish and Criollo expansionary efforts.[3] In fact, other Indian groups such as the Inca did not defeat them, nor did Spanish conquests. Not until the late nineteenth century did the army of the "criollos" finally humble the Mapuche nation in the War of Pacification, which the official history of Chile prefers not to name in hopes that the Mapuche have forgotten it.[4] "It's that they [the Mapuche] do not write it in books," Malú Sierra reminds us, "but they continue filing it away in their genetic memory. From generation to generation until the present, the horrors that they suffered are recounted around the hearth."[5] Again, similarly to the story told by the destitute My Father, [For the Homeland] relates a tale of loss of family, rights, dignity, and freedom, but not of memory— the one vehicle of resistance left the persecuted of Chile, whether indigenous, mestizo, or white.

In Chile as elsewhere in Latin America, awareness of issues concerning native peoples came to a head with the 1992 commemorative ceremonies surrounding the quincentennial of the European and Amerindian encounter. In Chilean contemporary literature written by women, Isabel Allende and Marcela Serrano—both middle-class whites with connections to the country's power elite— incorporate an indigenous element in their writing where previously they had not. In Paula (1995), Allende states: "I was born in August, under the sign of Leo, sex, female, and, if I was not switched in the clinic, I have three-quarters Spanish-Basque blood, one-quarter French, and a tot of Araucan or Mapuche Indian, like everyone else in my land."[6] Later in passing she again remarks on "the health and strength of our most recondite genes from Basque sailors and indomitable American Indians."[7]

The stereotypical role of maid attributed to indigenous women is found in the first few pages of the early Chilean novel La amortajada (1938)/The Shrouded Woman (1948) by María Luisa Bombal. Serrano develops the topic further in Antigua vida mía (1995) by including Marcelina Cabezas, a house servant of Mapuche and mestizo extraction who, reminiscent of the Indian nanny in The Nine Guardians by Mexican Rosario Castellanos, instructs the young Cayetena on Mapuche culture. Representative of Chilean social structure, the nursemaid in Ana María del Río's Tiempo que ladra (1994) is also "araucana."[8] Agata Gligo, originally from Punta Arenas, the southernmost region in Chile, includes in the plot of Mi pobre tercer deseo (1990) a project of recuperating the history of the exterminated Selk'Nam natives of that area.[9]

These authors' precursor, Chilean Nobel (1945) laureate Gabriela Mistral, was recognized for giving voice to native peoples, the marginal, and the dispossessed of Latin America when she wrote during the first half of the twentieth century.[10] Mistral was born Lucila Godoy Alcayaga (1889–1957) into a lower-middle-class family. Her father abandoned her mother and older half-sister while Mistral was still a child.[11] Left to support themselves in a rural Chile, the two women raised and educated the young Mistral whose later writing reflected the bonds she felt with those living in hardship.

Eltit too grew up with an absent father and was raised by women— her mother and grandmother, the latter of peasant extraction and unschooled.[12] This personal aspect may explain the recurrent God/ fatherlike figures in the author's writing. The inextricability of class and race consciousness as a burdensome reality for many in Latin America comes to light in an interview where Eltit refers to Peruvian writer José María Arguedas and admits that she has dragged a "dilemma" through life that has never stopped tormenting her.[13] "This dilemma has to do with coming from a poor background that left in me a social resentment that at this stage is incurable. . . ."[14]

In terms of how personal identity affected the writing of [*For the Homeland*], Eltit also remarked that "The privilege of this disconcerting biography seems to be that I incorporated in my psyche— and often in an unconscious form—multiple languages, syntax, perceptions that not even I recognize in myself. I am a mestiza, in that sense, bi or trilingual within my own language. That was what permitted me to tackle the novel."[15]

Indeed, a retrospective look at Diamela Eltit's production finds this novel to be her most biographic work, one in which personal contemplation of identity as a product of growing up in poorish neighborhoods leads her to ponder about a marginal sector of Chilean society that is ultimately linked to the homeland's indigenous roots.

Besides the issue of ethnic identity, another biographical aspect influential in the writing of [*For the Homeland*] was the death of the author's father on 31 December 1983, at a time when her first novel, *E. Luminata*, had been released and she had started working on her next book manuscript. Eltit has commented that she wrote [*For the Homeland*] while mourning her father's death, one whose violent nature she experienced as a double grievance. "Struck down, then, by the death of my father and by the violence of his death, I continued writing," she remarked, "but the writing, contaminated by the proximity of the sorrow, affected my syntax to a great extent. . . . The violated syntax brought forth the memory of my origin and from there, the different memories that inhabit me in larval form, and which in that situation became unblocked, took me by the hand— the hand that wrote. The title of that novel is [*For the Homeland*], an

epitaph associated with my father and a social epitaph in solidarity
with the numerous deaths occurring in the country from a violent
system that has extended a clandestine mourning across the length
of the [Chilean] territory."[16]

At the time, Eltit was referring to the persecution of political dissidence by Pinochet's paramilitary units.[17] During that period other
repressive regimes in the Southern Cone region—Argentina and
Uruguay, for example—similarly targeted poor and working-class
sectors which were rallying for better living conditions and whose
inhabitants were more likely to be associated with leftist movements
which opposed the bourgeoisie and the governments that traditionally protected this affluent minority. Violence against civilians was
part and parcel of the national reality in Chile and bordering countries during the writing of [For the Homeland].

As in E. Luminata, unconventional grammar and syntax, word and
page fragmentation, disrupted narrative, unassociated dialogue sequences, the use of neologisms, and slang in this second novel pose
difficulties that convey to the reader the crisis affecting a nation in
upheaval. But with such experimentation Eltit also proposes revolutionizing literary aesthetics; what this entails is, a "profound sociocultural change," observes Mary-Beth Tierney-Tello, which "must
clearly be undertaken at the linguistic and symbolic level."[18] For
Eltit, mainstream writing does not suffice to inscribe life at the margins (including the indigenous elements of Chilean nationality
evoked in [For the Homeland]) because minority sectors of society operate on a different symbolic order and communicate with a language and syntax other than conventional Spanish.

Precisely because Eltit attempts to present different Chilean cultural identities, "Her textual practice actively works to defy the authority of prevailing structures by breaking dominant codes of
gender and family identities, by violating class boundaries which
keep certain social groups muted and certain linguistic forms out of
print, as well as by refusing to comply with narrative expectations of
'readability' or 'intelligibility.' "[19] Although "readability" and "intelligibility" continue to pose challenges in [For the Homeland], unlike the anonymous, mute, and dispossessed characters of E.
Luminata who occupy a public square by night, Eltit gives more
structure to her second novel with a recognizable plot and identifiable protagonists whose actions are mostly confined to a neighborhood bar and a jail cell.

Public and private tragedy, that is, political circumstance and the
death of the author's father (patria and pater) become convoluted
in a novel where loss of the progenitor prompts the daughter/pro-

tagonist to launch an odyssey of self-discovery during whose course glimpses of a nation and its indigenous roots are revealed as well.

DRAWING CONNECTIONS WITH THE MAPUCHE INDIANS OF CHILE

From its opening paragraph the novel semantically alludes to language formation and origin:

> ma ma ma ma ma ma ma ma ma ma ma ma ma ma ma ma ma ma ma ma ma ma ma ma ma am am am am am am am am am am am am am ame ame ame ame dame dame dame dame dame dame dame madame madame madame dona madona mama mama mama mama mama mamá mamá mamá mamacho el pater y en el bar se la toman y arman trifulca. (9)

> [ma ma ma ma ma ma ma ma ma ma ma ma ma ma ma ma ma ma ma ma ma ma ma ma ma am am am am am am am am am am am am am ame ame ame ame dame dame dame dame dame dame dame madame madame madame dona madona mama mama mama mama mama mama mama mama woman the pater and in the bar they take her and brawl.]

As if pronouncing the first syllable of human utterance—ma ma ma ma—the narrator's evocation of the mother eventually includes the "pater," together they embody "mamacho," that is female (mama) and male (macho) as Eugenia Brito observes.[20] Both are relevant elements of Eltit's Chilean mother/fatherland depicted in the novel's title, a nation whose indigenous Mapuche people believe in a cosmological female/male duality reflected in a supreme being, Ngenechen and his wife Ngenechen kushe, and other minor deities also with female and male counterparts.[21] Thus, duality as a principal concept of Mapuche philosophy manifests itself in their notion of a divine Father and Mother.[22]

Reference to the indigenous race, a critical issue when broaching the topic of a Chilean homeland, appears in the first page of the novel where the mother is described as a bleached blond, "machi," and "india putita." The mother's bleached hair reflects inauthenticity created by the desire to erase racial features. The internalized perceptions of white superiority and the advantage of racial whitening is exemplified later in the text when the daughter, Coya, daydreams about another life as a blue-eyed blond:

Probé para atrás antes de ser Coya y reina y escogí un nombre paralelo,
padres alternos, barrios soleados. . . . Tuve una cara distinta a mí y fui
eslava . . . rubia . . . ojos azules y . . . dotada de piernas largas tal como
una atleta. . . . Cuando era rubia me miraban y me tiraban frases y la
mayoría quería casamiento conmigo. No concubinato, entiendan que
estoy hablando de leyes, de resortes legales. Porque rubia pude haberme
casado hasta el cansancio con testigos, padrinos, parientes. . . . (98)

[I regressed before being Coya and queen and chose a parallel name,
alternate parents, sunny neighborhoods. . . . I had a face different from
mine and I was Slav . . . blond . . . blue-eyed and endowed with long legs
like an athlete. . . . When I was blond they looked at me and flirted and
the majority wanted to marry me. Not concubinage, understand that I'm
talking about laws, legal ties. As a blond I could have married endlessly
with witnesses, members of the wedding party, relatives. . . .]

Coya mentally pictures a different bloodline altogether, one with another set of parents who can produce a white offspring whose features afford social benefits not available to women of color. The
protagonist's hopeless wish to be Other relates to Eltit's comment
that marginality breeds greater desires "precisely because you are so
far from satisfying them."[23] Self-acceptance does occur, however, as
the protagonist "returns" from her daydream and assumes her lot:

VOLVI
Pródiga y humilde regresé en mi mente: despacito las pisadas por el barrio y encantada con el barro saludé como siempre a mis vecinas, en toda
la cuadra me resigné. (99)

[I RETURNED
Prodigal and humble I returned in my mind: slow steps through the
neighborhood and delighted with the mud I, like always, greeted my
neighbors, on the entire block I resigned myself.]

Reference to the mother as "machi" is another indicator of indigenous culture embedded in the text. In Mapudungun, the language
of the Mapuche, the "machi" identifies the shaman in charge of the
physical and spiritual health of their people.[24] The importance of
the female vocation of "machi" will be analyzed later with respect
to the daughter, Coya. For now let us note the paradox of naming
the drunk and sexually depraved mother to the sacred role of
"machi," someone who rather than superiority over ordinary folk
incarnates physical and spiritual degeneration.[25] The epithet "india
putita" [little Indian whore] also elicits issues of gender, race, and
class at the root of any exploration of Latin American identity.

Symbolically, the novel begins with allusion to an Indian mother engendering a next generation. "[E]l palo papacito la empuja adentro y atrás," [Stick daddy pushes her inside and behind] the narrator remarks, "De juerga están y de farra" [They're having a blast and whooping it up] (9). The second page of [*For the Homeland*] presents a sketchy "origin" story of fetal consciousness and birth:

Cuando se revolvieron yo no estaba. Miento. . . . Yo casi estaba presente, por lo menos a medias. . . . ¿Qué hice? ¿qué dije? ¿por qué la mama no puja? . . . . "abre las piernas pa que me quepa el hueso y nuestros pelos se enreden en la maraña arisca y tenaz". . . . Ma ma ma me viro patas pa abajo y pido fuerzas pa la salida . . . (10–12)

[I wasn't there for their roll in the sack. I lie. . . . I was almost present, at least halfway. . . . What did I do? What did I say? Why does mother not push?. . . . "open your legs for bone to fit and our hair becomes entangled in the untamed, sticky thicket". . . . Ma ma ma I turn feet first and ask for strength to exit. . . .]

Undoubtedly in [*For the Homeland*], Coya's very name establishes a link between the Chilean homeland and Latin America's original inhabitants. Furthermore, the monosyllabic articulation of the opening lines of the novel (ma ma ma ma ma . . .) suggests a call for both a carnal mother and the earth mother of the Mapuche Indians of Chile. "Mapu" means land and "che" means people, thus the Mapuche are the people of the land. Early in the novel Coya plays with soil and states "la tierra es mía" (16) [the land is mine]. Given her name, the statement symbolically acts as a battle cry for an Indian nation which for centuries has fought the expropriation of their land. The name of Coya's friend, Rucia, which in the Chilean countryside usually means blond, also refers to a gray animal or gray-haired person,[26] and in this regard calls to mind Gabriela Mistral's reference to the Mapuche as "the formidable gray race, the spot of ashen eagles that lives south of the Biobío [river]."[27]

Nameless but clearly an important figure to the protagonist and the community, the father in [*For the Homeland*] corroborates Chilean anthropologist Sonia Montecino's portrayal of the indigenous father as cacique or political figure, family provider, and keeper of order, one who is a key person especially in the development of a daughter's sociopolitical consciousness.[28] The father is "almost heroic," notes Montecino, for he maintains the stability of the family and the community—a mediator of conflicts within and outside his household, the proclaimer of the communal *nguillatún* (the Mapuche religious celebration).[29]

In the novel, the father symbolically embodies Coya's male counterpart—the Inca who sheds his red Indian blood ("sangre roja aindiada," 29)—after Juan, one of his own men and contender for Coya's affection, contributes to his violent death by turning police informer. "Llegó, vino herido por el hampa y los guardias lo buscan" [He got here, wounded he made it through the underworld and the police are after him], Coya recounts her father's ordeal (33). Notably, a principal reason for Juan's betrayal stems from his jealousy of the unusually close father/daughter relationship, one that, reminiscent of the Inca/Coya noble couple, involves incest. Among the Mapuche, references to sexual liaisons vary among reports, but what remains consistent is that indigenous kinship systems include relationships considered incestuous by Judeo-Christian standards.[30]

[*For the Homeland*] presents Coya tending the wounded father with explicitly erotic, and almost ritualistic, gestures in the mixing of blood and bodies:

> Mí lo sanó cuando llegó sangrante. . . . Mí lloró. [L]a Coya, yo, se acordaba cuando llegó a la mesa y sacó su camisa, su prenda mostrando el pecho y yo deslicé la tira, despejada en vuelta y vuelta la carne abierta y saqué ahí mismo la prenda mía y torso a torso nosotros dos. . . . Besados, yo nada palabra supe qué decir, más que niñita al hombre mío, al padre mío que se bajó hasta mi pecho langüándome (sic) la sangre suya misma. . . . Mi boca se ponía en la de él y lo hinchado me enfebrecía y su pecho se pegó primero, al pezón mío primero hasta la punta en sangre. (29–31)

> [Me cured him when he arrived bleeding. . . . Me cried. Coya, I, recalled when he arrived at the table and took off his shirt, his garment showing his chest and I slipped off the strip, uncovering with each turn the open wound and on the spot I took off my garment and torso to torso us two. . . . Kissed, I not a word knew what to say, only little one to my man, to my father that descended to my breast licking off his own blood. . . . My mouth on his and the swelling excited me and his chest pressed first, to my nipple first to the bloody tip.]

Notably, this anomalous relationship is narrated in equally irregular Spanish where nonstandard grammar and syntax pose the marginality of this language vis-à-vis a protagonist whose indigenous name, Coya, connects her to an Inca patriarch, precisely the father and partner she attends to here.

In this section, the only one in the novel where the protagonist interacts with her father at length, Coya repeatedly refers to him as both child and lover: "como una niña mi amado" [like a little girl my loved one], "amado por mí" [loved by me], "como dos niñas fuimos" [like two little girls were we] (29); "mi amado" [my loved one], "l'amante mío" [th'lover of mine], "más que niñita al hombre mío" [more than a little girl to my man] (30); "mi amado" [my loved one], "niñita mía, muñeca mía" [my little girl, my doll], "amante mío, muñeca mía, niñita" [my lover, my doll, little girl] (32). In keeping with her role as Coya of Inca ancestry, the protagonist conceives of herself as wife and mother, a relationship that psychologically does not burden the daughter with the prohibition of incest since, as Coya, her psyche operates under the conventions of indigenous and not Spanish kinship structures.

But as with any of Eltit's texts, incest in [*For the Homeland*]—and, as we will examine at length in the study of *The Fourth World*—admits various interpretations, for besides the carnal aspect of incest linked to Coya as sister/wife to the Inca, and the obviously incestuous relationship with both parents, Eltit also aims at linguistic incest, that is, perverting cultured language and transforming "coa," Coya's other name and the vernacular of delinquents in Chile, into literary language.[31] As noted earlier, Eltit's attempt at inscribing a new aesthetics of the margins involves a sociocultural change at a linguistic as well as symbolic level.

The sensuous encounter between Coya and her father culminates at the end of the first section of part 1 (titled "se ríen" [they laugh]) which, from a Western perspective, begins with mention of improper parental conduct toward their progeny. "La mamastra la besa en la boca y su papá la besa en la boca: hostigan" [The stepmom kisses her on the mouth and her pop kisses her on the mouth: they harass] we read in the first complete sentence of the novel, thus bringing the topic of incest immediately to the foreground. The laughter referred to in the title of the section is directed at the daughter and mother as perverse public spectacle:

Sus dedos recorren mi columna y creo que me pide un baile. Sí, es completamente seguro que quiere moverse conmigo ahora que las copas la animan. No me atrevo delante de la gente, pero ella me ha escogido y acepto su mano en mi cintura y sus pechos oprimiendo los míos. Casi no puedo apoyarme en su hombro, es que me da, siento vergüenza cuando su pierna se mete entreabriendo las mías: no hagai eso, le digo, pero es inútil, no hay cosa que la detenga. . . . Se ríen de nosotras en el bar: Sí, salen de los reservados para la burla y por eso aplauden acompañándose de gestos extraños: empiezan a ofrecer plata. (19)

[Her fingers run up and down my spine and I think she is asking me for a dance. Yes, it's completely certain that she wants to sway with me now that the drinks cheer her up. I don't dare in front of people, but she has chosen me and I accept her hand on my waist and her breasts pressing mine. I can hardly rest on her shoulder, it's that, I feel ashamed when she introduces her leg between mine: don't do that, I say, but it's useless, nothing can stop her. . . . They laugh at us at the bar: Yes, they leave their reserved rooms to poke fun and they applaud accompanied by strange gestures: they begin to offer money.]

From the novel's outset, incest signals unconventional family life as defined within the kinship structures of most readers, thus [For the Homeland] calls for a different reading, a semiotics of the Other as unfamiliar, as outsider.

Given Eltit's knowledge of Inca culture and the name chosen for the female protagonist, the association between incest and an indigenous element is apparent in the novel. As Tafra notes, "incest also expresses a desire to return to one's ancestors in search of profound racial roots."[32] Eltit has stated that in regards to Coya she "worked with very obscure and little verbalizable perceptions that have to do with family relationships" in which "cultural repression pushes you toward the father and towards heterosexuality," yet, as depicted in the novel, she also wants to explore the primal desires toward the mother as first love object.[33]

Keeping in mind the indigenous links discernible in the novel, on a purely symbolic level the topic of incest can reflect a people's mechanism for cultural survival. As Mapuche armed resistance over the expropriation of native land escalated, "cultural resistance became entrenched in the communities. The Mapuche clung to them as occurred in other parts of the Americas, for they knew that this was the only way to protect their lands constantly under menace and to survive as an ethnic minority. Mapuche society closed in upon itself."[34] Thus, symbolically, incest in the novel thwarts interaction with outside forces that will pervert the clan—physically (through reproduction) and culturally. Early in the novel, the barrio, and more specifically the neighborhood bar, becomes the stronghold against invasion from a literal army of outsiders.

In terms of economic and cultural marginality, a parallel can be drawn between the situation of native Chilean peoples within mainstream society and that of the inhabitants of the community depicted in [For the Homeland]. Repeated references to "erial," "eriazo," "hampa," and "barro" identify an impoverished barrio where carousing and sexuality in the local bar serve as an escape valve for its patrons' precarious existence. Chile's political upheaval, especially in urban areas, tacitly surfaces in one character's wish for escape to the province for safety and peace:

Flora . . . quiere irse, pero a la provincia y hacerse cargo de la tierra, cuidar árboles, criar sus animales y olvidarse del barullo del país. Flora está como el total de la gente asustada y cree que allá lejos, recortada contra los cerros nadie podría darle alcance aunque la buscaran. Que quiere irse, que quiere irse, que quiere irse, les ha dicho a una por una:-
-Me voy a ir a mi casa, Coya.
-Me vuelvo a mi casa, Berta. (60)

[Flora . . . wants to leave, but for the countryside and take charge of the land, look after trees, raise animals and forget about the country's turmoil. Flora is like all frightened people and thinks that far away, sequestered in the mountains no one could catch up with her even if they searched for her. She wants to go away, she wants to go away, she wants to go away, she has told them one by one:-
-I'm going home, Coya.
-I'm returning home, Berta.]

Flora, a name evocative of Mother Earth, desires to return home to the countryside where she can come in contact with nature (land, trees, animals) and resume a rural lifestyle still in touch with an indigenous culture which communes with the land as a way of life and a source of identity.[35]

From the veneration of Mother Earth stems the importance of the mother, a role portrayed from the onset of [*For the Homeland*] and perpetuated in an array of ways, from the intimacy between Coya and her mother; to the voices of mothers in interaction with their estranged daughters, Rucia, Flora, and Berta; to the chorus of anonymous mothers that appear in nightmares as Madres 1, 2, 3, 4, 5, 6.

According to Montecino, the mother figure, especially the one abandoned with child, lies at the core of mestizo identity forged during the conquest and colonization when unions between Spanish men and Indian women seldom ended in institutionalized marriage.[36] Such alliances often resulted in high father absenteeism with a family commonly consisting of a single mother and bastard children (*huachos/huachas*).[37]

In keeping with the abandonment, illegitimacy, and female-only parent model which played an essential role in the formation of Chilean mestizo psyche,[38] Coya's friends, Berta and Rucia, express their resentment at being *huachas,* daughters without fathers and of single mothers who are burdened with the responsibility of family subsistence. "Mi mamá era muy pensativa conmigo, muy poco comunicativa y cuando le preguntaba por mi papá, ella me decía que en algún lugar andaba" (122) [My mom was very pensive with me, not very communicative, and when I would ask for my father she would tell me that he must be somewhere], states Berta. Her bitterness towards her mother shows when she says: "Le gustaba el vino y los señores que la abastecían. Yo en la calle para esas fechas, yo caminando. Yo golpeada muchas veces cuando se descontrolaba por el miedo de lo que me podía pasar en las esquinas y en el baldío de las reuniones" (122) [She liked wine and the men that supplied her. I in the streets during those days, walking. I beaten many times when she lost control fearful of what could happen to me on the street corners and in the wasteland of encounters]. The implication of prostitution suggests that the mother can do little to prevent a similar fate for her daughter.

Rucia, in turn, suffers a triple psychic blow for she is not only fatherless and probably illegitimate, but feels maternal abandonment as well. "Mi mamá era como un bicho, algo maligno y resignado" (134) [My mom was a bitch, wicked and resigned] the daughter remarks acridly. "Dejó a mis hermanos en casa de familiares, porque ella no se hizo cargo nunca, tenía una enfermedad que yo no creo" [She left my brothers and sisters with relatives, because she never took charge of them, she had an illness that I don't believe].

Her mother, however, explains her position as follows: "La dejé encargada y pagué religiosamente por su mantención. No tenía lugar para tenerla, no tenía salud para cuidarla, ni a los otros chicos tampoco. Pero ella era mi preferida porque fue la primera y la más dolorosa para salir. No comprendió nunca y se fue apartando, ensombreciendo y poniendo insolente" (136) [I left someone in charge of her and religiously paid for her support. I didn't have a place to keep her nor good health to take care of her or the other kids. But she was my favorite because she was the first and the most painful delivery. She never understood and began to distance herself, turning gloomy and insolent].

A strong female-centered ethos prevailed across all social classes during the Chilean colony when territorial wars or employment prospects prompted men to constantly be on the move while meantime women remained alone, for months and even years, in charge of a ranch and a family, one often raised with the help of female servants and relatives.[39] Rucia's mother in [*For the Homeland*] exemplifies that the mother, even when absent, is the parent who provides for the children's welfare. The mother figure—whether Indian, mestiza, or Spanish—emerged as the backbone of Chilean society early in national construction.

Although the novel's protagonist is not a biological mother, she bears the title of "madre de madres" [mother of mothers] (206–207), evocative of the queen or Coya as the highest-ranking female figure within the Inca hierarchy. Significantly, besides being invested with great dignity, the Coya of the Inca world ruled over the female population and was looked upon to intercede with the gods on women's behalf.[40]

In the novel, Coya's friends look to her as their leader. The power they attribute to her becomes obvious in prison when the incarcerated women ask Coya to intercede for them with Juan, their guard, in securing privileges such as extra blankets. "Todas ustedes me tienen cansada, me echan encima todos sus problemas" [I'm fed up, you burden me with all your problems] complains Coya at one point, to which Flora responds: "Lo único que se te pide es que consigas un poco de alivio, porque tienes el poder con el hombre es que te pedimos los favores" (265) [You are only asked to get us some relief, because you have power over the man we ask you for favors].

As far as privileges, in the Inca world young girls of extraordinary beauty were chosen for the special role of becoming *acllacunas* or Vírgenes del Sol (Sun Maidens) who, taken from their homes to live in cloistered residences called *acllahuasi*, were trained for various services to the Inca and Coya, including performing duties in connection with religious ceremonies.[41] [*For the Homeland*] parallels Coya to her Inca counterpart as the highest-ranking female in the community's hierarchy, at least while she is imprisoned. Moreover, given the allusion to the protagonist's nobility, the incarceration of the women elicits a travesty of the indigenous *acllahuasi*. The sacred Inca place of female confinement has turned into a prison in the novel, and instead of beautiful "acllacunas" the women of Coya's entourage are haggard, pestilent, and ugly. Whereas Eltit's narrative contains allusions to indigenous culture, the women's degeneration in its depiction reflects the extent of a peoples' decline in power and autonomy.

Degeneration is also reflected in the vice that reigns in the bar where Coya's family and friends socialize, get drunk, engage in perversion, and resist outsiders. A parallel can also be drawn here between this community's stifling marginality and that of the "indio" [Indian] in the "reducciones" or Chilean reservations. "Alcohol," observes Malú Sierra, "was, without doubt, the underhanded enemy that contributed efficaciously to the annihilation of the Mapuche."[42] Alcohol, the "remedy" that society offered the Indian to drown defeat, impotence, and despair, also ravages the nation's impoverished sectors as portrayed in [*For the Homeland*].[43] "Por causa del miedo se abren los bares . . . y se apersonan los fugitivos, los hambrientos, los apacibles seres que beben" [On account of the fear the bars open . . . and the fugitive, the hungry, the placid beings that drink appear]

observes the narrator. "Entonces se larga en serio la primera gran
borrachera" (76) [Then the first great drinking spree truly begins].
The bar acts as a refuge where the fugitive and hungry of the land
drink to alleviate their fear and despair.

Armed police raids of this community, whose members operate in
the underground resistance movement, allude to the overwhelming
persecution of the working-class poor during Pinochet's regime.
"Del hampa provengo. . . ." [From the underworld I come] states
Coya. "Por eso que destituyan y destruyan la patria, que den acabo
al país completo. . . . Aquí estamos más muertos que vivos, más asus-
tados que nadie, más inseguros, más animales mestizos" (142) [For
that reason let them divest and destroy the homeland, finish off the
entire country. . . . Here we are more dead than alive, more frightened than anyone, more insecure, more mestizo animals]. The oppression Coya voices on behalf of the mestizo population reflects a
chapter in contemporary Chilean history, but it is also historically
reminiscent of the persecutory campaign launched against the Mapuche by the government in quest of territory.

In her essay "El pueblo araucano," Gabriela Mistral pointed out
that "mestizaje" for Chile's "maternal race" remained the same or
worsened under the criollos than under the Iberians. "Mestizaje
would discover the way of breaking down the Araucanian fortitude
and of relaxing their tenaciousness giving free reign to their vices,
particularly their drunkenness in some occasions, and at other times
uprooting the Indians from their region in order to disperse them
and drive them mad with the loss of their land, directing them to
the famous 'reducción,' the well known 'reservation.' . . ."[44] Another
Chilean matriarch, the popular cueca singer Violeta Parra, records
in "Arauco tiene una pena" ["Arauca Bears a Sorrow"] how little
has changed for the indigenous population since Chileans (mestizos
themselves) oppress the Araucanos as the Spanish once did.

> Arauco tiene una pena
> más negra que su chamal:
> ya no son los españoles
> los que le hacen llorar.
> Hoy son los propios chilenos
> los que le quitan le [sic] pan.[45]
>
> [Arauco bears a sorrow
> darker than its cloak
> no longer are the Spaniards
> the ones who make it groan.
> Today the very Chileans
> are the ones who snatch its bread.]

[*For the Homeland*] depicts army trucks with armed soldiers taking part in operations described as "redada," "cerco," and "invasión" [raid, siege, and invasion], a discourse that suggests the escalating nature of the interventions in the barrio and concurrently describes the onslaught of government troops in Indian territory carried out a century earlier. "Toda redada se realiza al amanecer, cuando están profundamente dormidos, así obtienen mayor facilidad de desplazamiento" [All raids are carried out at dawn, when they are profoundly asleep, that way its easier for them to move around], remarks Coya, "En toda redada intervienen la sorpresa y la emoción. . . . Cuando se inicia una redada están las cuatro esquinas de la red estacadas en el suelo: Gritos, golpes, desórdenes son preferenciales" (50) [Surprise and emotion are part of all raids. . . . When a raid is initiated the four corners of the net have been staked into the ground: Cries, blows, disturbances are preferable]. The basic elements of a raid as described by Coya—the cover of night, surprise, violence, and a network of reinforcement to insure trapping the enemy—have changed little over time.[46]

For centuries the presence of the "huinca" or the non-Indian in Mapuche territory signaled the imminent violation of Indian rights, especially the usurpation of land; thus to date, distrust of the "huinca" remains the fundamental element of Mapuche resistance.[47] A parallel suspicion of outsiders is portrayed in the novel with the arrival at the bar of men who stand out because, unlike the inhabitants, they look like "eslavos" and "zarcos" (blue-eyed Slavs). "Porque era un zarco el que se ubicaba en la mesa. Los parroquianos lo esquivaban desconfiado: -Este eslavo nos trae mala suerte, dijo Flora. Pero nadie, ninguno de nosotros se atrevía a sacarlo, hacer presente el descontento y birlarlo a otro sitio" (58) [Because the one at the table was a blue-eyed Slav. The locals were distrustful and avoided him: -This Slav brings us bad luck, said Flora. But no one, not one among us dared kick him out, make known the discontent and dispatch him elsewhere]. In fact, rumor has it that a "zarco" seduced Coya's mother into leaving her family. One version of the story recounts:

La mamá no pudo retacarse cuando vio al zarquito yarcar por el barrio. El la olfateó en el bar y en todas las partes en que se desenvolvía, allí estaba el zarco sonriendo, hundiendo la mano en el bolsillo, pagando y sacando fotografías a diestra y siniestra. . . .
-Vámonos, dijo el zarco.
-¿Y por qué me iba a ir contigo?
-Este sitio no te sirve, estás arriba del nivel.

-¿Y mi familia? dijo ella.
-No sería la primera vez, ni la última.
Sumó mucho para convencerla. Ella como que se iba y no. Se fue porque
los consejos se pusieron sobre las otras formas.
-No te lleves nada, yo te compro todo nuevo.
Así se alejó dando un austero aviso y prometiendo noticias. (48)

[The mother could not hold back when she saw the young Slav gallivant
through the neighborhood. He sniffed her in the bar and everywhere
else, there was the smiling Slav, reaching into his pockets, paying and
taking pictures left and right. . . .
-Let's go, said the Slav.
-And why should I go with you?
-This place is not for you, you're above this level.
-And my family? she said.
-It would not be the first time, or the last.
-It took a lot to convince her. She was wishy-washy. She left because the
advice clouded the other things.
-Don't take anything, I'll buy you everything new.
That's how she left giving an austere notice and promising to stay in
touch]

Eventually the mother returns, only to permanently "disappear"
after a raid of the barrio. Throughout the novel Coya questions her
mother's disappearance and persists in looking and asking for her,
even when she is imprisoned herself and the search becomes but a
symbolic gesture of hope in reuniting with her mother.

Fundamentally, the nature of the disappearance and the lack of
information regarding the mother's whereabouts call to mind the
strategy used by Pinochet's regime, one that, incidentally, was especially harsh against Mapuche leaders.[48] On one level, the mother incarnates the fate of thousands of political dissidents in Chile. But
moreover, given the novel's coded indigenous elements, Coya's
mother, as metonym of Mother Earth, also represents the violations
of native peoples' rights whose ancestral lands were usurped by the
"huincas." Just as the mother is, supposedly, the very essence of the
family, the Mapuche "family" has been left without their Mother
(Earth or "mapu"), snatched by outsiders who, like the "zarco" in
the novel, used deceit and false promises to get their way with the
Indians. Notably, soon after the mother discovers the seducer's
fraud and returns home, she is forcibly taken from her family, a situation that, symbolically, suggests that when land could no longer be
obtained from the Indians through trickery, violent methods were
implemented.

Coya's designation as "machi," a Mapuche shaman, signals an important indigenous attribute. "[Y]o machi y madre de madres tengo en vigencia cada uno de mis conjuros" (206) [I Machi and mother of mothers have at hand every one of my incantations], Coya reminds herself as she is tormented by hallucinations in prison. In Mapuche society, where the vast majority of machis are women,[49] the female shaman distinguishes herself from regular Mapuche women because her ability to relate with the supernatural world through trance gives her great informal power and makes her a highly respected member of the community.[50] Although typically all Mapuche women are knowledgeable in the use of medicinal herbs, machis pride themselves in excelling over other women in this kind of healing especially since remedies are often revealed to them through "peuma" or dreams.[51]

This aspect of native culture appears in [*For the Homeland*] when Coya tends her wounded father using organic medicine as would any ordinary Mapuche woman or machi:[52]

Le di esa noche yerba para los males, le emplasté el pecho con matico, agüita de boldo, palqui puse en las tablas para que se le pasara el ardor, todas las plantas que sabía en sus puntadas. Tan bien que se portaba que no decía frito cuando molí matico en el pecho, rezándole al santito yo me pasé la noche con el pecho a la vista para ver el torso de ti dañado. (32)

[That night I gave him herbs for his ailments, I plastered his chest with "matico, agüita de boldo, palqui" I put on flat parts to alleviate the sting, all the plants I was familiar with on his stitches. So well-behaved that he did not say a word when I grounded "matico" on his chest, praying to the little saint I spent the night with the chest in sight to keep an eye on your injured torso.]

Besides applying her curative know-how, Coya spends the night in prayer. Her preoccupation with both physical and spiritual realms is characteristic of shamanism and reflects the religious syncretism born of mestizaje.

Dreams (peuma) and visions (perimontún), the mediums whereby the Divine good (ngenechén) and evil (kalku) communicate with human beings, constitute an important aspect of Mapuche life since it is through the oneiric realm that messages about personal and collective, positive and negative events become known.[53] Mapuche poet Leonel Lienlaf (whose book dedicates a section on dreams turned nightmares for his race) points out that his people, unlike Christians, do not need temples of worship because their religion is rooted in the unconscious.⁵⁴ Indeed, once under a trance and unaware of what she says and does, a machi undergoes spirit possession and communicates with the supernatural.⁵⁵

[*For the Homeland*] includes its share of dreams, visions, hallucinations, revelations, or apparitions which on one level allude to the nightmare Chileans experienced under dictatorial rule, but given Coya's identification as machi, they also reflect the different cultural mind-set that Eltit attempts to depict in the novel. In fact, the first set of visions occurs while Coya, after administering all the herbal remedies at her disposal, lies in wait at her father's deathbed. Although unclear whether the dreamer is Coya or her dying father, in the section titled "No te mueras" [Don't die], death manifests itself in a parade of six mothers (identified as Madre 1, 2, 3, 4, 5, 6), two of which torment their ailing son—Coya's father—by giving him a gun with instructions on ending his own life, a revelation where "armas y almas" [(fire)arms and spirits] (42) presage his violent death.

Also pertinent to the dreamworld, in another section titled "El cerco, el delirio, el cerco" [Siege, delirium, siege], the protagonist, who is both Coya and machi, experiences six visions while she, her mother, friends, and other patrons hold out in the bar as trucks of army guards close in on the barrio:

ABRIR LOS OJOS A:
        Seis visiones.
        Seis las versiones en que tuvieron la borrachera.
        Pasiones seis. (82)

[OPEN THE EYES TO:
        Six visions.
        Six versions of their drunkenness.
        Passions six.

As machi, Coya's inner eye, that is, her unconscious, needs to be receptive to the six visions triggered by excessive drinking and imbued with sensual passion as well as religious "Passion" in the Christian sense of suffering persecution—a plight common to both the Mapuche after Spanish arrival and Chilean nationals after the coup d'etat.

The persecutory policy of Pinochet's regime turned into a literal witch hunt for political subversives. In this respect, Coya's marginality as "machi" makes her a prime suspect for a police round-up. Those unfamiliar with indigenous culture would probably equate her to a witch. Under Pinochet, merely acting differently or looking out of the ordinary was oftentimes enough motive to be summoned to police headquarters for questioning. Many never returned home alive. The fear of communism in Chile during the military regime finds an analogy in the European witch-craze of the fifteenth, sixteenth, and seventeenth centuries. For instance, the accusation of witchcraft, was a "crimen exceptum," a crime distinct from all others for which few would escape death once on trial.[56] But since there was no real crime, ordinary laws "would not suffice for accusation and punishment. . . . The intent was to purify society" of such feared and perverted individuals.[57]

In Chile the State and not the Church served as the vehicle for purging society of undesirables. According to Jean Bodin, a sixteenth-century jurist and magistrate, the purpose of witch trials was "to strike awe into some by the punishment of others, to diminish the number of evil-doers, to make secure the life of the well-disposed. . . ."[58] Similarly, with the torture and extermination of dissidents, modern Chilean history can claim its own Inquisition.

Reminiscent of the prosecuted hags of old, Coya and the friends who share prison quarters are socially marginal women. As a "machi," Coya is the leading hag among them. She is respected and also feared. She is the healer, the wisewoman, the counterpart of the "curandera" found in Caribbean santería and spiritism. In the novel, incarceration has turned the women haggard in appearance. Significantly, Mary Daly points out that while definitions for "haggard" in the *Merriam-Webster Dictionary* include "untamed" when pertaining to hawks, "wild in appearance" refers to eyes or to a "wild-eyed" person. Obsolete meanings of the word "haggard" include "willful," "wanton," "unchaste," and used as a noun it once meant "an intractable person, especially a woman reluctant to yield to wooing."[59] These definitions describe various aspects of Coya's present looks, demeanor, and personality, including her incestuous relationship with her parents and her resistance to Juan's romantic advances in prison because she knows of his involvement in her father's death.

Two traumatic events, points out Montecino, mark the lives of Mapuche women.[60] Both entail great separation anxiety. The first, the death of the father, involves the loss of the person who provides economic stability and whose absence often means a change in status— for the daughter who assumes the mother role for younger siblings as the mother takes over the husband's tasks and for the family, which must contend with poverty.[61] The second, marriage, forces the daughter to leave the birth family and relocate to the husband's village.[62]

Not uncommonly, it is reported that the dead father returns in the daughter's dreams in order to let her know of his peace and give her necessary advice and guidance.[63] In the novel, specifically vis-à-vis Coya as machi, the dead father's appearance in vision number three illustrates the Mapuche's belief that the dead visit the living— often to remind them in dreams of their obligations:[64]

-Volviste, dije. . . .
-Llegué, me dijiste. . . .
-Ni la muerte, me dijo.
-Ni el crimen, le dije.
Y empecé a enumerar:
-Ni los golpes, por ejemplo, y seguí.
Mientras en cada uno de los hechos, él decía sí con la cabeza y entendí que el amor que te tuve iba allá lejos atropellando casas, baldíos e incluso fronteras mismas. (95)

[-You returned, I said. . . .
-I've come, you told me. . . .
-Not even death, he told me.
-Not even crime, I told him.
And I began to enumerate:
-Not even the blows, for example, and I continued.
While with each one of the deeds, he nodded yes and I understood that the love I had had for you went far, trampling houses, empty lots and even borders.]

Indicative of a cultural mind-set at ease with the supernatural, Coya shows joy rather than fear at seeing the apparition, yet aware that the army threatens the barrio and that the dead bring messages to the living, she tries to interpret the father's presence as a warning of an impending calamity:

[M]i instinto me indicó por algunos segundos que estaba en peligro, que si después de todo había llegado era porque mi madre y yo teníamos apenas unos segundos para el final. . . .
-No es verdad, me consoló.
Y su sabiduría me levitó. (96)

[For a few seconds my instincts told me that I was in danger. If after all that, he had come, it was because my mother and I had but a few seconds left for the end. . . .
-It's not true, he consoled me.
And his wisdom levitated me.]

Although the father's spirit dismisses any immediate harm, eventually Coya, her mother, and friends do end up in jail. And it is at the peak of physical torment during a torture session that Coya in her role as shaman calls forth the spiritual strength necessary to survive: "Yo queja a más no poder del daño, estropeo y maldad a mi cuero. Machacada, machi, mucho me asusto y hago un extremo intento cuando levanto penosamente un brazo y mis dedos intentan tocar el ojo azul, el cielo azul tan implacable para mí" (174) [I complain to no end from the hurt, damage and evil to my hide. Mashed, "machi" much I fear and I make an extreme attempt when I laboriously raise an arm and my fingers try to touch the blue eye, the blue sky so implacable for me].

As revealed by Coya's attitude and others' treatment of her in prison, she stands apart from the rest of the women. In this respect, the protagonist of [*For the Homeland*] too embodies a similarity with the female machi of Mapuche life. An outstanding characteristic of a machi, which differentiates her from other Mapuche women, is her liberty to voice her opinion and make her own decisions. Unlike ordinary women bound to the traditional role of wife and mother and the dictates of husbands, a machi can choose whether or not to marry and have children, which in any event becomes secondary to her role as shaman. "Machis rule themselves," says one informant,[65] which means that unlike other Mapuche women they do not answer to men or ask permission of their husbands to go off (sometimes for days) on a business call; rather, machis receive respect and reverence from both men and women, including their own husbands who help with those domestic chores that their machi wife is not obliged to do.[66] In fact, the "lonko," or community head, may call in a machi for advice concerning an important issue. Together, machis and lonkos (and during strife the "toquis" as leaders in war) are the traditional authorities in a Mapuche community.

From all indications in [*For the Homeland*], Coya and her father are looked to as community leaders who command the barrio's respect. Yet one must keep in mind that for all their local status, mainstream Chilean society considers them marginal. Eltit portrays a strong-willed female figure whose characteristics match those of a true-to-life machi—a respected, independent woman with a mind of her own who rules herself and thus is free to come and go as she pleases. The significance of this portrayal lies in the fact that outside Coya's immediate community she is simply another poor and voiceless Indian woman.

During her incarceration Coya begins to record the plight of the oppressed, and in this respect [*For the Homeland*] turns into a prison memoir of the same strain as the "resistance literature" that Barbara Harlow studies in her book by that title. When everything about detention threatens to control her life, Coya turns to what Michel Foucault calls the "power of writing," a method of subversion banned by prison authorities across time and geographic boundaries because of its empowering nature for inmates, especially political detainees.[67]

Marina Arrete P. observes that the writing of "History" manifests itself as a key component in Coya's search for identity,[68] that is, self and nation are inextricably linked in the novel. Hence the book's interpretation, whether based on oppression in earlier or recent Chilean history, must point out the text's questioning of official history as represented by Juan[69] —community member turned informer and prison guard. When Coya renders her own account of her mother's seduction, Juan insists on another version:

-No, dijo Juan. Ocurrió de esta manera anota:
La madre que era bailarina y experta, se vio seducida por el zarco quien no le dio tregua hasta convencerla y apabullar a toda la familia al decirle que ella era más.
Cedió fácil y partió sin problematizar el destino que estaba tomando. Dejó la carta sobre la mesa y parcó. (48)

[-No, Juan said. It occurred this way take note:
The mother who was a dancer and an expert, found herself seduced by the Slav who did not let up until convincing her and crushing the entire family by telling her that she was above them.
She gave in easily and left without questioning the path she was taking. She left the letter on the table and took off.]

Juan presses Coya not only to record his version ("anota" [take note], he commands), but to also acknowledge it as the official story: "-Reconoce, dijo Juan" (49) [Admit it, said Juan], to which she responds with noncomplicity: "-No, no reconozco nada, botemos esta papelería, es basura" (49) [No, I won't admit a thing, let's throw out this pile of papers, it's rubbish]. Later in the text Coya continues to reject Juan's official version. "Es imposible" [It's impossible], Coya insists, "Mi mamá jamás tuvo que ver con eslavos de ninguna clase" (66) [My mom never got mixed up with any Slav]. Accounts of what happened to the Chilean mother(land) vary depending on who is in authority to speak and record the story. Coya's writing in prison "emerges as another vehicle of resistance against the intent of domination represented by Juan."[70] But as we will next note, Coya's recording of her (people's) history, albeit significant, is rudimentary since indicators of ethnicity in the novel suggest an ancestry rooted in oral rather than written transmission.

MULTILINGUAL MARGINALITY: ORAL TRADITION AND THE EPIC

Orality remains the ancestral mode indigenous peoples use to perpetuate their culture and hand down their version of history.[71] While in prison, Coya—whose name marks her indigenous nobility, but who paradoxically represents society's marginals (women, the poor, the persecuted, the outcast, native peoples)—struggles to chronicle her story probably due not only to her limited skills but also because writing requires a different mind-set, and certainly a different discourse from oral language.

Berta, one of Coya's cellmates who helps with the editing, alludes to [*For the Homeland*] itself when she remarks on the challenges Coya's text poses for her as a reader: "[E]lla misma fue la que le dio coherencia y sentido a los papeles mal escritos que Coya le entregó. Le parecía imposible sacar algo legible de allí, pero sacrificó sus horas de sueño y rehízo lo escrito" (210) [She herself was the one who gave some coherence and made sense out of the badly written papers that Coya handed her. It seemed to her impossible to make out something legible from them, but she sacrificed her sleep time and re-did the writing]. Berta persists in her task because deciphering Coya's writing means disclosing an aspect of Chile's unofficial history that includes her and the other women prisoners. Let us keep in mind that published in 1986 under censorship and given the thematic exposé of national crisis, the novel would probably not have seen the light of day (and Eltit may have ended up behind bars like her protagonist) had it not been for the text's unorthodox writing. Hence, the reader must contend with character as well as linguistic marginality.

Breaking away from the erudite language associated with literature dates back to the first Latin American novel, *El periquillo sarniento* (1816). Its Mexican author, Joaquín Fernández de Lizardi, chose Castilian over Latin and moreover inscribed street language, that is, speech then not considered proper for "the realm of public writing."[72] As studied in the chapter on *E. Luminata*, graffiti, literally a form of public writing, can be associated with Coya's resistance writing in prison in as much as it is a clandestine operation, the grammar is poor ("papeles mal escritos"), it is attributed to the lower strata of society, the message is one of protest, and it serves as an escape valve under repression.[73] In order to record her orally-based culture, Coya appropriates writing, which, to use Rama's concept, traditionally belongs to the "lettered" elite. Ultimately, Coya's illegal writing, like graffiti, testifies to the "desire to exist more completely by leaving a tangible mark of identity."[74]

Eltit reminds us that in a Chile under dictatorship, government and self-imposed censorship shaped new ways of "how to say things and what to say."[75] At the time, "all literary production was altered" the author points out as she further explains the difference in the then emerging generation of writers, one rooted in the "torturous manner of naming the reality of daily life" during those years when the "tremendously repressive" nature of the novel in Chile paralleled political circumstance.[76] In order to break away from the standard structure of the national novel—symbolically subverting the political status quo as well—Eltit borrowed from different genres (something she had already explored in *E. Luminata*) and incorporated various types of languages which together composed a coded, and often obscure, discourse reflective of the communicative needs of a society affected by oppression.

The Mapuche philosophy about life—as something to be lived and not questioned because what counts is experiencing it, not deciphering its many mysteries[77]—may prove a useful approach for those readers who have a low tolerance for frustration. The emotional charge conveyed in [*For the Homeland*] is one aspect of the novel that can better be experienced than explained. Raquel Olea observes fluctuations or contradictions in narrative construction indicated by such phrases as "Miento," "Era al revés," "No, no fue así," "No, no era así" (10–11) [I lie; It was the other way around; No, it did not occur like that; No, it was not like that].[78] Other indicators of a challenging text include the use of alliteration ("Corrí Coa y Coya por la calle," 27), repetition of the same words or phonetically similar words ("pariste," "partiste," 75; "lama, llana, llama;" "barrio," "barro," "hampa," "apa," 29) as well as syntactic distortions.[79]

The abundance of language and the variety of techniques that rival the protagonist for the spotlight on the "margins" contribute to narrative complexity because they "disrupt any sense of signifying security or univocality."[80] Readers of [*For the Homeland*] must keep in mind that Coya is not a fully developed, well-rounded character that they can get to know, for, in fact, her role is representational. She embodies an array of identities and not surprisingly she speaks in many tongues. Brito remarks how the protagonist explores many language registries including Spanish when it was introduced into Latin America, Amerindian languages, and today's popular modes of expression—all of which constantly come into contact in the text but without forming any particular hierarchy.[81]

Throughout the episode where Coya tends her wounded father, for example, she uses poetic language with a baroque flair: "Esclava suya, corcel de sus piernas, sí, yo, jinete de su cabalgadura, él jinetera al hombro. No, pistola cruzada en el pecho, mi amante del pecho vendado la bala" (29) [His slave, courser of his legs, yes, I, jockey of his mount, he saddle-backed. No, pistol across his chest, my chest-bandaged lover the bullet]. The following passage illustrates the use of hyperbaton as diversion from modern Spanish syntax: "me muero de ti por pena del cuero, de la salud suya, yo la Coya entera la noche en vela, solos los dos y mío, aunque herido y reventado ceñudo también lo quise: pagar la cuenta suya puedo yo, esconderlo hasta el olvido a usté" (32) [I die from you for hide's sorrow, of his health, I the Coya the night entire on vigil, alone us both and mine, despite injured and exhausted scowling I too loved him: pay his debt can I, hide him until the forgetfulness of you]. However, alongside baroque discourse the reader also finds popular constructions such as, "Te hei jurado," "pa que," "Me dai más," "Lo hai sacado," "¿qué estai?" "ni haiga paz" (29–32), interspersed with formal, even foreign, structures: "l'amante," "L'amor," "l'cuerpo" (30–31). Given Coya's role as "machi," the linguistic distortions also suggest the mysterious invocations of a shaman. After all, she embodies the archetype of the "witch," a subversive figure in American, Latin American, indigenous, and even African cultures.

Besides the repetition of words mentioned earlier, internal rhyme reinforces the complexity of textual construction while creating a sense of orality.[82] Both repetition and rhyme are important elements in the epic genre, one embedded in Eltit's text as we will expound on later. The epic in turn is closely connected with myth and the oral tradition, a quality found in [*For the Homeland*] which links it to the indigenous method of transmitting culture. In fact, verbatim transcriptions into Spanish from Mapudungun illustrate to what extent word repetition occurs in Mapuche storytelling.[83] Because Mapudungun developed as a spoken and not a written language, punctuation is not used, thus, when read, it gives a run-on sentence effect similar to the result Eltit accomplishes with internal rhyme in the text. Shifts between poetic and popular language, which reflect Coya's identity as both noble and marginal, appear throughout the novel.

The book, which begins with an allusion to a maternal (ma, ma, ma . . .)—and conceivably Mapuche—bond, concludes with a multilingual celebration of marginality: "Se levanta el coa, el lunfardo, el giria, el pachuco, el caló, caliche, slang, calao, replana. El argot se dispara y yo" (278) ["Coa," "lunfardo," "giria," "pachuco," "caló," "caliche," "slang," "replana," all arise. The argot takes off and I.] As Djelal Kadir points out, these language variants fall outside "the institutionally sanctioned and grammatically lawful."[84] Therefore, the addition of "Mapudungun" to the above list seems natural for a book that Eltit admits writing with a dictionary of Mapuche terms.[85] The preservation of native language constitutes a stronghold of Mapuche resistance equivalent to the arsenal Coya's father is rumored to hide. Revolutionizing language in writing is one weapon Eltit wields in her struggle to insert the margins into the Chilean literary mainstream.

Let us recall that from the beginning of the novel Coya is associated with nonstandard language. She also identifies herself as Coa, the lingo in Chile associated with delinquents. In this regard Tierney-Tello lucidly observes that "Coya/Coa is a personification of language itself; she is 'dual y bilingüe.' "[86] Named as "Coa" from conception and acknowledged as "pariah" by her own mother, she, as both "Coa and Coya" (that is, marginal in language and identity), runs through barrio streets to get home to her father who is rumored to be headed there, wounded.[87] The need for bicultural self-affirmation awakens after "the tragedy" which, given the protagonist's multifaceted identity, alludes concurrently to several events: the conquest of native peoples, the 1973 military coup d'etat, and the death of her father.[88] "Esa noche de la tragedia, alguien acabó en mi nombre y desde entonces dual y bilingüe si me nombran Coa y Coya también" (22) [The night of the tragedy, someone stopped at my name and since then dual and bilingual if they call me Coa as well as Coya], the protagonist remarks. The loss of rights, liberty, and life is the common denominator in this Chilean "tragedy."

Coya, confined to a prison cell, incarnates the situation of political dissidents under dictatorship as well as the predicament of women guarded and sequestered by men like Juan.[89] Her confinement in terms of limited physical space, the uprooting from her community, and the loss of freedom likewise suggest the plight of indigenous peoples in Chile who, ousted from their lands, live within the boundaries of the "reducciones" or reservations. Although they are casualties of oppression, neither native Chileans nor Coya (novelistic embodiment of all marginalized Chileans) have relinquished memory—the vehicle for survival.

After suffering incarceration, torture, and all sorts of physical deprivation, memory remains Coya's last bastion of resistance which Juan, prison guard and symbol of the dictatorship's tactics, realizes he must usurp if he is to dominate her. Significantly, in this last attempt for control, Juan explicitly states his intention to "empty" her of all memory except for her ignoble period in confinement:

-¿Cómo puedes tener mi memoria? ¿Cómo puedes robármela? . . . .
-Aprendí, Coya, para eso me entrené todo este tiempo.
-¿Toda mi memoria Juan? ¿Toda completa?
-No entera. . . . Te dejo el encierro intacto, pero para atrás nada: Coya voy a parirte de nuevo, así como estás ahora, ajada, avejentada, calmada. (244)

[How can you have my memory? How can you rob me of it?. . . .
-I learned how, Coya, for such purpose I've been training all this time.
-All my memory Juan? Completely all of it?
-No, not completely. . . . I'll leave you with the incarceration untouched, but before that nothing: Coya I'm going to give birth to you anew, like you are now, worn-out, aged, calm.]

As we will see later, memory plays an important role in the epic, an oral form for communicating heroic struggle announced in the second part of [*For the Homeland*] titled "Se funde, se opaca, se yergue la épica" [The epic burns out, dims, flares up]. Given Chile's history, this reference in the novel summons the sixteenth-century epic *The Araucana* by Spaniard poet Alonso de Ercilla y Zúñiga who renders lyrically the confrontations between Spanish troops and the Araucan or Mapuche. Inevitably, Chilean readers will associate Coya's declaration—"Hay una épica" (273) [There's an epic]—with Ercilla's work, especially since the protagonist's name, her social marginalization, her loss of freedom in prison, and her spirit of resistance constitute cues of her indigenous identity.

Eltit has commented that she intended to make an epic of marginality with characters that were not merely survivors but combatants[90]—"survivors" and "combatants," two words that describe the history of the Mapuche people. In the novel Coya indeed emerges as an outstanding figure that incarnates one oppressed group's struggle for survival. Keeping in mind the "parodic and carnivalesque twist" in the protagonist's role as mythic heroine,[91] let us identify those components that would uphold Coya's proclamation of an epic.

Traditionally—with Homer—the epic has been a genre rooted in poetry, and despite the previously noted poetic qualities of [*For the Homeland*] it remains a novel. Similar to Eltit's avant-garde writing, in citing the case of James Joyce's *Ulysses*, G. J. B. Watson notes that "the survival of epic form into modern times is a live issue, and the

application of epic modes to modern experience . . . an exciting tribute to the longevity and adaptability of this most distinguished of
literary kinds."[92]

The epic mode in its early manifestations shows an affinity with
mythology since myths developed as a way of explaining man's environment, that is, the phenomenon of nature, and his experience in
dealing with the mysteries of daily life. Unexplainable forces of nature (winds, sunrise, sunset, hurricanes, lightning, thunder, volcanic
eruptions, earthquakes) for example were commonly attributed to
the will of specific gods. The "machi's" close relationship with natural forces and the underworld ties her marginal figure to a mythic
tradition. The word "mythology" from its Greek derivation "mythos," a tale, and "logos," an account, could be defined, Alexander
S. Murray explains, as "an account of tales" that relates "the origin,
character, and functions of the ancient gods . . . the origin of mankind, and the primitive condition of the visible world."[93]

Hugh Fox explores one connection between myth and the epic
that bridges the "ancient Old World" with the "ancient New World"
of the Americas and points us towards Ercilla's confrontation between the Spaniards and the Araucans in Chile. According to Fox,
the voyage or journey motif found in classic epics refers back to a
remote time, lost to memory, when a voyage across the ocean to
South America actually took place. "We're back to *The Argonautica*,"
remarks Fox, "and its sequential similarity to its Amerindian counterparts."[94] Fox has compared a multitude of Amerindian, Asiatic
and Mediterranean myths and found strong evidence of mythological connections among them for they all speak of a voyage during
which a hero overcomes trials in an unknown land (sometimes expressed as the underworld) and eventually succeeds in returning to
his homeland.

In regard to Fox's contention of an ancient transatlantic encounter, [*For the Homeland*] contains an epic aspect connected to myth
insofar as Coya embodies Chile's Amerindian roots and, as we shall
point out later, she also encounters outsiders, in the form of an oppressive state that launches her on a journey which entails surviving
and returning home alive.

What is meant by "myth," of course, can be ambiguous perhaps
due to fluctuation in cultural relevance. Myth in the life of a Mapuche shaman, for instance, diverges drastically from a Eurocentric
reader's notion of myth because the functioning of our society no
longer relies on origin stories or exemplary models for explaining
the world of nature and human behavior. Mircea Eliade points out
that "the Greeks steadily continued to empty 'mythos' of all reli-

gious and metaphysical value. Contrasted both with 'logos' and, later, with 'historia,' 'mythos' came in the end to denote 'what cannot really exist.' "[95]

In primitive societies, however, sacred stories were part and parcel of a peoples' religion and ritual celebrations. While in general myth has come to mean fable, invention, and fiction, for archaic peoples "myth" denotes a true story, one that is cherished because of its sacred significance.[96] Among the many explanations of myth, Eliade's version, worth quoting here at length, incorporates the sacred nature man originally bestowed on it:

> Myth narrates a sacred history; it relates an event that took place in primordial Time, the fabled time of the "beginnings." In other words, myth tells how, through the deeds of Supernatural Beings, a reality came into existence, be it the whole reality, the Cosmos, or only a fragment of reality—an island, a species of plant. . . . Myth then, is always an account of a "creation"; it relates how something was produced, began to *be*. Myth tells only of that which *really* happened, which manifested itself completely. The actors in myths are Supernatural Beings. They are known primarily by what they did in the transcendent time of the "beginnings." Hence myths disclose their creative activity and reveal the sacredness (or simply the "supernaturalness") of their works. In short, myths describe the various and sometimes dramatic breakthroughs of the sacred (or the "supernatural") into the World.[97]

In the sense that myth recounts the "beginnings," let us recall that [*For the Homeland*] begins with Coya's conception.

The divine aspect of myth, however, eroded "in later times of higher civilization and greater refinement, when the origin of the gods as personifications of natural phenomena was lost sight of" and mythic "stories came to be viewed as disgraceful" and were even ridiculed in plays, thus eventually discrediting the faith in the gods.[98] With the abandonment of myth as the realm of the gods and the supernatural, man's life and glory became the focus of action and in the scheme of things he emerged as the epic mythic hero. Hence the evolution from the irrational/supernatural aspect of myth to the rational/human nature of the epic.

As a basic mythic pattern evident in much of epic writing across national boundaries and time, a hero leaves home on some kind of voyage or quest, and a set of trials must be endured and overcome on the journey that concludes with a return home. On the last page of the novel we read: "El fuego, el fuego, el fuego y la épica" (297) [The fire, the fire, the fire and the epic]. And for a successful return home Coya announces: "-Se abre el bar, mujeres. Lo abrimos, lo administramos con jerarquía" (279) [The bar opens, women. We open it, we manage it with hierarchy].

The epic is the genre of great crisis generally expressed through the image of combat and warfare.[99] "It may be coincidental," remarks Tom Winnifrith, "that Virgil, Dante and Milton wrote their epics after a grueling civil war, in which their emotions had been heavily involved."[100] In exploring the meaning that Homeric poems had for fifth-century B.C. poets and their audiences, John Gould associates the epic with what Jean-Pierre Vernant calls "le moment tragique," the birth of tragic drama. It is the moment in Greek history when debate, doubt, and conflict began to invade the belief-system of ancient Greeks.[101] By the time of Aeschylus, social and political change had "brought about a radical break with many fundamental strands in traditional thinking about human experience."[102] As an expression of the times, around the fifth-century the notion of epic began to shift from individual super feats to more contemporary experiences of war.[103] For example, when a play portrays the Trojan War the audience hears not just of particular heroes but about the miseries of war conditions suffered by the mass of men who fought.[104] In the novel, Coya and the women (like the female chorus of Greek dramas) imprisoned with her are symbolically victims of a nation's history (both the Spanish Conquest and the dictatorship's war against subversives). They represent the dispossessed, Chile's marginalized sectors.

The epic is about heroes, but most of all about survivors (the hero makes it back home alive). The myth pattern and circumstance given to epic are repeatedly present in [*For the Homeland*]. Reminiscent of the downfall of Troy, after the fall of the bar under fire Coya is forced to leave home and enters prison, a figurative land of the dead, a descent into the underworld where monsters in the form of torturers put her through hell. Coya's vision quest is to make it out alive. In order to survive she must endure psychological and physical trials that are barbaric. Although undoubtedly a patriarchal domain, prison in the novel is populated by women with Coya as the masculinized heroine, a devouring mother who deviates from prevalent models of femininity and figuratively castrates Juan, her oppressor.[105] Tafra observes that by disarming Juan, Coya decenters the phallus, which means a decentering of the logos as well.[106] As we will study in the next chapter, this symbolic appropriation of male power is also present in *The Fourth World*. In that novel the female twin usurps the Word, displaces her twin brother as narrator, and takes the sexual initiative in what develops into an incestuous relationship.

In Greek drama women did not have a role per se on the stage, but their situation was nevertheless portrayed in epic form because, as Gould highlights, "[W]hen a fifth-century dramatist wants an image of the human suffering of war, all war, it is to the women of Troy that he instinctively turns, as Euripides did in *Hecabe, Andromache* and *Trojan Women.*"[107] Moreover, parallel to Eltit's depiction of the ordeals of incarceration, "Euripides can present the treatment of the Trojan captives by the Greek victors as itself the act of 'barbarians': 'it is you Greeks,' says Andromache in *Trojan Women,* 'who have devised barbarian cruelty.' "[108]

"Barbarism" can certainly describe the methods Pinochet's state apparatus used against detainees in Chile. The figure of the Latin American dictator surfaces when in *Prometheus* Zeus is read as a "tyrant who has just seized an arbitrary power with the backing of his kinsmen and whose 'court' is thronged by lesser gods who owe their powers and privileges to him."[109] In *Imaginación y Violencia en América,* Chilean critic Ariel Dorfman contends that given the history and (geographic, political, social) realities of Latin America, its literature inherently portrays violence engendered by or committed against, usually, the protagonist who commonly dies a violent death.

Coya can be included among the Latin American protagonists that, immersed in a harsh life/death predicament, pose themselves the following questions: "How do I survive in this world, how do I maintain my human dignity, how do I liberate myself, how do I use this violence instead of it using me?"[110] As with the marginal community in [*For the Homeland*], Dorfman identifies a vertical type of oppression or violence committed against those who do not have the power to fight back such as women, the poor, the native, the black. Unlike the Naturalists, Dorfman observes, contemporary writers focus on characters that rebel in a variety of ways so that even if they do not succeed in the struggle themselves, others to follow may attain liberation.[111] The epic genre fits right in then with the theme of "civilización y barbarie" portrayed in the Latin American narrative of the first half of the twentieth century, and which has made a comeback in contemporary fiction especially on the theme of dictatorship. The return to barbarism that Dorfman points out reflects a return to the violence of Latin American origin and conquest.[112]

Clearly, the cities in many of the novels dealing with the Southern Cone during the 1970s and 1980s, including [*For the Homeland*], have become jungles where man hunts down his adversary and political subversives are persecuted like animals. For this reason the protagonists embody an almost supernatural sense of struggle, an epic dimension for overcoming the forces and the world that attempts to

exploit them.[113] In contemporary Latin American novels "civilization" overflows with barbaric acts of torture. The violence perpetrated against Coya and her friends is symbolically committed
against the whole of Chile, and given the protagonist's name, by extension symbolizes the centuries of cruelty towards the indigenous
peoples of the Americas. Hence, figuratively, the survival of Chile's
dispossessed including that of its native communities rests on Coya's
resilience and liberation. Coya can be read as Chile—indigenous
Mother Earth and modern nation.

Besides identifiable motifs that include a journey, grueling trials,
a return home, and a warlike atmosphere of violence, "orality"—an
outstanding feature of Mapuche culture and a predominant aspect
in Eltit's novel—likewise connects [For the Homeland] with the epic
genre. Singing or recitation was the realm of the ancient bard who
characteristically is portrayed entertaining the nobles at feasts.[114]
The bard himself depicted in the lays of the Iliad and Odyssey was
considered divine in the sense of possessing the favors of the gods
who inspired his singing. In this regard, when the novel is elevated
to epic status, Coya's favored rank as machi, one who possesses special spiritual powers, parallels that of the ancient bard. In classical
epic the bard, the seer, and the healer of diseases, considered public
workers, carry out functions that parallel those of the machi of Mapuche culture. Coya is the one in the novel to narrate the predicament of her community, and as machi she is both prophet and
healer who tends her dying father with all the herbal remedies of
her vocation. Both bard and machi are masters of "some craft which
can be of service to the community at large."[115]

"In general," comments Penelope Murray, "the bard is described
sympathetically and in terms of respect, even though he is not always
treated respectfully by the characters within the poems."[116] Coya's
relationship with friends and family reveals yet another parallel with
the epic bard. While on the one hand she distinguishes herself as a
respected figure, sometimes feared by the other women, at times
those close to her also harass her. Coya as machi, like the bard who
is "famous and respected because of his art" can also trace a connection with the "aristocracy," but this does not mean that they [machi
and bard] do not maintain a close "association with the people."[117]
Thus the bard is attributed with both divine and profane links.
Among the epithets (renown, faithful, hero, honored by the people)
used for bards in epic poems which can also apply to a machi, that
of "faithful" often appears associated with a "comrade" or "com-
panion," usually of lower rank than the bard or hero himself. Coya's

friends indeed fit this description as comrades or companions of a lower status, at least in the hierarchy of prison life.

Memory is another theme that alludes to Eltit's intention for an epic motif in the novel's construction. For a bard, oftentimes blind and living in an oral culture (in this respect like the Mapuche), memory was of vital importance.[118] Notably, the bard is divinely inspired to sing and recite stories by the grace of the Muses, and Mnemosyne, the goddess of memory (and especially the memory or recollection of great events), was the mother of all the Muses.[119] Thus when the poet/bard was possessed by the Muses he drew "directly from Mnemosyne's store of knowledge."[120] Let us recall that Juan, as jailer and representative of an oppressive regime, threatened to usurp Coya's memory, a fact that connects her to such epic characters as Homer's Odysseus and James Joyce's Bloom, both menaced in like manner and "linked by having to voyage through dangerous seas, literal in the case of Odysseus, a metaphorical sea of matter in the case of Bloom" and a psychophysical sea of torment for Coya notably because hers entails a voyage of self-discovery.[121]

Given the importance of memory in mythology, it is not surprising that in Indian myth an amnesia-sleep motif equates to ignorance, captivity, slavery, loss of self, and death, while the recuperation of memory (anamnesis) is a prerequisite for immortality.[122] Part of prison life for the women in [*For the Homeland*] means being subjected to sleep-inducing drugs that keep them asleep or groggy, alter their memory, cause delirium in some, but above all strip them of control, so they become malleable inmates. Blindfolding or symbolically blinding the captive is the first step toward immersing her in ignorance and disorientation that leads to "the fall of the spirit" and true bondage.[123]

We had noted previously that "prison" in the mythic theme of the novel represents a descent to the underworld found in Greek mythology and is comparable to the amnesia motif of Indian myth where "[t]he fountain Lethe, 'forgetfulness,' is a necessary part of the realm of Death."[124] Notably also, in Greek mythology Hypnos (sleep) and Thanatos (death) are twin brothers. Since the ability to remember means to live forever, Juan's attempt to empty Coya of her memory aims to strip her not only of Self, but of the vast cultural memory that she embodies as Coya, machi, and "madre de madres," that is, her peoples' ethnic identity. Through myth, ritual, and customs, which require memory for the transmittal of oral culture, the Mapuche of Chile have labored to keep their way of life from dying. Apropos, George de Forest Lord reminds us that Homeric poems "could be memorized and passed on through the race unaltered from generation to generation. The *Iliad* and *Odyssey* preserve not only the history of outstanding men and women from remote times; they also incorporate the code of an entire culture."[125]

Coya struggles doubly in prison in her quest for self-discovery (who is she?). After all, her father was killed and her mother has disappeared. Suddenly she finds herself orphaned, perhaps one more "huacha," an identity rooted in the Spanish conquest. Hence, her motivation to stay alive is complex because it also includes a quest for communal survival. Borrowing de Forest Lord's words, in [*For the Homeland*] "the narrative pattern relates both the success of the hero in search of himself and his success in restoring or preserving his culture."[126] Becoming motherless and fatherless means losing the parents as bulwarks of one's biological origin and cultural roots. The transformation of the hero, or a rite of passage, is part of the basic dark mythic journey and detectable in the novel for Coya is a stronger person as a result of her hellish ordeal. While in prison she stands out as a leader of women and vows to make it out alive, which she does. Coya has defeated the dark forces of forgetfulness and death incarnated by Juan, the threshold guardian (literally the women's guardian/guard in prison) who mandates tortures symbolically reminiscent of ancient human sacrifice to the gods.[127]

These mythic/epic characteristics of the novel are not devoid of connection to modern Chile for they bridge the gap in thematics between the contemporaneity of Pinochet's Chile and the antiquity of the Mapuche nation. Moreover, textual construction inextricably incorporates a generic play between the written/novel/modernity and the oral/epic/antiquity modes of narrating the Chilean nation. Coya's torturous trials in prison remind us of the journey that many Chileans underwent as a result of the persecutory policy of the state apparatus during the military regime. Myths tell of the horrors that lurked everywhere in primordial times, the wrath of the gods was placated with human sacrifice, and man feared the omnipresent unknown. This scenario can be easily transposed to the state of terror that blanketed many sectors of a militarized Chile under Pinochet. The dictator and his secret service were the omnipresent forces, the monsters menacing society. Many Chileans succumbed under barbaric treatment. And then the nation was asked to forget, to erase the eighteen years of terror from the collective memory and work towards democratic transition and reconstruction, as if a large portion of the population had not lived in a hell, an "underworld," for so long. The novel's revelatory quest intends to inscribe those horrors of a nation's history specifically so that it is not lost to memory.

As the title suggests, this memorial narrative project is for "la patria," [the mother/fatherland].

Thus Eltit's [*For the Homeland*] is a modern, female-centered, multilingual/genred, and marginal rendition of a national epic evoking, but inevitably diverging from, Ercilla's classic composition. In the section "Vencedores y vencidos" ["Winners and Losers"] (also reminiscent of Spanish/Mapuche relations) the narrative of native women's part in their people's epic battles parallels the hardships of prison life experienced by Coya, the women of her group, and many in Chile. The female epic featured here wields procreation as an important weapon in the fight for group survival: "han parido, han parido hasta el cansancio" (259) [they have given birth, labored to exhaustion]. Moreover, in Eltit's epic, not male warriors but brave women and specifically mothers (as is the case in recent Southern Cone history) embody native peoples' plight in the face of persecution:

Han emigrado:
   Portando, llevando en las espaldas los vástagos. Han cruzado pantanos, altiplanos, cumbres moderadas huyendo de la invasión y acurrucadas sobre los arenales con las piernas abiertas y la sangre: el niño, la niña bañada con agua fría en el río al alba. (259)

[They have emigrated:
   Carrying, bearing their offspring on their backs. They have crossed marshes, high plateaus, moderate peaks fleeing from the invasion and huddled over the sands with open legs and the blood: the boy, the girl bathed with cold water in the river at dawn.]

Women have fought and traveled alongside men, often the very ones that have victimized them: "Solas, solas, solitarias reclutadas al rifle, al caballo en ancas, el inca, el cacique que las perturbó. Reductas al fin pariendo y mezclando la sangre con blancura . . ." (259) [Alone, alone, solitary recruits at gunpoint, on horseback, the Inca, the cacique that perturbed them. In the end reduced to giving birth and mixing the blood with whiteness . . .]. Victims of historical circumstance and gender, the last line of the quote suggests native women's birthing of the whiter mestizo race.

Coya also Coa, pariah, Indian, and mestiza along with the other incarcerated women embody the hybrid nature of the Chilean nation, a hybridity symbolically portrayed in the various genres of [*For the Homeland*]'s textual construction. Eltit's contemporary epic pays tribute to Chilean indigenous peoples whose spirit of struggle against oppression echoes in the voices of those who in recent history fought dictatorship. Coya proclaims an epic in an effort to keep a nation's memory alive and to insert its social, political, ethnic, and cultural margins into the Chilean literary mainstream.

4

El cuarto mundo: A Dialogue
in Gender Differences

In *EL CUARTO MUNDO/THE FOURTH WORLD,* AS IN [*VIGILANT*] AND [*WORK-ers of death*], Eltit continues to develop the dysfunctional family introduced in [*For the Homeland*]. However, in these books the author's concern for underprivileged groups concentrates on the situation of females within the Latin American family. Likewise, the topic of "lo indio" paramount in my reading of [*For the Homeland*] also appears in *The Fourth World,* but not until quite late in the story. The racial struggle noted in the previous chapter shifts its focus in this novel to the common battle between the sexes within a patriarchal society where being born female, for most Latin American women, means a life shaped by oppression and marginalization.

The Fourth World presents gender inequities as a map from which to draw analogies for other exploitative behavior occurring in Latin American territories. And since, as Tafra has succinctly noted, all of Eltit's discourse ultimately reverts to a reflection on literature itself, the chapter explores how the status of Latin American women writers compares to the cultural inscriptions of their male counterparts.[1] In the study I also argue that women writers' inferior standing vis-à-vis men's formidable power parallels the historical position of Latin America in the face of imposed Spanish colonialism and North American imperialism.

In Chile today more women writers are taking part in female networks to alleviate the isolation that naturally comes with their craft and as a show of solidarity in the face of an establishment that regards men as the authorities in virtually all matters of cultural endeavor.[2] The overwhelming majority of literary critics are predominantly middle-class male intellectuals who have authored books, and their opinion carries much clout when promoting—or discrediting—a writer's work. They clearly control cultural production as judges in literary contests or directors of special projects vested with the power to grant or withhold scholarship awards and funds. Men

121

also compose the majority on editorial boards with control over publication of book manuscripts, which most likely a man will critique once released in book form.

Against these odds, Diamela Eltit has emerged as a writer of cultural consequence. In 1990 she was appointed as Chile's cultural attaché in Mexico City, where she lived until 1994. While in Mexico she traveled to Cuba in 1992 to serve as judge for a La Casa de las Américas literary contest, and she is often called upon to appear in culturally related functions in Santiago and elsewhere in Chile. But recognition in her homeland has come slowly for Eltit who rejects the restrictions of conventional writing. As we have studied thus far, transgression and exclusion go hand in hand in Eltit's work and apply to both the marginal characters that populate her novels as well as to the writer herself.

Transgression has been at the core of Eltit's novelistic themes since the publication of her first book, *E. Luminata*, with its disregard for traditional narrative, syntax, and lexicon as well as its focus on social outcasts. Likewise, neither writing nor characters in her second novel, [*For the Homeland*], conform to mainstream practices. Reading becomes easier with this her third novel, *El cuarto mundo*, published in 1988 and translated as *The Fourth World* in 1995. In fact, Eltit admits that she consciously wrote the book "como una señorita" [as a lady], that is, properly adhering to the rules of grammar.[3] As already noted, the earlier narrative innovations prompted Chilean critics to point to Eltit's enigmatic and obscure style, thus contributing to pigeonholing her work as too difficult to understand.[4] Exclusion from the general book market was born of Eltit's unorthodox writing, but only in part because in the 1980s the Left in Chile had taken up the banner as representative of the political opposition and boycotted any work not explicitly denunciatory of government repression by labeling it as avant-garde and elitist.[5]

The Fourth World speaks to such exclusionary practices carried out by and against Latin American writers. The novel's emphasis on gender issues underscores the prejudice against women as females, and by extension, as writers. Women's functions, both physiological and cultural, are inscribed in the novel in a parallel agenda of sexual and textual reflexivity. Eltit marks her writing—*E. Luminata*, [*For the Homeland*], *Sacred Cow*, [*Vigilant*]—with female (pro)creative capacities highlighted in the plot of *The Fourth World*, one where readers run the risk of semiotic shipwreck in the watery womb, the menstrual flow, or the bodily fluids of human copulation. Reading in the first part of the novel calls for an exegesis of amniotic space, the site from which a female perspective vies to insert its biological as well as literary creation into mainstream writing tradition.

While focusing on *The Fourth World* this study draws parallels with *Christopher Unborn* by Mexican novelist Carlos Fuentes in the hope that critics will delve further into the transnational dialogue between the two novels which I touch on here.[6] In their respective books Eltit and Fuentes not only incorporate a male fetus as narrator but include a female twin as well. Although Fuentes published the original Spanish version, *Cristóbal Nonato,* in 1987, a year before *El cuarto mundo* appeared, Eltit was not aware of Fuentes's book, as she wrote hers in Chile.[7] Latin American writers may share a language and a cultural tradition—as the siblings in the novels share the womb—but unfamiliarity with each others' writings is common, even within national boundaries.

Both novels depict exclusionary practices that reflect gender bias and insinuate the fe/male perspective of the individual writer. Admittedly, besides a few similarities (a narrating fetus, a set of twins, evidence of the author's gendered perspective), *The Fourth World* and *Christopher Unborn* are otherwise worlds apart. After all, Eltit remains marginal compared to Fuentes, who enjoys notoriety in Mexico as well as abroad and whose books are automatically published, promoted, and incorporated in the canon. However, through a self-reflexive lens, Eltit's novel invites readers to ponder such discrepancies. One aspect of this reading of *The Fourth World,* in dialogue with *Christopher Unborn,* illuminates the gendered relationship between siblings in and across these novels as well as among their respective authors as representatives of a family of Latin American writers.

More so in *The Fourth World* than in *Christopher Unborn,* scrutiny of the twins' experience within their nuclear family suggests an analogy with fellow writers of a literary community where female peers abound at the margins in terms of publication, readership, name recognition, market profitability, and cultural status. In the first part of *The Fourth World* the behavior of the fetuses calls attention to primordial gender roles which the female protagonist attempts to subvert when, shortly upon birth, she realizes the inequities she faces. The sister's struggle for recognition within a family that reveres her brother at her expense illustrates, by extension, the situation of women writers who for generations have witnessed a literary establishment tout the accomplishments of men while they—the sisters—remain shrouded in anonymity. Read as an analogy, the campaign of transgression launched by the rebellious female twin in the text serves as a platform from which to address the exclusion of women's contributions to literary history.

IN DIALOGUE WITH CARLOS FUENTES' *CHRISTOPHER UNBORN*: WHEN PATRIARCHY REACHES INTO THE WOMB

The Fourth World begins with a tale of female vulnerability and male sexual aggression: "On April 7 my mother woke up with a fever. Sweating and fatigued, she moved between the sheets closer to my father ever so painfully, hoping he would come to her aid. Inexplicably and without compunction, my father possessed her, forcing her to submit to his desires. On that April 7, enshrouded in my mother's fever, I . . . was conceived" (3). No doubt from a female perspective, the novel begins with a rape, albeit its implied legality within marriage. "Afterward, when it was over," comments the fetus, "she had a dream infested with feminine horror" (3).[8] In the Spanish text "fui engendrado"[9] reveals the voice of a male fetus, one who not only possesses the words with which to narrate his biological conception even at this preverbal stage of development, but from the outset of his creation story includes the mother's rape, the fundamental "feminine horror" which burdens female existence universally.

Featured prominently, the female body—not stereotyped as either voluptuous, sexy, or ever ready for lovemaking but rather as frightful and ailing with sunken eyes, aching joints, feverish, consumed by thirst, soaked with perspiration, and trembling spasmodically[10]—renders tribute to human frailty and the toll of human conception. Eltit further develops in [*Workers of Death*] the mater dolorosa depicted here who suffers not for someone else—the son—but physically herself. Despite the wife's deteriorating health, the husband in *The Fourth World* insists on his copulative rights and a second child is conceived following another incident of sexual aggression. "The next day, April 8. . . . ," comments the brother, "my father engendered my twin sister" (3–4). Unlike the male, the female fetus does not narrate her own conception; thus the male's right to speak for the other is established in the mother's womb—notably, a space subject to patriarchal assault. The male fetus's accession to language as narrator places him immediately within the Symbolic order described by Jacques Lacan in his linguistic theory.[11]

Lacan identifies three inextricable components—the Real, the Imaginary, and the Symbolic—in the structure of the mature human psyche. The Real—which we will come back to later—encompasses lived experience, incidents and events affecting us in daily existence. If one considers the full range of humanity's past experiences, "The Real in Lacan . . . is simply History itself."[12] Development of the

Imaginary (not having to do with imagination but with image) has been named by Lacan as the "mirror stage," that phase between six and eighteen months when a child makes the connection between self and the image reflected in the mirror, a reflection that prompts the "I" of the subject to come into being.[13] The mirror as object produces the subject's double, a twin. Prior to this stage of development a child does not differentiate between self and mother/caregiver.

In the novel, the "Imaginary" stage occurs figuratively in the womb when the male fetus, although lacking a mirror, discovers the difference between himself and his double—the twin sister. In Lacanian terms, the male fetus of *The Fourth World* begins life with a mature psyche structure (he is aware of his existence, has the ability to distinguish between himself and others in the family, and possesses language know-how)—indeed a being superior to his female sibling.

The narrator of *Christopher Unborn* is also male, and one who initially speaks from an undefined space, but a site that turns out to be the father's testicles. "Ay dios! Out I come . . . I lounged God knows how long in my father's pruny cave . . . until this moment when this man decided to do what he is doing: throw me off balance, tear me off by the roots, nip me in the bud and ejaculate me . . ." (9). By contrast, the male narrator's experience in Eltit's novel is entirely uterine. Notably, each author situates the narrative voice in a fe/male procreative body, which suggests inscription of their own gendered perspective.

The absence of dialogue in the first part of *The Fourth World* means that only the male narrator voices his thoughts.[14] In both novels neither male fetus has been born and each is identified as logocentric, in possession of the "Word" with which to relate a world where male supremacy rules.[15] From the womb they witness the patriarch's sexual prerogative and the mother's subordination. As noted, Eltit's novel opens with a scene of twice-fold marital rape, a subject often introduced but skirted in Latin American women's writing since orthodox Catholic teachings consider sex a conjugal obligation. But social consciousness on the topic and its literary inscription are changing. Chilean writer Marcela Serrano, for example, addresses this type of abuse openly in her novel *Antigua vida mía* (1995), where a middle-class female protagonist kills her husband after several violations; although a scandal rocks the city when she pleads guilty, she is absolved by the courts.

The husband in *Christopher Unborn* is as adamant about sexual intercourse as the male spouses of Eltit and Serrano's novels, but Fuentes presents a humorous situation that dilutes the seriousness of the matter. The wife in *Christopher Unborn* questions her procreative duty and her husband's resolution that she not only produce a male child but must deliver him on 12 October 1992 in order to qualify for a contest in commemoration of the discovery of America. From a male perspective the seductive skills of the husband are too much for the wife to resist and she willingly subordinates her wishes to his. "You'll see, Angel, my mom told my dad," recounts the fetus. "You'll see, he'll be born when you want, I swear to you my love, I'll have him for you on time, sure I will . . . I swear I'll give you a son because that's what the rules say, that's it, I'm no longer demanding the kid be a girl, no Isabella, only Christopher, just as long as you go on whispering into my ear what you've always said to me, honey" (11). In Fuentes's novel, the patriarch's triumph over a reluctant female body (made to procreate at his will) parallels the Spanish conquest of America and the rape of native women. This saga of violence against women played a part of Chilean history as well, but in contrast to Eltit's and Serrano's novels, in *Christopher Unborn* the husband's verbal playfulness during coercive coitus will more likely amuse than outrage readers.[16]

The respective male fetuses of *Christopher Unborn* and *The Fourth World* observe an external world in which parents behave according to gender socialization; fathers demand sexual compliance and mothers act out of fear of displeasing the husbands. As Jean Baker Miller points out, in relationships of inequality, subordinates know that "their fate depends on accommodating to and pleasing the dominants."[17] The wives in Eltit's and Fuentes's novels show signs of submissiveness, passivity, and dependency generally adopted by women in order to avoid conflict with those who have the power to harm, punish, or in some way make life disagreeable for them.

In keeping with this defense mechanism, the mother of *The Fourth World* presents an image that masks her true personality. At first naive, the fetus comments: "my mother had few ideas and her lack of originality irritated me the most" (5). Later he recognizes his misjudgment and says, "Cognizant of events happening around me, I discovered that my mother would lie to my father, a behavior that she had learned well and which was simply a strategic move to perpetuate his illusion of power" (7). In order to cope in an undesirable marriage, the mother plays by the rules of gender, which means repressing the true "self." "While I should have figured it out from the beginning, especially given the nature of her dreams," remarks the fetus, "I had let myself be deceived by her apparent sincerity" (7).

In *The Fourth World,* the male fetus serves as a voyeur of sorts since he is in a position to witness parental behavior that would otherwise be hidden, especially to children. As a woman, the mother has thoroughly internalized her feminine role. For example, although unauthentic, she demonstrates an interest in fashion and physical appearance. "Frankly, she was indifferent to wearing apparel or jewelry," observes the fetus, "it was my father who imposed his desires on her. By consciously submitting to them, she hoped to not only please him but also humiliate him" (7). Her inhibited desires surface as fantasies that "prompted strong guilt and, at times, triggered excessively hard self-punishment" (7). From the womb, the fetus witnesses the mother's attempt at atonement for this guilt by "fasting for several days at a time" (7) or "taking on tasks that she hated to do" (8), like caring for sick elderly people and blind children.

The mother's self-inflicted punishment specifically involves the body and corresponds to cultural dictates traditionally affecting females. Prolonged fasting not only implies abstaining from the physical pleasure of eating, but it also reveals an obsessive preoccupation with dieting, one that calls to mind anorexia and bulimia as predominantly female ailments. In Serrano's *Antigua vida mía,* a busy professional singer faces this issue with her teenage daughter who manifests dissatisfaction with her mother's public role and vies for attention by developing anorexia. In the patriarchal household of Eltit's novel, managing her food consumption may be the only control the mother can exercise, especially over her body. In fact, the fetus observes that his "father did not approve of her dieting" (8), perhaps the very reason why she persists. Whether the wife's dieting serves as atonement for her fantasies or whether her agenda— subconscious or not—aims to subvert patriarchal control, the matter nevertheless focuses on the female body, traditionally a repository of repression as well as object of the other's gaze.

The mother's volunteer work is another aspect of her life that links women to cultural dictates involving the body. Washing the elderly and cleaning the infected eye sockets of blind children may be another form of doing penance, but they are also tasks generally rendered by women and subordinates. Since disposition toward affiliation and service to others are not innate but learned by females, the mother has internalized gender roles—at least to the extent that she feels she must pretend to care about others. Notably, the fetus observes that his father's admiration for her charitable work prompts the mother to relate detailed descriptions of her activities while hiding her true aversion from him.

But aversion to the body is also manifested by the husband who, as a devotee of the beauty cult ("culto de la belleza," 19), avoids sexual intimacy with his wife because her pregnant body repulses him. The husband's selfishness as well as his sexual orthodoxy is revealed when the fetus realizes that his father is incapable of satisfying his mother sexually during the pregnancy. While Eltit's novel attributes the wife's sexual dissatisfaction to the husband's copulative inability ("no era capaz," 19), in *Christopher Unborn*, Fuentes by contrast presents the husband's planned affair with the young Penny López (356, 358) during his wife's pregnancy as a parody of "machismo," a cultural tenet that condones rather than condemns men's marital infidelity. While in *The Fourth World* a feminine perspective underscores the husband's lack of sexual ingenuity during pregnancy, in *Christopher Unborn* rejecting the wife's body for another's is not posed as the husband's inability to satisfy her; on the contrary, his affair is touted as a means of relieving his penned virility.

With the parents as models, the fetuses in each novel begin to assimilate the complexities of power relations between the sexes. But the learning process is not limited to the external world, for they each share the uterine space with a female twin. Significantly, the narrating male fetus in *Christopher Unborn* does not discover his sister's existence until immediately before their birth, which occurs in the antepenultimate page of a book that exceeds five hundred pages. The female's passivity and silence throughout the novel mark her erasure from the plot; she has been altogether displaced from the brother's narrative monopoly.

Unlike the twin sister in Fuentes's novel, in *The Fourth World* the female fetus makes her presence known. From conception she seeks corporal proximity with the brother although he does his utmost to evade closeness. The female yearns affiliation while the male desires autonomy. In this regard the twins reflect common female/male behavior that antedates the socialization that awaits them upon birth. On the other hand, without established rules in the womb, the fetuses act on personal desires instead of adhering to social convention. For example, since the female fetus has not yet learned the practices that correspond to her gender, she is the one who unabashedly pursues proximity with the male until he finally gives in to an encounter. "[E]very time I moved, the currents of the jostling waters would push her forward and, on two occasions, she crashed into me," narrates the male fetus. "I remember these moments as offensive, even threatening" (6).

Complaint about harassment, typically voiced by females as subordinates in a male dominated society, is here communicated by the male fetus who, in discovering sexual difference while rivaling for

space in the womb, alludes to the penis envy Sigmund Freud attributed to women. "Even though I was repulsed by her oppression, I
allowed her to approach me and, *when we rubbed together, she would
rant and rave with envy.*"[18] However, in Eltit's novel the male's narration does include what Freud disregarded in his texts—the clitoris
and female orgasm. "I felt her [trembling] so hard that the turbulent waters hurled me against the surrounding walls,"[19] he recounts,
"Unable to recover in time, I felt her approach me again, with such
frightening impulses, and rub impudently against my incipient but
already established modesty" (10). Such a statement reveals female
sexual autonomy that breaks with traditional archetypes of femininity and masculinity. She not only approaches the male for intimacy,
but he mentions recognizing her tremors—"conocidos temblores"
(18)[20]—apparently existent prior to and independent of the encounter with her male sibling. Implicitly, Eltit debunks penis envy
and genital lack ascribed to women by Freud and instead inscribes
the clitoris—the female sex member which, because it can produce
orgasms without male complicity, has been erased semiotically from
literature.[21]

Moreover, when a uterine encounter between the twins does take
place, it is the male fetus that shows signs of passivity and modesty
traditionally characteristic of females. This behavior, defying social
gender constructs, is remarkable considering that the male conquest of females is an important component of "machismo," or the
cult of virility, prevalent in Chile as well as in the rest of Latin
America.[22] In the womb the female fetus of Eltit's novel exhibits an
unrestrained and precocious sexuality. Contrary to the conventions
of "marianismo," it is she who initiates the male sexually. "Feeling
harassed but not knowing why . . . I tried to push her away," explains
the brother, "but the friction of her obsessive rubbing back and
forth paralyzed me. I surmised that it was preferable to let her satiate
her curiosity . . ." (10).

At this stage of development the twins serve each other as mirror
in the womb, site for a new gender order in which the male contemplates his twin and sees his feminine self. Inversely, the female fetus
sees her masculine self reflected in her male twin. This new "order,"
however, identifies the masculine self as innately withdrawn, modest,
and yielding while the feminine self manifests the outgoing, confi-
dent, and dominant side of human nature. This twist in gender attributes, existing only in the socially uncorrupted space of the womb,
mirrors the animal world where the female, in her capacity to conceive offspring, instinctually seeks out the male for insemination.
The sister also deviates from the stereotype of feminine weakness

even though at the time of conception the male fetus points out her fragility. "My sister was weaker than me, which, of course, was due to the chronology of our conception; nevertheless, the differences between us were still greatly disproportionate" (6), he comments. But contrary to his statement, when the time of birth arrives it is the female child who exerts tremendous physical effort in paving the way out of the birth canal. In fact, the male twin admits not lifting a finger to help ("Yo no hice el menor esfuerzo," 22).[23]

Suzette A. Henke laments the dearth of women's fiction writings— American as well as European—which "articulate the problem of reproductive reality" and "woman's reproductive vulnerability."[24] Why, she asks, do—even feminist—writers shy away from concerns about such topics as contraception, venereal disease, and pregnancy? As I expound further in the chapter on *Sacred Cow*, Latin American literature discloses little by way of writing that reflects female physiological consciousness. Indeed, female bodily functions have been marginalized or excluded from literary inscription, but Eltit is one writer who works toward rectifying erasures of the kind. As North American feminist ideologies started to trickle south two decades ago, Latin American fiction with plots about women's experience as wives and mothers became more common. But the physical trepidations of female fertility and maternity, which Henke finds lacking in Western women's literature, went largely excluded in Latin American women's writing as well. Eltit's focus in *The Fourth World* on life in the womb coupled with constant subversion of gender stereotypes underscores a female-centered perspective intent on setting apart social gender constructs from those aspects of female existence which truly distinguish women from men.

Maternity, both in its biological and psychological dimensions, first appears in the novel embodied in the twins' mother, for whom pregnancy prolongs the disempowerment of the initial spousal aggression. In *The Fourth World* details of the physical and psychological experience that comes with pregnancy help correct the exclusions Henke reprobates in women's fiction writing. "Her body underwent a transformation that overpowered her," says the male fetus. "We would frequently feel her hand touching her tense, stretched skin, probing herself, caught between obsession and dread" (9). Narration makes clear how anxiety-provoking pregnancy can be— especially for a first-time mother who may not know the workings of her body or have access to prenatal information. "[A]ttempting to visualize the biological process going on inside herself" (9), although understandable, is psychologically draining. Extraordinary physical symptoms reflect this woman's state of mind. "Living in a state of agitation," remarks the fetus, "my mother lost part of her hair, and almost lost control of half of her face and the capacity to focus at a distance" (9). Fear and pain, experienced by the pregnant mother, combine to portray a disturbing "sacrificial" attitude reeking of biblical doctrine and "marianismo" (a Molotov cocktail serving as the culture's opiate for its women):

> Her back felt like it was practically splitting down the middle and the expression on her face, covered in a rash, revealed excruciating pain whenever she tried to move.
> She would think about death as the final phase of her biological undertaking and, strangely, she was ever so serene about it. She firmly believed that every mistake, every detestable act of her life, would receive adequate retribution because of her relentless suffering. She was also steadfast in her belief that she was giving up her body in exchange for her soul. Suffering from pain, her flesh had paid for her wrongdoing.
> Her heart, pounding rapidly, thumping hard and even skipping beats, seemed to sound a death knell. . . . She could feel that her own gestating creation was destroying her. (12)

The text suggests that, weaned on church teachings, the mother has internalized sex as "her wrongdoing" for which pain during pregnancy and birth becomes the tithe levied against her—while culpability does not touch the husband. Such phrases as "excruciating pain," "detestable act," "relentless suffering," "giving up her body in exchange for her soul," contribute to a sense of physical as well as psychological martyrdom.

From impregnation to birth, violence envelops human conception in *The Fourth World* and, as we will see later, in [*Workers of Death*] where aggression becomes an unavoidable part of a mother's existence. Nancy Houston's observations on the mutual exclusiveness between war and motherhood point to a "social contract" in which "women are required to breed, just as men are required to brawl."[25] Whereas killing and birth are mutually exclusive from Houston's perspective, it is not so in Eltit's text where biological labor is depicted as a battle fought in and against the mother's body:

> We were provoked into trying to survive at all costs; instinctively, my sister tried to flee by placing her head in the tunnel. Our world turned to chaos, enmeshed in organic turmoil and cellular revolt. My mother's entire physiology was put on alert: blood began to trickle down through the opening.
> My sister lashed out with fury, pounding hard against the stubborn-

ness of her mother's bones. I was alarmed, too, and in response to my
sister's panic, I doubled up and awaited the dramatic spectacle.

My sister's wild behavior seized me with fear. I thought that both our
bodies would be destroyed in the violence. The tension mounted for
hours. (13)

A semiotics of war (survival, instinct, chaos, turmoil, revolt, on alert,
blood, fury, pounding, panic, wild behavior, fear, violence, tension
mounting for hours) underlies textual construction of biological
labor where the womb-turned-battleground becomes the primal
space for bloodshed.

Birthing, like war, can leave physical scars as well as psychological
trauma that are often erased or veiled under the glory of the outcome. Among the signs of a marked female physiological consciousness, the text includes evidence of pre and postpartum depression
as yet another aspect of female experience. The son narrates that
with a second unwanted pregnancy, his mother "took refuge in apathy" (23), "she let herself be dragged down by an insipid feeling"
(25), she felt that "Her life had no meaning or security anymore"
(25), it was not unusual that "she would collapse into a state of mel-
ancholy" (28), all of which indicates that she was "immersed in a
serious personal crisis" (28).

In several respects the circumstances surrounding birth are notably different in *Christopher Unborn*. First, there is no description of
the mother's birthing experience as narrated by the male child in
Eltit's novel. Also, despite sharing the same womb, in Fuentes's text
fraternal contact is nonexistent between the twins. As already observed, the female's presence goes unrecognized until the moment
of birth at the conclusion of the novel, thus snuffing any possibility
for her inclusion. Moreover, the role granted the brother as protec-
tor of a defenseless female and hero in the battle to enter the world
testifies to a glorification of male supremacy (even if intentionally
parodied by Fuentes). Without any evidence of female participation,
the novel concludes with the spectacular birth of the twins. "A child
is being born. . . . He comes into the world holding the hand of a
little girl whose eyes are closed. The boy has his eyes wide open. . . .
He emerges from the belly of his mother as if he were crossing the
pacific sea, carrying the girl on his shoulders, saving her from death
by water" (531). *Christopher Unborn* underscores the lack of fraternal
interaction and when contact does come to light, albeit temporarily
during the birth, the male is born as protagonist and hero—no
blood or pain is represented in this symbolic rather than biologic
birth. This exemplifies how an author's representation of birth can
marginalize, in essence dismiss, a female reality par excellence.

By contrast, in *The Fourth World* the female child singlehandedly tackles the birth odyssey, an undertaking that her male sibling does not participate in but openly takes advantage of. In Eltit's text both siblings confront the same life experience, but the female works much harder than her male counterpart in achieving their goal: birth. Thus, in Eltit's novel the birth scene highlights the privilege with which the male child comes into the world. The disparity in effort plants the seed of contention, which soon thereafter harms the sibling relationship that had developed in the cramped space of the mother's womb. After the twins' birth the characteristics exhibited in the womb change, and the siblings begin to conform to culturally designated male and female traits. For example, the female, once assertive—even audacious—becomes passive in her new environment. The brother is surprised by her "seemingly docile nature"; "As she lay next to me, her body was always subordinate to mine," he remarks (14).

Symbolically, the female's aspiration to satisfy and mold herself to the other starts in the cradle. The brother confirms the sister's subordinate role when he discovers physical pleasure. Whereas he says, "I soon became dependent upon my self-generated excrement: fascinated by its rhythmic production, I would roll about in it, feeling its soft, warm texture. I yearned to bury myself in it and experience from deep down inside the profound nature of pleasure," [his] "sister found consolation in her beauty. She learned to transmit her pleasure to others and, in that way, experience pleasure herself" (15). Yet the sister's apparent docility turns out to be merely a strategy for achieving the affirmation that she desires—a case of powerlessness engendering pretense.

Similarly, her brother presents a false image of himself when he becomes "intentionally unsociable" (14). Although he outwardly communicates aloofness, he yearns for contact with his sister in the cradle as much as he once had evaded her in the womb. "If my extremities reached out for her but didn't find her in the crib, I would begin to wail, for my fear—seemingly more intense than life itself—was always stronger than my hunger," he confesses (13). But the public persona that he presents corresponds to the socially constructed characteristics of male autonomy, which conflict with his true emotional need for relationship. Thus, once born both children show gender traits consistent with social conventions; the female child no longer asserts herself and the male fosters detachment when in fact he craves intimacy.

Whether spotlighting the parental or sibling relationship, the male child's narration in the first part of *The Fourth World* evidences

how predetermined gender classifications promote the inauthenticity that causes strife between the sexes. In the case of the twins, a
major rift occurs when the brother falls ill and the mother displaces
him from the shared cradle to her own bed. She fusses over the son
round the clock while neglecting the daughter who devises ways to
attract attention. "Relegated to the other side of the room, my
sister. . . . would alternate between sweet smiles and a sharp, irritating whine that my mother simply ignored.[26] She came to know hunger and the stinging of her excrement and urine" (19), admits the
brother. As the male child observes, the sister's clever antics to get
the mother's notice—including "prolonged cooing," "incessant
gurgling," and early "crawling on all fours"—does not produce the
desired attention (20). Yet once the brother's fever breaks, he remarks that: "happiness and pride overtook my mother like a hurri-
cane" (20). Whereas the sister works at earning attention, the son is
gratuitously the object of pride and jubilation.

Jealous of her brother and determined to achieve recognition, the
sister prepares "a marvelous trick" that leaves the brother "pale
with envy and feeling like a failure" (20). As he recounts, "[S]he
looked at my mother straight in the face and, in clear fashion and
without stuttering, spoke her first word" (20). But her accomplish-
ment, far from producing maternal validation, on the contrary, provokes rejection. Not only does the sister estrange her brother, but
also the father, a strong believer in male superiority, feels defrauded
that the daughter begins to speak first. Consequently, the mother
tries to protect her son from the father's scorn by bestowing him
with her full dedication. Thus, despite the sister's linguistic development, she does not receive due recognition because, symbolically,
with control of the Word, she has usurped the male's cultural domain.

Accession to knowledge has always been risky business for women.
The cover of the original Spanish text reproduces a fragment of Jac-
ques-Louis David's *Cupid and Psyche* of the Cleveland Museum. According to myth, Psyche was happy with her husband Cupid, but
because of his restriction that forbade her to lay eyes on him, she
was unsatisfied with their arrangement of a strictly nocturnal relationship. Eventually, Psyche's curiosity brings on punishment to herself and misery to both when one night she lights a candle to
contemplate Cupid, who awakens, reproaches her severely, and immediately abandons her. For women the message rings clear: Stay in
the dark for if you seek enlightenment you run the risk of rejection.
The twin sister's incursion into language meets with disapproval be-

cause, like Psyche, she unveils what the patriarch wants to keep from females—knowledge.

THE FEMALE WRITER IN A MALE DOMAIN:
ON THE MARGINS OF THE THIRD WORLD

In *The Fourth World* the girl's struggle to achieve recognition within her nuclear family suggests an analogy of women writers' situation within the literary establishment. Even though writers may share a field and kinship (like Eltit's twins who share the mother's womb), nevertheless, public homage continues to be disproportionately unequal according to gender.[27] The following words by the brother about the relationship with his sibling also speak to the lack of kinship between men and women writers: "We were practically strangers. . . . in truth, we were silently, provokingly defiant of each other" (21–22).

Analogous to the mother's domestic duties in *The Fourth World*—which trap her in the home with little opportunity to enter the more lucrative labor market—the work of women writers is often left out of the literary canon altogether or marginalized under categories that label their books as "literatura femenina," thus pigeonholing them for "feminine consumption" and virtually ensuring their exclusion from mainstream literature. It may be argued that there have been exceptions to the above scenario, such as the Chileans Gabriela Mistral and Isabel Allende. But in reality the canon has recognized their work because it falls within the parameters expected of literature written by women. Moreover, neither writer posed a challenge to the canon of their time. Mistral produced mostly poetry (the genre traditionally considered acceptable for women) centering on themes about love, maternity, and service to mankind which conformed to the role Latin American society designates for women. Not withstanding that Allende has become the most widely published and read Latin American female author writing today, she established her literary career with *The House of the Spirits* (1982), a novel that pays tribute to her grandparents (a severely patriarchal grandfather and his loving, faithful wife), dabs in magical realism patented by male precursors as far removed as Alejo Carpentier and Gabriel García Márquez, and denounces the now historic dictatorship in Chile. Neither Allende's themes nor writing style posed any challenge to or presented reason for objection from the consecrated literary canon.

In Mexico, the disregard for Elena Garro's novel *Los recuerdos del porvenir* (1963)[28] reflects quite a different reader reception than Allende's because Garro's use of magical realism anticipated its proliferation in the prose of Latin American male authors of the late 1960s and 1970s. Also, Garro's focus on the conflict between church and state in Mexico leading to the Cristero Revolt (under the presidency of Plutarco Elías Calles, 1924–28) constituted transgressing the male realms of politics and history, this practically two decades before Allende's treatment of the military coup in Chile. Outside the acceptable scope of feminine literature, Garro's book was ill-fated because it stepped out of the canon's bounds (for women) on two counts—literary technique and topic.

By contrast, the overwhelmingly positive reader response given to Mexican Laura Esquivel's book *Como agua para chocolate: Novela de entregas mensuales con recetas, amores y remedios caseros* (1989)[29] presents the other side of the coin. The novel, quickly made into a major movie, brandishes a plot flourishing with magical realism and features a protagonist who dedicates her life to cooking, suffering, and waiting for the man she loves. Evidently, recognition is granted women writers who do not wander off too far from the boundaries of mainstream literature marketed to appeal to a female readership.

From the family presented in *The Fourth World* readers can glean a call for the eradication of the pigeonholing that interferes with true kinship among brothers and sisters and, by analogy, excludes peer writers from the literary canon. In the novel, the female child takes advantage of the mother's involvement with a newborn sister and works to reestablish fraternal ties with her twin severed during socialization. In fact, she literally makes a travesty of traditional gender constructs. "Seeking to capture real-life situations, we would play every possible role," admits the brother, "if I was the wife, my sister would play the husband while we watched the other rise blissfully to our ideal condition" (24). Harmony as an ideal condition comes about through agreement and inclusion; thus true understanding of our fellow brothers (and sisters) is possible only by joining with the other, ideally achieved by literally becoming the other, albeit temporarily.

The female twin's efforts to flout conventions in the first part of the novel flourish in the second part where she definitely usurps the Word and completely displaces the brother as narrator. Significantly, she debuts as narrator in part 2 by proclaiming a gender transformation: "My brother adopted the name María Chipia and, like a transvestite, became a virgin . . . " (69). Adoption of this name suggests rejection of a "macho" identity. In Hispanic culture not only is virility incompatible with male virginity, but macho behavior often includes the deflowering of females. Symbolically, the brother's turning into a virgin suggests a female sensibility not in keeping with patriarchy's "order of things."[30]

Transvestism affords gender fluidity by allowing an individual to virtually experience both realms simultaneously. As a cross-dresser, a biological fe/male appropriates the social persona of the opposite sex while maintaining her/his own. S/he literally crosses and blurs gender lines. In the novel's exposé of gender inequities, transvestism emerges as a root metaphor for the ideal brotherhood of Latin American writers that Eltit envisions. In essence, the collapsing of traditional literary and gender (as well as class and racial) categories suggests Eltit's wish-fulfillment fantasy as a writer. "One of the most consistent and effective functions of the transvestite in culture," writes Marjorie Garber, "is to indicate the place of what I call 'category crisis,' disrupting and calling attention to cultural, social, or aesthetic dissonances."[31] "Transvestism creates culture,"[32] Garber also notes, a third culture "which questions binary thinking—female/male; white/nonwhite; dominant/subordinate—and introduces crisis."[33]

The military coup that for eighteen years interrupted the long history of democracy in Chile indeed constituted a national crisis. Chilean critic Nelly Richard observes that transvestite-inspired artistic expression (photography, video, literature, theater) exploded under dictatorship in a country of opposing images: domination and submission.[34] Richard sees the two faces of the Chile of that period embodied in the figure of the transvestite; on the one hand the military machine imposed a discourse that heightened identifications with virility and the rhetoric of power, while on the other, like a woman, Chile was forced into obedience and silence under threat of severe punishment, including disappearance, incarceration, torture, and death.[35]

Textual construction in *The Fourth World* reflects the divisive nature of Chilean reality under dictatorship. As a member of a family in crisis the male twin asks: "When did a fissure occur inside me? I began to see the world split into two, and the gap in between threatened to swallow me up" (26). He further admits that his world "had fallen apart" (26)—words that could allude to the internal turmoil associated with an identity crisis of someone who has pondered about his "hybrid nature" (16), but that could also suggest symptoms of anxiety caused by the persecutory campaign of a military regime. Signs of phobias convey that the character borders on mental instability:

> I was terrorized by the thought of losing a leg in a race or an arm by just moving it; that my tongue would fall on the floor if I said something. I thought my pupils were going to gyrate uncontrollably outside their orbits and explode into a thousand pieces, leaving me blind.
>
> I was so terrified that I suspended defecating for fear of losing my intestines. So, I reduced my activity to the point of partial paralysis.
>
> Fear's continual presence had pitted me against a world bent on destroying me and itself. Having become extremely sensitive, I also became the most propitious victim of this potential sacrifice. (26)

The terms "terrorized," "terrified," and "fear" specifically applied to bodily trauma implicate dismemberment (losing a leg, tongue, eyeballs, intestines) and the torture of dissidents in Chile during the dictatorship. Those governed by a repressive regime often experience "partial paralysis" as a consequence of living in "fear's continual presence" for they know that they too could disappear and become a "victim of this potential sacrifice." Likewise, the obsessive parental vigilance of the deviant twins in the second part of the novel suggests the other's gaze as a mechanism of repression under dictatorship.[36]

Given the political climate of a Chile affected by fifteen years of military rule at the time the novel was published, the character's personal "fissure" (fisura) imbricates national circumstance. When defined as "A separation into subgroups or factions,"[37] the term "fissure" calls to mind the reality of Eltit's textual family, one that, like a political body, divides into two factions: the father protects the youngest sister, María de Alava, while the mother sympathizes with the twins. Furthermore, their fundamental differences simulate those that divide traditionalist and revolutionary party lines. On the one hand the father, as embodiment of tradition, molds María de Alava into his image and begets "a conventional person," who, according to the male twin, "justified everything she did with the same reasoning as our father's" (29). Fashioned to idealize the father, the youngest daughter's imaginary games "would always end the same way," observes her male sibling, "hugging her in his arm, the figure of my father would carry her to safety. She would pretend he was some hero—a sailor, a watchman, a captain, a gladiator" (50). Moreover, Western binary conventional thinking reduced "her necessarily to two opposing poles: success or failure, goodness or badness, life or death" (51). On the other hand, quite removed from the orthodoxy displayed by the father and María de Alava, the mother's adulterous affair and the twin sibling's incestuous relationship severely undermine the traditional nuclear family as stronghold for propagation of patriarchy. Tension between tradition and change, which threatens to destroy this family, reflects the situation of a Chilean nation fraught with political dissension rooted in the fear of the social reforms heralded by the socialist government of Salvador Allende.

Crisis implies a disruption of—and often inspires hope for change in—the status quo, a situation familiar to Eltit the writer who challenges the establishment with a hybrid body of work, which analogous to the transvestism of the twins, confounds cultural tradition. Symbolically, the female sibling's scandalous behavior in *The Fourth World* suggests a call for "sisters" to assert themselves in the struggle for equal admittance into the privileged literary brotherhood. In the novel, the female twin vies for fraternity by appropriating the mother's socializing task and molding her brother according to a new order absent of the cultural conventions that had divided them at birth. "Little by little, my sister reconstructed my identity, watching me obsessively and transferring her knowledge to me," concedes the brother. "She forced me to separate my body from my thoughts and to distance myself from the world around me" (27). Distance here suggests breaking away from gender strictures that sustain the patriarchal "order of things"—as Eltit's Spanish version reads.

In the second part of the novel, the female twin turns narrator and pseudo-mother, thus juxtaposing literary creation and procreation. Her assertiveness in defying patriarchal dictates contrasts with her younger sister's emulation of the father. And unlike the mother, the twin daughter is not tormented by sexual fantasies but rather sheds all inhibitions and commits incest as the ultimate transgression. She freely satiates her sexual appetite with her brother and together they conceive a child whose development coincides with part 2 of the novel. Each sexual encounter, incestuous and therefore taboo, symbolically stimulates a literary task deviant from the mainstream. The twin sister's relationship with the brother suggests that bringing about a change in the reign of power requires transgression of the established "order of things."[38]

Of course, historically, men have been the ones to shape world "order," whether in the domain of economics, politics, class, culture, or family—even human psychology. Lacan's Symbolic order serves us here to elucidate the child's encounter with the Law of the Father and the prohibition of incest. This order of the psyche registers the realm in which human beings make the connection between language or the signified (the word "mother") and the signifier (mother, the person). Unlike in the Imaginary stage where the child recognizes others visually as in a mirror, the Symbolic constitutes the world of abstraction where symbols—names, words, that is, language—stand in for those objects or persons not within vision's range. Whereas in the Imaginary stage the child's relationships were immediate (requiring the other's presence), in the Symbolic these are mediated through language. A child's accession into language occurs during the Oedipal period, one in which, as Anika Lemaire explains, "the child moves from the immediate, non-distanced relationship with its mother to a mediate relationship thanks to its insertions into the symbolic order of the Family. . . . In the Oedipus, the father plays the role of the symbolic Law that establishes the family triangle by actualizing in his person the prohibition of union with the mother."[39]

The incestuous sibling relationship in *The Fourth World* highlights a disregard for the Law of the Father as a strategy in the sister's bid for kinship and accession into culture. According to Lacanian theory, the position of the father takes on the value of Law only insofar as the mother recognizes it. If she questions his authority then the child remains subjected to the mother and her desire.[40] If, on the contrary, the mother does recognize the father both as a man and as the representative of the Law, the subject (child) will have access to the "Name-of-the-Father" (son of . . .) and with his given name assume a place in the symbolic law of the family.[41] Of these two possibilities, let us consider how the former situation—rejection of the father's Law—illustrates a new order in Eltit's text.

Soon after the birth of the twins, the male child narrates how the mother physically displaces the patriarch as both husband (by imposing an extended period of abstinence) and as father figure. According to the male twin's observation: "As far as my mother was concerned my father had no part to play in our lives, except for the simple hellos and good-byes. In fact, my father meant nothing to her" (17). Also, as noted previously, in the second part of the novel the female twin not only displaces the brother as narrator and thus accedes to the symbolic order of language, but she also substitutes the mother by taking on a pseudo-mother role with respect to her male twin. In this new family structure the pseudo-mother does not recognize the Law of the Father and consequently—as evidenced by the incestuous relationship—the son remains subjected to her (sexual) desire. But even prior to the incest, the male sibling, as the father's namesake, literally dismisses identification with the Name-of-the-Father. "When he called me," the son recounts, "I would turn toward him, not as a way of responding to him but rather to see if he was talking to himself" (14). His reaction stems from the biological mother's spurning of the Name-of-the-Father, when out of revenge, she secretly names the son María Chipia.[42] Likewise, at the end of the novel, the child/book born out of the twins' rejection of father-rule will in turn remain subjected to the mother, who marks it with her own name: diamela eltit.

In 1987, a year before the publication of *The Fourth World*, Eltit commented on the relationship between the body and the text and expressed her interest in generating "a sexed text, genital, even, and threateningly obscure and pubescent."[43] The author's words illuminate the sexual motif as constant in *The Fourth World*, especially the obsessive copulation between the twins in part 2. Eltit implies that gender influences her writing, not only in its production but also in how it will be judged in the marketplace. Her statement regarding obscurity suggests a search for a style that challenges the reader while presenting a fresh "pubescent" approach.

The unbridled sexual encounters that the sister initiates throughout part 2 of the novel metaphorically suggests the vast creative energy expended by Latin American women writers in their effort to subvert a patriarchal order that ranks their work second-class, a production largely relegated to a literary periphery. Eltit spoke out on the topic of marginality in 1987 in the inaugural address of the first International Conference on Latin American Women's Literature ever to meet in Santiago, Chile. "We convene . . . for the first time in our country a conference on literature produced by Latin American women and this implies a political gesture, but a complex political gesture addressing history as power, the history of literature in whose long and sustained narrative a fine, but strict spatial division has been traced that limits the female textual body."[44] Eltit's fiction promotes eliminating the limits traditionally placed on sexual/textual female expression if women are to gain a foothold on gender equity and begin to redress literary history's erasure of female contributions.

Eltit also recognizes that "women are not the only minority group facing diverse power issues; there are ethnic, sexual, as well as economic minorities that likewise contend with parallel obstacles and conflicts."[45] Undoubtedly the margins are by no means reserved for women, but historically females have been afforded less opportunity to abandon the periphery. With respect to her craft, Eltit recounts that she has experienced the effects of discrimination, albeit camouflaged in different ways. "The label 'no se entiende' [cannot be understood], that, when applied to some male writers, could entail a compliment, a challenging text," Eltit notes, "in my case has become a determinist and exclusionary slogan. . . . [pejoratively meaning] "too intellectual."[46]

A decade ago Susan Bassnett referred to the 1970s boom in Latin American literature and reminded the literary community that "the explosion of international interest in Latin American writing . . . has made García Márquez, Fuentes, Cortázar, Vargas Llosa etc. familiar household names for European and North American readers, but nothing comparable has happened with women writers."[47] At the time Bassnett also noted the strategies of exclusion practiced by literary critics. She cites one Latin Americanist who in his study of contemporary novelists compared their position to that of the Modernists, of whom José Martí had said in 1893: "It is like a family in America."[48] "A family it may be, but a family made up entirely of fathers, brothers and sons," Bassnett argued.[49]

Since then, men critics have begun to redress the exclusion pointed out by Bassnett. In the case of Eltit, Djelal Kadir dedicates a chapter of his book *The Other Writing: Postcolonial Essays in Latin America's Writing Culture* to her work. Likewise, Chilean critic Guillermo García-Corales includes Eltit, along with her well-established male peers José Donoso and Antonio Skármeta, in *Relaciones de poder y carnavalización en la novela chilena contemporánea*; and Juan Carlos Lértora, also Chilean, has edited *Una poética de literatura menor: La narrativa de Diamela Eltit.*

Tradition shows that the scope of human experience—that which Lacan calls the Real—has been recorded mainly by and about men. Hence from a feminist perspective, Jameson's equating "The Real in Lacan . . . [as] History itself"[50] would instead be rewritten thus: The Real in Lacan . . . is simply *His story*. Feminist criticism and fiction illustrate, as they attempt to redress exclusions of old, that women's—Real—existence, their lived experience, traditionally has been relegated to his story and thus excluded from history except as appendages to Name-of-the-Father (mother, daughter, or wife of). Significantly, Eltit includes a gamut of (psychological and physiological) female experience and ends *The Fourth World* with her real name, thus stamping it as her story.[51]

As a female-centered narrative *The Fourth World* also presents the theme of literary vocation from a feminist perspective, but its discourse does not exclude but rather includes the (male) other. For example, from the novel the reader can glean that, regardless of gender, marginality affects Latin Americans as a family of peoples. Repeated references made in the text to "the most powerful nation in the world" and "the sudaca brotherhood" suggest that, beyond national borders, a Latin American "brother" who writes may also be discriminated against and stamped a "sudaca," a pejorative term used in Spain to identify a person from—Sud América—South

America.[52] Therefore, Eltit's text includes the other's marginality as well. One can conjecture that having suffered personally the injunctions placed on women's words and deeds, the author identifies with society's marginal elements.[53]

Fuentes, in turn, excludes the participation of the (female) "other." In *Christopher Unborn* the quartet called the "Four Fuckups"—orphans that roam the streets playing for alms—are pariahs in Mexican society and parallel the "sudaca brotherhood" of Eltit's novel. Notably, however, the fourth member of Fuentes's the "Four Fuckups," La niña Ba, is female, identified with a generic (niña) incomplete name (Ba), and invisible to boot.[54] Fuentes thus includes the female while at the same time annulling her presence; he symbolically inscribes the girl's exclusion in the text. Made mute and invisible, the female twin in *Christopher Unborn* is thus erased from the plot.

The Fourth World presents a dysfunctional family in the process of breaking up, but dialogue still takes place. On a symbolic order, Eltit's "sudaca brotherhood"—which includes the "other's" participation—represents a Latin American family of nations. Only by pulling together will they be able to guard against foreign intervention. "[A] tribute could free us permanently from the most powerful nation in the world, which had put a curse on us," advises the younger sister. "[O]nly brotherhood could propel that nation into crisis" (83–84). Although nowhere is that "powerful nation" identified, Eltit implicates the two governments that historically have exerted great power over Latin America: Mother Spain and Uncle Sam. On the one hand, the author slyly indicts Spain by employing the pejorative term "sudaca" with which Latin Americans are marked on the peninsula; on the other she also incriminates the United States by referring to "the most powerful nation in the world." Given the allusions to such foreign powers, the novel makes a call for an alliance of Latin American nations.

LATIN AMERICAN BROTHERHOOD: SPANISH COLONIALISM AND NORTH AMERICAN IMPERIALISM

On a metatextual level the dialogue established here between *Christopher Unborn* and *The Fourth World* transcends the national borders of Mexico and Chile when one considers the countries' common history of Spanish colonialism and North American imperialism.[55] The title of Fuentes's novel reminds us that its raison d'être is the commemoration of the Spanish legacy in the Americas.

Those "Fuckups" and "sudacas" of each respective novel appear practically anonymous because they are likely marked with the social stigma of an indigenous bloodline. The negative connotation that "sudaca" carries in the land of the Spanish colonizer stems not merely from a geographical vanquished "Sud América," but a genealogical territory where Spanish and Indian blood forged the mestizo, the half breed.

Chilean essayist Jorge Guzmán observes the extent of denial that surrounds the racial designation of "mestizo" in his country when he says that Chileans do not even conceive of such a racial category. "We [Chileans] are not that, they say annoyed,"[56] notes Guzmán. In fact, according to Guzmán, in Chile there is no consciousness or— because it has been so repressed—validation of miscegenation, what the author calls "mesticidad" or also known as "mestizaje."[57] In this regard, the mother's rape as the initial scene of *The Fourth World* and the husband's sexual coercion of the wife in *Christopher Unborn* symbolically inscribe (Spanish) male aggression towards the (indigenous) female as a reminder of Latin American national origin.

In keeping with Eltit's attention to marginal segments of the population, she implicitly acknowledges the Chilean mestizo in the "sudaca brotherhood" often mentioned in the second part of *The Fourth World*. However, the author goes further when the discursive "we" makes allusions to the "indio" erased from Chilean literary tradition. Unlike the use of terms such as "india" and "machi" in [*For the Homeland*], readers of this novel glean an inscription of indigenous presence only from allusions, which, as literary recourse, illustrate the repressed isssue of race in Chilean national identity that Guzmán points out. For example, the twin sister remarks: "We are savagely prepared for extinction" (87),[58] a declaration suggestive of both the image (of the savage) the Spanish construed of the native peoples of the Americas and the (extinction) plight most indigenous groups suffered at the hands of the colonizer. Shortly thereafter she says "[W]e both know which is the only way to delay our extinction and the humiliation of our race" (90). Of course the pronoun "we" and its possessive form "our" refer directly to her twin brother, but markers such as "extinction," "humiliation," and "race" suggest inclusion of the marginalized "indio."

Indirect references to the brother's physical appearance identify him as sporting hair "down to his shoulders" and a painted face.[59] And moreover, the sister once comments that her brother "performed a beautiful ritual in which he turned arid white,"[60] thus implying that he is not by nature "white" (or "blond," the actual term Eltit employs). Routine references to dance as ritual and as a form of paying tribute likewise allude to a key aspect of indigenous culture.[61] Figuratively reminiscent of the conquest, the female twin observes that, "Outside, the young sudacas are hovering around the bonfires and a familiar sound fills my ears: the hooves of horses. I hear horses' hooves" (96).

Chilean critic Eugenia Brito points out that Eltit's writing inscribes what occurred five centuries ago as model of contemporary society.[62] The hooves of the conquistador's horse when transposed to modern Chile recall the mounted police of Pinochet's regime assigned to break up street rallies. With this leap forward in time, the text can also be read for signs of a "poetics of disenchantment," a designation Chilean critic Guillermo García Corales applies to a number of novels published during the 1980s that, in addressing the dictatorial period in Chile, question the effects that the confrontations between authoritarian forces and the resistance had on the nation's collective unconscious.[63] "The voices inside me are telling me to sharpen our discontent," states the twin sister, "This sudaca discontent, red and bloodthirsty" (80).[64] Textual evidence indicates that this profound "sudaca" dissatisfaction voices anti-imperialist as much as antimilitary sentiments in a Chile where national armed forces ousted a democratically-elected government with the aid of Yankee intelligentsia and capital because the United States vied to protect the foreign investments of North American businesses.[65] Anti-imperialist and antimilitary sentiments prevail in a region where, as Heraldo Muñoz points out, "widespread Latin American perception tends to associate the U.S. government with unpopular authoritarian regimes that repress efforts to promote socioeconomic transformations and democracy . . . [because] the fact is that, alleging 'security reasons,' Washington repeatedly has ended up on the side of dictatorial regimes, or else has kept silent while 'friendly regimes' murdered, tortured, and exiled thousands of dissidents."[66]

A brief reflection on the Chilean national situation during the presidency of Salvador Allende will elucidate key passages in *The Fourth World.* In 1971 the Chilean decision to nationalize U.S. property in the copper industry, without compensation for the expropriations, marked a significant gesture towards economic nationalism and a challenge to the U.S. investor community and to U.S. policy in Latin America. Although Allende's predecessor, Eduardo Frei, had "felt compelled to begin to 'Chileanize' copper, and the idea of nationalization of copper was no surprise to the U.S. policy makers,"[67] nevertheless, during Frei's administration "the United States had presented Chile to the world as a 'showcase' country—an example of what the Latin countries could do with U.S. technical and economic assistance."⁶⁸ But when the Chilean political leadership actually instituted measures to halt exploitation of national resources by large U.S. mining concerns such as Anaconda and Kennecott, assistance by way of loans, until then routinely granted by the World Bank, the Inter-American Development Bank, and the Export-Import Bank, went unapproved.⁶⁹ Such actions made it clear that "the 'international' lending agencies are mere appendages of the U.S. government."⁷⁰

Indirect references to U.S. imperialism figure prominently in the second part of *The Fourth World*: "[O]ur house is under siege because of the voracity of the most powerful nation in the world" (87). "I am a victim of a tumultuous political plot against our race. They persecute us with the force of their scorn" (89), declares the twin sister, a statement that points as far back as the Spanish conquest and as recently as the 1973 United States–backed coup d'état.

Once President Salvador Allende was deposed, U.S. business interests regained a foothold and thrived in Chile under Pinochet's military regime, but, as the last pages of the novel hone, at the cost of selling out the country to foreigners:

> With the hope that money will fall from the sky, every kind of rhetorical discourse is heard. . . .
> Their voices waver, especially the old and greedy, as they squabble over the money that falls from the sky but vanishes into thin air. They sell the wheat, the corn, and the willow groves for nothing, while the young sudacas who planted them look on. Sweat is for sale. Frantic merchants shriek at the buyers, who astutely lower the prices to buy up everything, including the sellers themselves. The money from the sky returns to the sky and the sellers even sell what doesn't belong to them. . . .
> Only the name of the city remains, because everything else has been sold on the open market. Amid the anarchy of supply and demand, the last items are auctioned off, amid accusations of sham and fraud.
> Adultery has perverted the city; the city prostitutes itself, giving itself away at any price to any bidders. The transaction is about to conclude and the contempt for the sudaca race is clearly printed on the money falling from the sky. (113–14)

U.S. "credit diplomacy" during periods of friendly relations with Latin American countries (equated to "the money that falls from the sky" reiterated in the text) lures Latin American nations to fall prey to imperialism, but falling out of favor surely means ("the money from the sky returns to the sky") economic catastrophe.⁷¹ Along with a depiction of those who sell their homeland to foreigners, *The Fourth World* includes the sentiments of others who reject alms in the form of (foreign) economic aid: "Once a young sudaca stuck out his hand and I put a coin in it, he refused it. I can still see his sunken eyes, like yours. Perhaps it was a fever. He spoke about the brotherhood. He talked a long time about it" (111). One can conjecture a call for unification under the banner of economic nationalism as a key step towards social revolution in Latin America. Given the United States' record for manipulating Latin American nations to act against each other, a "sudaca brotherhood" envisions a united hemisphere in the effort to curb U.S. hegemony.[72]

In light of the above reading that points to textual inscription of a common Latin American origin (based on colonialism and a more recent history of imperialistic control and dictatorship), Raymond L. Williams's observation that *The Fourth World* "is not concerned with the broad historical truths elaborated in *One Hundred Years of Solitude* or *The Death of Artemio Cruz* . . ."[73] illustrates how women's literature continues to be relegated to the shadows of the "masters." A tradition of such marginalization may be why, despite rallying for a "sudaca brotherhood," the female twin in Eltit's novel finds a need to transgress patriarchal Law. As noted, her transgressions include deviating from literary convention. At one point in part 2 she says, "María Chipia asks me to expose my secret. I violate it by saying: 'I want to create a terrible and annoying sudaca work.' "[74] She later implies sibling complicity in subversion when she asserts: "We have done terrible and outlandish things" (83). Reiteration of the term "terrible" (from the Latin terribilis from terrére, to frighten) warrants review of its meaning, which includes "causing great fear or alarm," "extremely formidable," "extreme in extent or degree," "unpleasant; disagreeable," and "markedly objectionable"[75]—all expressions judged suitable by many readers and critics to describe Eltit's literary production. Surely from her first incursions into the literary scene Eltit aimed to—and accomplished—"creat[ing] a terrible and annoying sudaca work."

Considering the sexual/textual link in Eltit's writing, the comment could well refer to the narrative innovations and the thematic taboos which both Latin American women and men writers have posed in their literature. The "we have done" that the twin sister utters includes and recognizes the brother's participation. The obsessive copulation of the twins in *The Fourth World* suggests that, symbolically, the child conceived incarnates the creative literary labor of this sudaca couple. "[W]e spent from dawn to dusk finding each other until we became fused. The child was suffering and we integrated that suffering into ourselves without guilt, without anxiety, and without evil. It was a tribute to the sudaca species. It was a manifesto," narrates the twin sister (108). The manifesto, textual product of the couple's sexual alliance, illustrates the link between literary creation and procreation. Given the sexual/textual paradigm at work in the novel, once the biological gestation comes to term, the mother/narrator's labor ends with the birth of the child and the conclusion of *The Fourth World*.

A similar parallel exists in *Christopher Unborn*. Not only does the book end with a birth, but the male fetus, as sole narrator, implies all along that his gestation is linked to plot development.[76] But in contrast to Eltit's novel, throughout Fuentes's text the fetus directly addresses the reader as "Elector," which explicitly conveys someone with authority (to elect). It also implicitly takes for granted readers who will "elect" the text at hand. The suppositions of authority and readership could not be made by Eltit given her precariousness vis-à-vis the canon.

The Fourth World ends as follows: "Far away, in a house abandoned to brotherhood, between April 7 and 8, diamela eltit, assisted by her twin brother, gives birth to a baby girl. The sudaca baby will go up for sale" (114). Instead of the boy heralded all along in the novel, a girl is born. A girl is born because, as symbol of a woman writer's production, her gender influences the value and success ultimately registered at the marketplace. As a female reader, I ask myself at the conclusion of the novel: Isn't Eltit's baby girl destined for failure? If the most powerful nation in the world considers Latin Americans underdeveloped—a notion that labels them as Third World—then where do doubly marginalized Latin American women stand, if not in that Fourth World of Eltit's title?—a world even further removed from the literary periphery already occupied by their Latin American brothers.

In the hierarchy of nations according to their degree of development, the "Fourth World"[77] is a further subdivision of the "Third World,"[78] which usually identifies the technologically less advanced nations of Africa, Asia, and Latin America. Generally characterized by very weak and largely agrarian economies, poorly fed, rapidly growing, and illiterate populations, these nations typically have unstable governments, and until recently were mostly controlled by Western nations through some form of colonialism. Eltit's novel suggests that the position of Latin American women with respect to Latin American men parallels that of "Fourth World" nations, lagging even further behind the already disadvantaged "Third World." The twin sister in *The Fourth World* presents a subversive female posture given the fact that Latin American women when compared to men generally are not (economically) self-sufficient, receive less schooling, have little control of their bodies and reproduction, and have a subordinate status within society that resembles that of colonized peoples.

In keeping with her agenda for representing marginal groups, *The Fourth World* illustrates that in a hierarchy of power, (Latin American) women—whether within their biological, literary, or political families—endure far more marginalization than (Latin American) men. Eltit's novel registers on a symbolic order what Bassnett pointed out in her literary criticism: "The family of male writers . . . has sisters, daughters and mothers who are emerging from their attic rooms and speaking in voices loud enough to be heard by all."[79]

Voicing a female perspective, the twin sister in the novel appropriates the mechanisms of power by usurping the brother's role as narrator, but she accomplishes this without invalidating or excluding his participation in their creative endeavors. By contrast, let us recall the overwhelming proof of exclusion of the twin's female counterpart in *Christopher Unborn.* As pointed out earlier, in the second part of *The Fourth World* the female twin does not monopolize the narrative, but rather engages in dialogue with her siblings. In fact, transgression of the incest taboo, metaphorically, points to the level of necessary collaboration between the twins/writers; together their cooperative venture produces a child/book. Despite the pigeonholing that will affect the novel's marketability, the fact that it will go up for sale marks a first step out of the "Fourth World" designation, a literary periphery within which women traditionally have been confined.

Eltit, embodiment of a "Fourth World" league of writers herself, concluded her address before the 1987 International conference on Latin American Women's Literature by asking for inclusion into the public forum and literary history.

> Latin American writing needs to actively convey its difference and fully participate in the culture in order to democratize it, and in this way, work within a democracy to guarantee equilibrium, especially with regard to the solitude that besieges literature. . . .
> That is why today we speak not of one hundred but of almost five hundred years of solitude that calls for a reparation in order to allow the female textual body to inhabit the mainstream body of history.[80]

To rectify the wrongdoing, *The Fourth World* presents defiance and collaboration as fundamentals for a re-elaboration of a new order that recognizes the marginalized Latin American body in all its diversity—sexual, racial, economic, and political.

5

Vaca sagrada: A Feminist/Postmodern Novel

OVER THE YEARS ELTIT HAS REITERATED THAT EXPLORING THE VERY mechanisms of writing is what continues to drive her literary production. "I am not too concerned with themes," she says in another interview. "What preoccupies me is how to say things. That is my great struggle. I can't say much about my books because I'm not too sure what they're about."[1] After writing *The Fourth World* "as a lady," Eltit maintains the semblance of a conventional plot in *Vaca sagrada* (1991)/*Sacred Cow* (1995), yet reverts to the textual obscurity of her first novels. The postmodern qualities examined in this analysis of the novel will affirm Eltit's writing continuum at the margins of Chilean literature.

In previous chapters the erotic antics of E. Luminata, the introduction of birthing in *For the Homeland*, and its further development in *The Fourth World* serve as examples of Eltit's attention to the female body. In *Sacred Cow* the author treats menstruation in an unconventional manner within heterosexual relations. Yet despite the centrality in which Eltit typically places the female body in her novels, she insists that what interests her most is not the biological body, but the body of writing, particularly one in crisis.[2] However, in an apparent contradiction, Eltit also theorizes about creating an aesthetics of blood (one necessarily founded in the body), which we will explore at length in this chapter.

While, as discussed earlier, from a feminist perspective *The Fourth World* admits an interpretation regarding the status of women writers vis-à-vis their male counterparts within national borders and Latin American territories, *Sacred Cow* instead calls attention to the mechanics of writing itself. This exegesis of *Sacred Cow* will draw from feminism and postmodernism in an attempt to shed light on female bodily functions and textual artifice, two significant elements in a novel that shows signs of crisis mainly through contradiction and ambiguity.

Within a body of work characterized by its resistance to interpreta-

150

tion, *Sacred Cow* culminates a series of novels that feature "disruptive aesthetic strategies" associated with postmodernist literature and limited readership.[3] Notably, in Eltit's subsequent novel, *Los vigilantes* (1994), she opts for a linear and a much more conventional narrative. But before examining specific narrative devices in *Sacred Cow,* Deborah L. Madsen and Mark S. Madsen suggest points of comparison between postmodern narrative and current technology's hypertext system which may prove helpful in approaching Eltit's novel.[4]

A hypertext is formed by a number of links that connect (visual, audio, or written) texts—called nodes, cards, articles, or pages—to a central document that serves as a database. In a hypertext, readers navigate their own narrative path through the data by choosing at each node, card, article, or page which link to pursue next, depending on which text is most germane to their interests.[5] In contrast to an individual text with a linear structure, and hence a narrative form, a hypertext document is composed of a network of smaller interlinked informational units. The nonlinear, fragmented narrative of *Sacred Cow* reminds us of the flexible organizational data in a hypertext.

Reading Eltit's novel resembles the movement through a hypertext system insofar as it obliges the reader to seek sense-making links, that is, to make intratextual narrative connections or mental cross-referencing. Hypertexts like much postmodern literature undermine the notion of a unitary narrative and encourage a multiplicity of readings. Such "hypertext" descriptives as "a complex network of textual elements," "non-sequential writing," and "multiple pathways of expression" apply to *Sacred Cow* as well.[6] Also, readers of hypertexts and postmodern texts face similar difficulties. In the case of a large hypertext with a complex network of links, readers can become "lost in cyberspace" for they can "lose track of where they have been and where they are going."[7] Similarly, the reader of *Sacred Cow* can easily get lost in the various story lines, which like hypertext links or tangents constantly defy the conventional notion of a unified plot. "I have lost the train of reason, of names, and all my stories are unraveling," Eltit's narrator/protagonist admits in the opening page of the novel (2). In essence we are dealing with a self-reflexive, but also a self-marginalizing, text.

Not only multiple stories but also lack of control over them sets the stage for textual instability characteristic of postmodern literature. The first line of *Sacred Cow* reads: "I sleep, I dream, I lie a lot" (1). From the onset the narrator/protagonist warns the reader about the uncertainty of the text, both as an unconscious (I sleep, I dream) as well as a conscious state (I lie). "I'd already acquired the habit of constant lying," stresses the narrator/protagonist later, "given the slightest encouragement I'd launch into some fabrication that inevitably led to endless problems since I frequently forgot what I'd said, and more than once was brought up short, faced by my own contradictions" (2). The confession serves as a "caveat lector"—reader, you will be dealing with a narration affected by lies, forgetfulness, and contradictions. Manuel's acceptance of her lies could be read as an implicit invitation for the reader to play along. "He knew about my lies and didn't seem to care," remarks the narrator/protagonist about her lover, "I . . . got used to a kind of complicity. It wasn't an understanding exactly, in the sense of a pact; more like a game . . ." (3). The underlying message suggests not taking the text too seriously since fiction is ultimately lies disguised as truth and most like a game in which the reader willingly participates as the author's accomplice.

"Truth" is questionable in the postmodern text. For Gerald Graff "postmodernism may be defined as the movement within contemporary literature and criticism that calls into question the traditional claims of literature and art to truth and human value."[8] Postmodernist literature has been called antiliterature for its self-parody and its "ironic view of its traditional pretensions to truth, high seriousness, and the profundity of 'meaning.'"[9]

Evidently self-parodic, in *Sacred Cow* the existence of the text itself becomes dubious when at the conclusion of the novel the female narrator reveals waking to the realization that she would write (what we have just finished reading?). In retrospect, advertising the lies at the beginning of the novel calls attention to them as textual artifice and is an early indicator of metafiction, another aspect common in postmodern texts. "When I lifted my head I realised what it was about them that I had to write" comments the narrator/protagonist about the characters, "I would write about them from the lonely safety of a room in my house. I got up in the pitch dark and looked for the proofs I'd kept. There were the tapes, the letters, the photographs. There we were, captured in a boxful of artifacts . . ." (106).

The postmodern text shows disrespect for itself when it calls into question its very existence. Notably, in its self-reflexiveness the (yet unwritten) text denies itself while at the same time vesting the characters with tangible evidence of existence (tapes, letters, photographs). Postmodernism hinges on incongruity which, when used as a narrative ploy, underscores how a text as cultural artifact can reflect our times. Concretely, how does postmodernity translate into the age of flux, instability, insecurity, uncertainty? This is what Ihab Hassan sums up as "indeterminacy," that is, "all manner of ambiguities, ruptures, and displacements."[10]

In North America, more so than in Latin America, the predictable life and gender patterns of several decades ago are on very shaky ground or no longer hold true. As late as the 1950s most people in the United States could expect (or were expected) to grow up, be schooled, marry, reproduce, work, and retire at a predictable age and probably within their home state or even their birth community. Division of labor and sexuality were also predictable; men were breadwinners, women homemakers, and both were (supposedly) heterosexual. However, by the 1960s the increased momentum of the women's, black civil rights, Chicano, and gay liberation movements in the United States propagated awareness of sexism, racism, and homophobia, hence challenging the traditional order of things.

More recently, corporate downsizing or restructuring has eliminated the "company man" and job security. The high mobility of today's North American family undermines the sense of neighborhood and community that comes from people knowing each other for generations. On the subject of family, divorce is one destabilizing factor that has affected large numbers of people in modern times.

To the south, economic and political volatility for decades has marked Latin America as an unstable region. Historically, this has translated into (im)migration and exile, destabilizing factors that account for much of the mobility of Latin Americans. Not corporate downsizing but disappearance of a breadwinner due to political repression explained the sudden precariousness of many households in the Argentina, Chile, and Uruguay of the 1970s and 1980s. These were also times of violence, displacement, and great uncertainty for much of the population of war-afflicted El Salvador and Nicaragua.

On many continents information technologies now contribute their share to the general malaise of insecurity. The Internet facilitates anonymous communication, and identity becomes guarded and uncertain. Computer viruses may strike anyone, at any time. E-mail users wonder about the privacy of their correspondence. World Wide Web publishing raises the issues of authorship and accountability. Television, movies, and video games reflect the violence that threatens our sense of security daily—on the street, in our cars, at home. Not surprisingly, the term "anomie" has come to describe the tenor of postmodern times.

LITERARY ARTIFICE IN *VACA SAGRADA*

In the literary realm, postmodernity often manifests as ambiguity and incongruity at various levels of textual construction: narration, characterization, plot, language. Narrative shifting, for instance, contributes much to the obscurity of *Sacred Cow*. The unidentified narrator/protagonist begins the novel with a first person account (which in the Spanish version reveals that she is a female). From her we learn some aspects of her relationship with Manuel, who has emigrated with his wife from the south of Chile. The introduction of another male character, Sergio, sets the scene for a conventional love triangle between the female narrator/protagonist and the two men. But plot familiarity and reader comfort level are soon shaken when, in a "disorienting turn," chapter 3 introduces a new story line about someone named Francisca and switches to a third person narration—a shift that sets a pattern for alternating chapters.[11]

In chapter 5 the narrator introduces a retrospective story line that features Sergio's adolescent relationship with a classmate named Francisca. Otherwise a linear third person account, this story is periodically interrupted by a dialogue between Francisca and an unidentified dying person—later disclosed to be the grandmother who raised her.[12] Moreover, each of the dialogue fragments is followed by a brief parenthetical aside that, from the content, appears to inscribe Francisca's interior monologue concerning her ailing charge. But such an assumption becomes questionable when several chapters later the parenthetical inserts appear again. This time, direct address highlighted in quotations—"Stop it, don't keep moving. . . ." (76), "Don't look at me like that. . . ." (78), "No, I don't like it like that. . . ." (80)—suggests a conversation (of which only one side is revealed) rather than Francisca's silent reflections.

Textual ambiguity intensifies with subject shifting at the level of sentence construction: "*Francisca* resists, anchored to the head of the bed with all *my* strength, thinking of the masterly articulation of the knee."[13] Has the anonymous narrator/protagonist here slipped and revealed that she herself is Francisca? In retrospect, like Francisca, the narrator/protagonist mentions an ill grandmother when narrating periods of her youth.[14] Yet there is also a hint of another Francisca: "She thought back to that other Francisca, the one that had been there before, but she failed to reconcile the two images" (13). Typically postmodern, *Sacred Cow* presents characters whose identity cannot be pinned down.

Readers traditionally have understood "character as locus of an essential identity," an identity marked by individual idiosyncrasies as well as universal qualities of human nature, which by their very essence cut across historical difference and cultural specificity.[15] In postmodern texts, characterization, as a process that establishes a character's identity, is compromised with the breakdown of plot pro-

gression, or the elimination of plot altogether. Plot affords characters a forum as well as motive for action and interaction through
which much of their identity is defined. "Postmodern narrative,"
observes Docherty, "insists on offering the merest fragments of character, without ever allowing for a fully coherent construction of an
identifiable whole; it is, as it were, like a series of torn photographs,
a photo montage. . . ."[16]

Although I would not go so far as Graff to say that "in postmodern
fiction, character, like external reality, is something 'about which
nothing is known,'" indeed not enough is known about Eltit's characters to form any significant profile.[17] Instead, the reader is left to
gather and assemble pieces that do not fit together to complete the
narrative puzzle of *Sacred Cow*. Characters remain elusive, in flux,
identity is fluid, as if confounded with others, split, unstable at best.
Not surprisingly, the term "schizophrenia" recurs in postmodern
discourses as varied as art, economics, literature, and architecture.
A case in point is the identity conflation of Francisca, the narrator/
protagonist and Ana (the latter's cousin).

As previously noted, the first indication of unstable subject identity occurs when the narrating "I" figure merges with Francisca
("Francisca resists, anchored to the head of the bed with all my
strength . . ."), thus planting the seed for the suspicion that Francisca and the narrator/protagonist could be one and the same person. Both can also be linked to an ill grandmother. But if the
individuality of the narrator/protagonist and Francisca can be confused, Francisca and Ana too share certain characteristics that fuse
them.

From the narrative segments about Francisca, the reader concludes that she is a physically abused woman in a dissatisfying yet
codependent sexual relationship, a profile that could easily match
the one given of Ana in her destructive relationship with Sergio. "I
haven't mentioned in my account that Sergio and Ana were
lovers . . ." remarks the narrator/protagonist towards the end of the
novel; "It was their common unhappiness that was the real bond
which kept them in that alarming relationship" (94–95). To further
reinforce the coincidence between Francisca and Ana, "Sergio and
Ana had known each other almost since childhood" and "He met
Francisca at school" as adolescents, eventually becoming obsessive
lovers.[18] Exemplary of postmodern self-less-ness, the narrator/pro-
tagonist could be Francisca, who could be Ana and all three women
converge in their sexual involvement with Sergio, the seminal grout
binding this mosaic of female characters. "The postmodern self is
no longer a coherent entity that has the power to impose (admit-

tedly subjective) order upon its environment," notes Hans Bertens, "It has become decentered, to repeat Holland's phrase. The radical indeterminacy of Postmodernism has entered the individual ego and has drastically affected its former (supposed) stability. Identity has become as uncertain as everything else."[19]

Along with narrative shifting and character instability, plot fragmentation, as another postmodern ploy operates in *Sacred Cow* to challenge the conventional assumptions of a unified, chronological, plausible, and retraceable story.[20] Symptomatic of postmodern plurality, the novel presents a semblance of stories, all the more confusing because, as the narrator/protagonist forewarns us in the opening page, her stories are "unraveling," literally coming apart, no longer holding together as a whole. Although on the one hand as a postmodern text *Sacred Cow* urges the reader to reconstruct its loose story lines, on the other it inherently resists order and structure to the extent that the futility of such effort is confirmed when in a metafictional reflection at the end of the novel the narrator/protagonist (now also writer) admits creating "the illusion of a real plot" and furthermore refers to her story as a "farce," defined by its improbable plot and characters, a ludicrous, empty show, a mockery. For Sandra Garabano "attempting to grasp the action in *Sacred Cow* would be to break the reading contract proposed by Eltit from the publication of *Lumpérica* in 1983."[21] Nevertheless, let us look at some salient features of the plot/s.

Sacred Cow is another of Eltit's urban novels, female-centered and heterosexually oriented insofar as it revolves around the principal female characters—the narrator/protagonist, Francisca and Ana—and their sexual involvement with a man, often identifiable as either Manuel or Sergio. With the exception of Francisca, who remains tangential to the other two women's kinship, the action can be diagramed as three (love) triangles in which only the narrator/protagonist remains constant. At different points in the narrative, character interaction can be mapped as follows: narrator/protagonist—Manuel—Sergio; the narrator/protagonist—Ana—Sergio; and the narrator/protagonist—Ana—Manuel. Nonetheless, as with other aspects of the novel any affiliation is questionable. "[M]y fondness for lies made me invent a love affair we'd never had," admits the narrator/protagonist (4–5).

The plot featuring Manuel's relationship with the narrator/protagonist is heavily invested in the theme of political repression, as already noted, a recurring topic in Eltit's writing and one that distinguishes Latin American postmodern literature from that of the United States with apolitical, ahistorical leanings. Identified with the

South, meaning Chile's rural region, Manuel is detained there with his entire family upon returning home from the city (a common denomination for the capital, Santiago) where he had been involved with the narrator/protagonist. Offering neither details nor motive for an arrest of such magnitude, the text counts on the reader's familiarity with recent Chilean history, and hence the assumption that the novel's action takes place during Pinochet's military regime (1973–90) when such occurrences were not extraordinary. In light of this time frame, the novel's narrative disruptions, character ambiguity, and plot fragmentation are reflections of the shattered lives of Chileans, the obsession with national identity, the political divisions, the economic disparity, and the senseless violence that impacted the country during the dictatorship. Within this context the novel's incoherence—what postmodern discourse terms "aporia"—makes perfect sense as it captures the mood of that time.[22]

Another principal plot features Francisca, her relationship with Sergio, or the insinuation of other male partners. Parallel to the victimization implied with the arrest of Manuel and his family, Francisca's story suggests domestic violence as yet another form of abuse of power. Although apparently unrelated, both stories (the narrator/protagonist–Manuel and Francisca-Sergio) are linked by the political climate at the time of one's arrest and the other's battery as well as by the silence surrounding both incidents. Politically specific, the narrator/protagonist defies "curfew" to attend to the beaten Francisca and once at her side feels overcome with "panic" about the situation, a sentiment frequently voiced in Chilean literature written during or about the dictatorship.[23] Given the novel's stifling atmosphere, one asks if eroticism, as another major theme in the narrator/protagonist's story, is not somehow also linked to national politics, if her promiscuous lifestyle of seduction, adultery, sexual experimentation, and drinking is not an attempt at subversion, an acting out against patriarchal dictates when protest against political repression is not possible. Such links, albeit subtle, of seemingly separate stories blur plot boundaries and urge the reader on in quest of other connections, connections that require textual scrutiny, often prove false, and dissipate at any turn of the page.

Sacred Cow's literary quagmire of narrative shifts, character instability, and plot fragmentation is immediately detected at the level of language where contradictions, often within the same paragraph, betray what Cornier Michael terms the "postmodern impulse." "I was no longer bleeding. I knew I had stopped bleeding when I gave up expecting it to start," asserts the narrator/protagonist, only to add immediately, "I was definitely bleeding, I went on bleeding . . ." (98).

Reality is not only in flux, but it changes radically; what is true at one moment is no longer so the next—a situation that correlates with national experience, where Chileans literally went to bed under a democracy and woke up to military rule the next day. "I was in mid-crisis when I met Manuel," remarks the narrator/protagonist. "For some time I'd been struggling between euphoria and melancholia, both equally impossible to alleviate" (2). Again, the contradictory shift in emotion—from euphoria to melancholia—underscores at the level of language a personal crisis indicative of other textual— and by extension, national—instabilities.

Unlike *E. Luminata* and [*For the Homeland*] where neologisms, jargon, inverted syntax, palindromes, and general wordplay exemplify language itself in crisis, language in *Sacred Cow* presents a semblance of reality, yet one that is undermined constantly. As Garabano remarks, the language machine operating in the novel is "for lying, concealing or seducing us," not for communication—after all, "sense in this novel always remains in suspense."[24]

In *Sacred Cow* like in other of Eltit's novels, language plays double duty in its socioaesthetic function. Overtly or as subtext, Chilean political circumstance appears as a historical present in every book. In the novel at hand, such words as "crisis," "craziness," "risk," "chaos," "tension," "upheaval," and "disorder" (appearing among others such as "death," "terrors," "dangers") describe postmodern writing as well as the state of Chilean affairs in the 1970s and 1980s. The fear evoked in chapter 4 of the novel, and in much of Latin American literature set during military rule, brings up the (post-modern) topic of the unrepresentable.[25] "There is no way to describe in detail what those days were like," the narrator/protagonist affirms, supposedly referring to the dictatorship, "because days like those cannot be contained in words. . . . It was all inside my head, and at the same time it was only out in the world. . . . Death took hold in the least expected places, death remained everywhere invisible" (15).

The insufficiency of language to depict "that nightmarish life that one lived without trivializing it," remarks Eltit, "is a dilemma for a writer. I tried to work the ambiguity (and surely I will die doing it, because I won't ever be able to do anything else) inherent in speaking about that dreadful atmosphere. . . . [that] if you narrate it, you will fall short. You have to leave it open because it's so difficult [to recount]."[26] In a tacit connection between language and politics in the novel, the narrator/protagonist's admitted obsession with "lying" reflects the mechanism that drove Chile's official discourse during a dictatorship, which constantly fed the public "lies" for "truth." So too the frequent assertion/negation shifts in the narrative point to the conflicting discourses in Chile, where, for example, citizen groups claimed gross human rights violations while the government denied any wrongdoing; or vice versa, authorities accused political dissidents of committing subversive acts against the state while objectors insisted that the arrested and disappeared were not terrorists.

AN AESTHETICS OF BLOOD: MENSTRUATION AND AIDS

Inscribing female experience is another function of language in *Sacred Cow,* one that calls attention to feminist/postmodern intersections. Postmodernism's appeal for the popular (including marginal spheres wherein figures the subaltern) accommodates feminism's focus on women as an oppressed group—a gendered category much in debate by feminists themselves in the United States in the advent of strong discontent among members from minority groups who could not identify with white, middle-class, Anglo women. But that is an old story from which stems today's acceptance that feminism cannot articulate or represent a stable subject identified as "Woman" given gender's intersection with racial, class, ethnic, and sexual modalities.[27]

In this regard, female characters in *Sacred Cow* respond to subject instability characteristic of postmodern writing as well as to feminism's recognition of women's heterogeneity—among and within themselves. As an example of Woman as unstable signifier, the novel's main character is narrator, protagonist, writer, lover (that is, desiring subject) and object of desire, friend, cousin, nursemaid, and worker, who happens to be poor, ill, fearful, and moreover at times indistinguishable from other female characters, principally Francisca and Ana. More succinctly, postmodernism and feminism intersect on questions of representability. In practice, however, the rift between postmodernism and feminism has occurred in the execution. Whereas postmodern aesthetics distorts, and in this sense misrepresents, reality by way of fragmenting subject, voice, and plot, feminism has generally concentrated on faithfully depicting women's varied realities given "the pervasive cultural condition in which women's lives were either misrepresented or not represented at all."[28]

Eltit salvages the postmodern/feminist rift in *Sacred Cow* by inscribing female bodily experiences within a postmodern textual body, and in so doing feminism and postmodernism intersect while undermining the Chilean mainstream literary canon on two fronts—aesthetic and thematic. In the novel, menstruation is a female-centered theme, and one that may be read figuratively as a postmodern text for, as Susan Brownmiller points out about menses, it is "a disruption of everyday routine" in the sense of requiring extra measures of care and precaution, it is an "untidy event" that "forces women to pay minute attention to the innerworkings of the body."[29] Indeed, postmodern writing is about textual "disruptions"; "untidy" and "disorderly," its reading requires "extra measures of care" and the reader must "pay minute attention to the innerworkings" of the text.

Elizabeth Grosz's hypothesis that in the West the female body has been constructed not only as lacking a phallus but also "lacking self-containment" precisely because a female's corporeal flows lead to a representation of women as a leaking, seeping, formless, uncontrollable, and ultimately unstable being, suggests a corollary with the fluid aspects of postmodern writing, starting with the inability of critics to "contain" a definition of postmodernity itself.[30]

In Eltit's writing postmodernism and feminism intersect on the margins of these very practices because she takes both to extraordinary limits. For example, not only is the accumulation of postmodern devices in *Sacred Cow*—as well as *E. Luminata* and [*For the Homeland*]—exaggerated such that it produces a cryptic writing, the inscription of menstruation, abortion, and eroticism, beyond depicting female reality, contributes to what the author has called an aesthetics of blood.

From the first page of *Sacred Cow* jumps the juxtaposition "I lie a lot"/"I bleed a lot," one repeated so as to draw reader attention— "I bleed, lie a lot" (1). Both lying and bleeding reinforce the novel's postmodern underpinning. Lying and a bleeding wound normally can be controlled, but not so in the case of the narrator/protagonist who confesses her obsession for lying; she literally cannot stop lying any more than she can stop her menstrual flow. Moreover, belonging to the realm of the postmodern, lying destabilizes the text with doubt, falsity, and uncertainty, a terrain shared with menstrual bleeding insofar as irregular or missed cycles conjure false or uncertain pregnancy or menopause, two aspects of female experience in themselves fraught with "indeterminacies." Grounded in postmodernism and an "aesthetics of blood," *Sacred Cow* is an unreliable text and one often out of control. Eltit herself has said that the text got away from her and acknowledges that the narrator went astray in the novel, but that does not seem to distress her for she attained a world where the symbolic is most important.[31]

Blood emanating from a female body as a consequence of menstruation, birth, abortion, or a wound points to a body politics— biological and social—operating in the novel. Let us not forget that the—beaten, tortured, executed—bleeding and often disappeared Chilean body became a rallying point in the ousting of General Pinochet's military junta. Parallel to the Chilean people in the throes of political repression, the bleeding female body (whether menstruating, birthing, aborting, or wounded) insinuates a vulnerable state. Unquestionably, Eltit's biological body is never apolitical. Jo Labanyi, who presents a critical dialogue between *Sacred Cow* and Julia Kristeva's *Powers of Horror: An Essay on Abjection,* notes "the uncomfortable relationship" that the novel establishes "between the female body and political horror."[32]

Anthropological studies have found that across many cultures the menstruating woman has been considered unapproachable in the sense of both holy and polluted, what the Romans called, "sacra," sacred and accursed.[33] In this regard, the novel's very title insinuates this sense of a sacred female body as well as the political figure of General Pinochet. He is Chile's "sacred cow," venerated by some and hated by others, but nonetheless a national institution. Moreover, on a symbolic level, Eltit's *Sacred Cow* conjures both early men's fear of the magical nature of menstrual blood in its connection with women's procreative power and a nation's fear of a dictator's power.

To continue with the body/politic parallel, menstruation and political repression share the realm of taboo[34]—both phenomenons can be associated with blood, silence, prohibition, and subversion. A precious body fluid, blood may symbolize life or death, the latter of which is tied to menses, the time during the ovulatory cycle when the potential for new life is minimal. In recent Chilean history, political repression, represented in the novel by the arrest of Manuel and his family, inherently suggests bodily harm, bloodshed, and disappearance, a situation that, like menses, seriously compromises human life. Notably, during her menstrual cycle the narrator/protagonist engages in sexual intercourse with Manuel, the very man whose life is later threatened by arrest, an incident surrounded by silence and stigma much like the rarely articulated subject of menstruation. Given the taboo aspect of intercourse during menstruation, the narrator/protagonist's remark—"We never spoke of the blood" (7)—calls to mind the official secrecy on the issue of the disappeared despite the fact that mass persecution and detention constituted a national bloodbath during General Pinochet's regime.

The body/politic parallel is also suggested in chapter 4, titled "the enigma of the city." When the narrator/protagonist attempts to articulate fear (read political repression) as a life-transforming experience, her memory immediately reviews various bloody incidents. The first blood image transports her back to childhood when, running from some imaginary enemy, she falls on some glass and gashes her leg open. For the narrator/protagonist fear and blood are related.

From that recollection of bodily harm, memory jumps to the family bitch, "bleeding and howling," "dragging herself along on her belly leaving a trail of blood behind her," in "labour, moaning like a woman in pain" (16–17). At the time, the young girl witnesses the animal's agony until her ill, prostrated grandmother, sure that the bitch would die with the litter still inside, asks her to help with the delivery. But, following the grandmother's orders, the child playing midwife is forced to turn executioner and drown the female pups. Given the novel's political subtext, the child's impotence vis-à-vis the powerful grandmother provokes the reader to ponder the circumstance and mind-set of a torturer/executioner. "I wasn't sure I could do it," recalls the narrator/protagonist, "But I did. . . . It was the three little female pups that I drowned, unable to stop crying as I held them under the water" (18). This disregard for life conjures the prevalent tenor of the dictatorial state, and moreover captures the general devaluation of female existence in patriarchal societies.

From Labanyi's perspective, "the bleeding female body is also associated with dissolution of the self in the form of death," and it is this "invisible sense of death which infiltrates the boundaries of the self" and "triggers [the] sequence of childhood memories. . . ."[35] This critic also notes that, "The novel insists on the bleeding female body as an image, not of fertility, but of disintegration and death."[36]

Significantly, another scene where fear, blood, and ultimately death coalesce features an abortion procedure. "I was amazed by the coldness of the woman and the incessant pecking of her instruments," recalls the narrator/protagonist. "She lifts up one hand and I see her white glove soaked in blood. It is impossible to describe the terror at the sight of the instrument she is holding" (19). In a different context this last reflection could describe the reaction of a victim of torture upon spotting the tools of torment. Hence, it is not surprising that memory of fear and blood leads the narrator/protagonist back to the reality of Manuel's arrest and all its implications of jeopardy to life. "When Sergio told me that Manuel had been detained in the South, I experienced a void, a hiatus. . . . I thought of death," comments the narrator/protagonist (20).

Typical of Eltit's writing, the female body acts as springboard for insinuating the scars of the Chilean unconscious and recuperating what the author herself has called "the body of History."[37] In *Sacred Cow* the narrator/protagonist's body literally becomes a slate for inscribing psychological and physical agony suffered by those in some way victims of political repression. After the arrest of Manuel and his family the narrator/protagonist cannot reconcile sleep. "It was now that I began to learn to do with very little sleep—with so little that all my muscles went into spasm," she confesses. "It was either my sleep or their death. I thought that if I were to stay asleep they would die by the hundreds.[38] I felt as though I was falling apart . . ." (22). For the narrator/protagonist, the stifling atmosphere of the repressive state in which she lives literally translates into a physical struggle for the breath of life: "My muscles no longer worked properly and my breathing had become very faint from lack of sleep. My breath began to come very slowly, it cost such an effort to breathe through the night" (39). In a section worth transcribing at length, the narrator/protagonist paints a picture of a body in physical crisis:

> Out of the blue my body began to betray me. . . . Deprived, chronically anorexic, I began to feel permanently sick. Manuel was in detention in the South and I could no longer visualise his shape. . . . Hunger pursued me and distanced me yet further from the tangible world. . . . Mentally I veered towards disgusting things to eat. I found I was beginning to fantasise about worms, left-overs, rotten food, until I picked up a piece of decomposing meat and ate my way slowly through it. . . . Afterwards an attack of vomiting left me helpless for a few hours. I desperately wanted to rid myself of the burden of this unfair penance and asked Sergio for help to make it through the night. I was worn, beaten, and begged him to keep me company in my struggle against the destiny of my nights. (46)

The narrator/protagonist seems to suffer from survivor guilt and hence punishes herself by doing "penance" as reflected by her anorexia, permanent hunger, and purging. Let us recall that the mother in *The Fourth World* similarly manifests self-punishment in her dieting and her volunteer work with sick elderly people and blind children. In *Sacred Cow* the narrator/protagonist associates her menstruating body with the fate of the detained, letting her blood flow without restraint as a reminder that she is alive and as a symbolic umbilical cord that sustains those threatened with extinction. "Manuel was in detention in the South and with my blood I suspended his sentence for one more night," she comments (22). Ultimately, however, the flow of blood, and specifically menstrual blood, carries a stronger connotation of death than of life: "And the blood kept coming, every month the blood came; and by then blood had lost all association for me but its irrevocable connection to death" (22).

Notably, anthropological findings coincide in that cross-culturally, menstruating women, albeit not necessarily unwelcome by them, have been excluded from ordinary life in their communities (barred from planting, harvesting, threshing, cooking), secluded from their families (often in special huts), stamped pollutants, and considered dangerous subjects.[39] The deliberate separation from mainstream society of a particular group finds an extreme corollary in the treatment of political dissidents under an authoritarian regime where, as in the case of Chile, those considered ideologically dangerous— read, espousing communism or terrorism—were not only physically removed from their home, place of employment, or public thoroughfare, but they became the lepers in society, frequently among their own kin.

Significantly, in their examination of the public speeches delivered by General Pinochet and reproduced in Chilean newspapers, Giselle Munizaga and Carlos Ochsenius note his reference to "contaminated groups," and they observe that specifically the Popular Unity government is portrayed as an "agent which contaminates everything it touches (the country, the State, citizens, people's conscience. . . ."[40] Public rhetoric about political dissidents and Judeo-Christian dogma concerning menstruating women intersect on the notion of contaminating agents.

Concerning bodily emissions, the Bible specifies that "When a woman has a discharge of blood that is her regular discharge from her body, she shall be in her impurity for seven days, and whoever touches her shall be unclean until the evening."[41] Remnants of ancient beliefs are still manifest in modern society, where menstruation is, with few exceptions, linguistically off-limits and physically kept secret with paraphernalia packaged neatly and made compact, disposable, flushable, spill-proof, and odor-free.

Clearly, in *Sacred Cow*, Eltit subverts the "cleanliness is next to godliness" of the collective unconscious with a narrator/protagonist who deliberately displays her menstruating body, observes its flow, stains herself, scrutinizes the dried blood, and furthermore engages in sexual relations during its course. Subversion also lies in the fact that menstruation, as the one excuse that scores of women throughout the ages have used to deny men sex,[42] seems precisely to be the narrator/protagonist's excuse for sex. Given Hispanic culture's predominantly Judeo-Christian heritage, sexual intercourse during menses pushes transgression into the realm of taboo. "You shall not approach a woman to uncover her nakedness while she is in her menstrual uncleanness," dictates the scripture on the subject of sexual intercourse.[43] Ignoring this law brings severe consequence to both parties who "shall be cut off from their people."[44]

Needless to say, the literal interpretation of such punishment for transgression of biblical doctrine is long outmoded. Yet as previously noted, certain aspects of ancient times do linger in modern society. In this regard, Jean Lipman-Blumen draws from art to explain the legacy of ancient civilizations in contemporary gender images. "In pentimento fashion each succeeding civilization paints over the canvas of previous cultures, yet earlier images of masculinity and femininity bleed through even the most contemporary gender role portraits. These ancient images form the nucleus of full-blown control myths that shape behavior, values, and attitudes."[45] Not surprisingly, among the control myths discussed, Lipman-Blumen identifies "Control myth #5: Women are contaminated and contaminating."[46]

To use Lipman-Blumen's pentimento analogy, in *Sacred Cow* the political subtext "bleeds through" many aspects of the novel. For instance, when Eltit evokes biblical tenets in transgressing myths that once served to control the fe/male body, she also covertly undermines the military regime's public rhetoric which, formulated to gain control of the country, drew heavily from religious discourse. A clear example of this is presented by Hernán Vidal, who examines the junta's "La Declaración de Principios" [The Declaration of Principles], a document "published in four languages—Spanish, English, French and German—on March of 1974" to justify military rule in Chile.[47]

Let us keep in mind that although *Sacred Cow* was Eltit's first novel written without the military in power, by the same token Chileans had lived with the junta's rhetoric for almost two decades when the novel was published in 1991. Vidal observes that in its missionary-like design "The Declaration of Principles" corresponds to a mythic discourse rooted in Scholasticism, at times reproducing the canonical language of the Spanish Reconquest, a discourse first adopted in Chile by certain Catholic sectors that sympathized with the fascism of Gen. Francisco Franco in the Spain of the 1930s.[48] More specifically the document mentions "human spirituality originating in God," "the nation's soul," and "our Chilean and Christian tradition," while it refers to the previous administration as responsible for "the fall," countless "vices," an "illegitimate," "immoral" socialist government that "does not recognize human sacredness." As Vidal remarks, the military junta proposed to "redeem" Chile.

From the patriarchal perspective of the military junta (which pigeonholed women in the most conventional roles)[49] and Chilean society in general (which in matters of gender remains provincial), Eltit's female characters would need redemption for they incarnate the "fallen," "immoral," "vice"-ridden woman. For example, the inebriated, sexually promiscuous, adulterous, and perverted narrator/protagonist of *Sacred Cow*, who, to boot, is a liar, does not correspond to the traditional Latin American Marian model and as such portrays a subversive female figure who revels in an erotic life free from cultural inhibitions:

I learnt that I could use Manuel's body in ways I had never imagined. I gave myself up to the subtleties of his skin, to the erogenous zones of his flesh. Ah such nights, such afternoons. . . . Manuel always naked. Moaning naked at my side, begging me to excite him further. . . .

We followed every whim . . . nothing could restrain us. Not even my blood. I stood upright with my legs apart and my blood ran down over Manuel. . . . We looked at the red stains on his body, on the sheets—the blood streaming from the slit between my legs. Manuel begged me to taint him with my blood. And I surrendered it to him: fully erect he explored me to elicit and enjoy the viscous liquid. (6–7)

Here Eltit deviates from the standard image of blood during heterosexual intercourse as a sign of defloration, the event in which, from the Judeo-Christian pure/impure distinction, a man literally and symbolically "soils" the virgin.[50] Instead the narrator/protagonist "taints" Manuel. As alluded to earlier, depicting sexual intercourse explicitly during menstruation disdains cultural sensitivities and defies the linguistic restraint traditionally observed in mainstream literature in Chile, even when the inscription of menstruation is not new and no longer shocking.

Among Chilean writers, Isabel Allende includes the topic of menstruation in *The House of the Spirits* (originally published in 1982 and practically a decade before Eltit's *Sacred Cow*, 1991), but she presents it within the parameters of popular attitudes, that is, as a disruptive, painful, messy, unwelcome event that, in the novel, moreover turns out to be a great embarrassment for Alba who, as participant in a student protest, is in a university building under siege by police when the untimely flow begins.

[T]he pain in her abdomen was becoming unbearable and the need to take a bath with running water was beginning to obsess her. . . . Alba felt a warm viscous liquid between her legs and saw that her slacks were stained with red. She was swept with panic. For the past few days the fear that this might happen had tormented her almost as much as hunger. The stain on her pants was like a flag. . . . When she was little, her grandmother had taught her that everything associated with human functions is natural, and she could speak of menstruation as of poetry, but later on, at school, she learned that all bodily secretions except tears are indecent.[51]

Pía Barros also addresses culture's (negative) affects on women's attitude towards menstruation in the short narrative collection *Signos bajo la piel* (1994). Reminiscent of Alejo Carpentier's temporal regression in "Viaje a la semilla," in "Las reglas del juego,"[52] Barros presents the treatment of menarche in the lives of six adolescents, starting with a modern-day teenager and spanning back to before the arrival of the Spanish in Latin America when menstruation was celebrated by indigenous women in fertility rites. Through the proliferation of words such as "shame," "dirty," "secret," "indecencies," "punishment," and "sinful" in addition to various myths and prohibitions associated with menstruation throughout the ages, Barros depicts the damage culture inflicts on the female psyche.

Radically different in her approach, Eltit displaces shame and traditional attitudes, connects the female menstrual flow with sexuality, and in so doing involves men in an erotic economy that in a phallocentric culture recognizes pleasure only in the transmission of seminal fluid.[53] "Manuel begged me to taint him with my blood. And I surrendered it to him: fully erect he explored me to elicit and enjoy the viscous liquid" (7), remarks the narrator/protagonist in the previously cited passage. Here Eltit not only inverts the notion of women as receptacles that receive men's flow, but she decontextualizes menstruation from the realm of the reproductive.[54] "The first issuing forth of sperm, the onset of nocturnal emissions, signals coming manhood for the boy, the sexual pleasures and encounters fantasized and yet to come," points out Grosz, "but the onset of menstruation is not an indication at all for the girl of her developing sexuality, only her coming womanhood."[55] Clearly, in Eltit's novel womanhood is by no means synonymous with maternity, for the narrator/protagonist engages in sexual encounters precisely during menstruation when conception is least likely to occur.

In *Sacred Cow*, sex and fear are the predominant motivating forces that drive the characters' coupling; nonexistent is the conventional romantic female/male relationship where sexual attraction leads to love, courtship, marriage, children, and family life. The novel presents conflict-ridden and even abusive human relations. One gets the impression that the abundance of desire and sexual activity is, considering the repressive political subtext, a manifestation of the desire to live, to feel alive. The narrator/protagonist and Ana, for example, not only engage in various sexual encounters, but also take turns bedding Manuel and Sergio in a sort of competitive female exchange of men. About Ana's tale of her "one perfect night with Manuel,"[56] the narrator/protagonist remarks, "On the verge of tears I had to listen to every last syllable of Manuel's words, struggling as he moaned. Are you moaning? Yes, you are. I know that moaning, it has always been there, between my legs, my most precious belonging."[57] Ultimately, sex in the novel seems to mean little to the characters, rather it is somewhat of an addiction that is difficult to give up even when pleasure has disappeared, it becomes an end in itself without the possibility of a meaningful connection with the other.

Noteworthy, one of the first things Hernán Valdés mentions when reflecting on the coup d'état in *Tejas verdes*, his personal testimonial on surviving detention in Chile during the dictatorship, is that because the military overthrow shattered intimate relations, men and women who had until then only known each other in the context of friendship or work, finding themselves suddenly unattached as a consequence of their partner's exile, disappearance, death, or general instability, ended up in bed as a way of fighting fear, insecurity, solitude, and depression.[58] *Sacred Cow* portrays the characters' need for, yet their failure in, love relationships, a situation supported by the postmodern text's fragmented nature and enigmatic connections.

Given the promiscuity of human relations in Eltit's novel, coupled with a revelry in menstrual blood during sexual intercourse and the author's proposal for an aesthetics of blood, today's reader, in an age of AIDS, cannot help but consider points of connection between the sexual exploits of the menstruating female, the bloodshed of politically persecuted Chileans, and the AIDS-afflicted, who, for starters, mainstream society likewise prefers veiling in silence, classifies as agents of contamination, and considers deviant.

Although I realize that I am lumping three disparate groups, nonetheless, its members, broadly speaking and within their respective circumstance, are all marginals. Sexually active women (in a strict, patriarchal society), political objectors (in a repressive Latin American context) and AIDS victims have been affected—even ostracized—by public attitudes that judge their behavior—shameful, unsafe, and therefore—punishable. A decent person was not one of "them," as Susan Sontag remarks of the stigma once attached to the cancer patient.[59]

In an interview, Eltit commented that "the female body is a moral territory"; so is, we might add, the body infected with AIDS.[60] Not surprisingly, in a patriarchal society the sexual practices of women and gay men become a question of moral weakness and indulgence which carry the imputation of guilt.[61] The sexual desire of (menstruating) women and homosexuals is transgressive. Despite varying reasons—and again, taking into account particular historicity—sexually active women, political dissidents, and the HIV- or AIDS-afflicted have been categorized as members of a "risk group," and especially the latter two fall into the ranks of pariahs because of their—real or perceived—association with delinquency—whether it be political activism, terrorism, the use of illegal drugs, or sexual perversion.[62]

Considering the historical, if implicit, context of *Sacred Cow* (again, whose very title for Chileans infers Pinochet), Eltit's notion of an aesthetics of blood cannot but evoke death, death as a correlation between one or more of the groups identified thus far. After all, menstruating women, political dissidents, and AIDS sufferers are all representatives of potential victims—be they the unborn, the disappeared, or the terminally ill. Phrased another way, there is a slight chance that conception of life will occur during menstruation, that the life of a disappeared political objector and an individual with AIDS will be spared—death looms as the greater probability.

Death as a consequence of political persecution in Southern Cone countries during the 1970s as well as from the AIDS virus starting in the decade of the 1980s constitute human catastrophes that, once no longer contained within the private sphere of the family as isolated tragedy or within particular community sectors at risk, turned into state crises and crossed national borders to become issues of international concern. As with any of Eltit's fiction, the reader should keep in mind that she was formed as a writer during a period in Latin America when military regimes ruling Argentina, Chile, and Uruguay imposed a reign of terror that today can be compared with the human devastation wreaked by the AIDS virus.

In their study on AIDS, Graciela Biagini and María del Carmen Sánchez point to a report by the AIDS Institute at Harvard University that comments on the extraordinarily serious problem and vulnerable position of developing countries, among them Latin America, which lack the resources to keep up let alone stay ahead in the fight against AIDS. Reminiscent of the discourse about political prisoners and the disappeared in Latin America, the issue concerning the state's responsibility to insure human rights and dignity for its citizens comes up in regard to AIDS patients who, besides facing moralizing attitudes, experience grave shortages of public clinics and hospitals that, already impoverished, cannot provide adequate care or meet the demand for bed space for those in the last stages of the disease.[63] By not instituting aggressive measures to tackle the AIDS crisis, are Latin American governments in essence allowing another kind of national genocide?

In *Sacred Cow* the menstruating body of a sexually active female acts as springboard for conjuring (blood) connections with broad sociopolitical issues. How can the threat of AIDS not come to mind in a text whose author has voiced an attempt at creating an aesthetic of blood, a text wherein characters come in contact with the bodily emission of others, including blood, saliva, semen, tears, vomit? "To remember his hands," reflects the protagonist about Manuel, "his tongue, his saliva, his spilled juices, his energy encouraged by the wine" (6–7). Keeping in mind that for Eltit the reader "activates" and "works" a specific text, she has also stated that she "cannot disconnect that which is erotic and even sexual from the social."[64]

As a casualty of political repression, Manuel shares things in common with victims of AIDS, especially since no one is immune to either calamity. Although certain groups—for example, members of particular political parties, social activists, and union organizers— were more prone to persecution under the dictatorship, as certain groups—drug users, hemophiliacs, homosexuals—are more likely to contract AIDS, by and large any one can be struck down.[65] Panic spreads fast when the "risk group" is potentially anyone and everyone.

The exact number of people who disappeared in Latin America at the hands of brutal military regimes will never be ascertained— and from all indications neither will the casualties from AIDS.[66] In yet another commonality, both political repression and the AIDS virus create a sort of human chain of fatalities. As with AIDS where one person could infect many others, so too one person under torture can implicate a few who in turn name others—ad infinitum. Paradoxically, the very tragedy that renders individuals powerless turns out to give them, albeit macabre, some control over their predicament. As one Chilean HIV carrier put it, "this virus gives us power."[67]

As noted thus far, menstruation, political detention, and AIDS intersect on the axis of fear, shame, secrecy, contamination, and taboo. In *Sacred Cow,* Eltit subverts the cultural construction that typically hides so well the menstrual bleeding of the female body that it seems not to happen at all.[68] This camouflaging stance was reflected in the attitude many Chileans once held about the disappeared and more currently it extends to a Catholic Church that some accuse of hypocrisy when it acts as if in denial of the social reality of AIDS.[69] A nonchalant attitude about AIDS would be alarming given the high incidence in Santiago of premarital (and in a "machista" culture probably extramarital) sex, conduit for the spread of the disease among heterosexuals.[70]

As late as 1996, AIDS in Chile was yet to be assumed within a national consciousness since most Chileans at the time continued to relate the AIDS-infected body with an imported body with foreign features and one practically invisible and not televised to the masses.[71] The degree of influence the Roman Catholic Church exercises in the Chilean media became obvious in April 1997 when two television stations, the Television Corporation of the Catholic University and Megavision, half-owned and managed by a devout businessman, Ricardo Claro, refused to air two commercial spots commissioned by the Chilean Ministry of Health in conjunction with Conasida (Comisión Nacional del SIDA) as part of its campaign to educate the public on the precautions to take for the prevention of AIDS.[72]

This incident turned into quite a polemic in Santiago with politicians, members of the medical community, and other public figures backing then Chilean President Eduardo Frei in his call for putting an end to censorship in the country. His accusation of hypocrisy pointed out that primetime soap operas aired by these same stations portray pre- and extramarital affairs widespread in Chilean society.[73] But when pressed to justify their decision, the stations only indicated that the spots were not in line with their editorial philosophy, which in translation means that suggesting the use of condoms is not an acceptable alternative from the perspective of a Catholic Church preaching premarital sexual abstinence, procreative sex within marriage, and conjugal fidelity.

What the Catholic Church was willing to negotiate was the idea of integrating "JOCAS" (Jornadas de Conversación sobre Afectividad y Sexualidad—loosely translated as Encounters for Conversations about Affection and Sexuality) into the formal school curriculum.[74] The three-day encounter (officially it was not a sex education program) emphasized morality, in essence the advocacy of virginity and sexual abstinence until marriage. Notably, the revised 1997 JOCAS program banned the exhibition of any form of symbolic or illustrative sexual activity and the distribution of condoms—despite evidence of the high incidence of pregnancy out-of-wedlock among teenagers and young adults.[75] The Church's unrealistic "it shouldn't happen" approach to the sexual practice of Chileans resembles the "hide it and it doesn't happen" attitude that Olea noted with respect to menstruation in the cultural construction of the female body.

Eltit's unreserved, even unconventional, female-centered depiction of sexuality in *Sacred Cow* should be appreciated within a national context where the dominant posture on this issue is often vastly discrepant with reality.[76] What distinguishes Eltit among contemporary Chilean writers is precisely an unwillingness to uphold the status quo, a reluctance reflected in her choice of themes as well as in a postmodern style which, she acknowledges, has limited her readership. Paradoxically, it is through postmodern writing, characteristic for resisting mimetic representation of reality, that Eltit's themes prove quite in check with reality. In *Sacred Cow* the adolescent affair between Francisca and Sergio—depicted in chapter 7 as "the ten nights of francisca lombardo"[77]—is one example where portrayal of sexual practice teeters between modern attitudes prevalent in Chilean society and traditional conventions the Catholic Church wants to maintain. In this respect too, Eltit's postmodern style reflects the ambiguities of the national reality.

As the story goes, Sergio meets Francisca in school, becomes totally obsessed with the girl, and spends the school year fantasizing, "possessing her in every way he could imagine" when after stalking her for days he realizes "that Francisca, though only fourteen, already had a vice that he was happy to satisfy" (25). Raging hormones on both sides eventually lead these young people to a sexual relationship, but one clearly burdened with traces of an underlying puritanical socialization. For example, after summer recess, Sergio, convinced that "Francisca had held a man between her thighs," felt "an uncontrollable rage" (28) fueled by the fact that "it seemed to him that she was brazenly flaunting her shamelessness" (29). Sergio's reaction evidences a cultural double standard where sexually active males have difficulty condoning the same behavior in females. "Francisca has had a man this summer, he thought, and the sentence went on echoing to the rhythm of his loathing" (29), because Francisca, as object of desire, is now a fallen woman, "a girl who had lost the race before she'd even begun" (31).

On Francisca's part, she acts in an apparently liberated way, but not surprisingly, given gender socialization in a patriarchal culture, her inner voice betrays a guilt-ridden conscious. In an illicit sexual encounter suggested by "a twenty-five watt bulb in the room," the Francisca who recalls her desire with a remark such as "I wanted his tongue, I desperately wanted his tongue, I longed to swallow his tongue," is also the Francisca who immediately clarifies that "none of this was me, it was the animal in me with its huge pink tongue,

baying to get out" (50). In light of this refutation, Francisca's repeated allusion to sexual drive as "animal" instinct through such
phrases as "my greedy animal self," "The hidden animal in me,"
"What animal? It was me," and "I shall growl like an animal"[78] does
not express a positive, uninhibited sexual self-image, but rather
demonstrates the internalization of cultural gender tenets that
deem aggressiveness and lack of restraint attached to nature and untamed Eros as inappropriate for females.[79] Also inappropriate would
be the sexual promiscuity implied when Francisca says, "Tonight
you are just another and I let you in like just another, as you know,
with my legs spread" (54).

Such culturally improper behavior for a female explains, in part,
self-loathing thoughts evident when Francisca refers to "the evil
within me, evil that I am"[80] in a chapter that amply reflects the incompatibility between pleasure and guilt, between modern and traditional values:

> In those punishing years I needed strength to keep those hands from
> creeping between my legs to touch me. What pleasure it gave me, I al-
> most came with the man's hand in the park. . . . I didn't have the
> strength to resist all those hands that tried it, I couldn't cut short my
> ultimate pleasure. . . . Don't let it happen to me, don't let it happen, I
> said, don't let it happen to me again. So I pressed my legs together, sit-
> ting on the sofa, until the throbbing began. I wasn't sure, and all I did
> was to sit on the sofa with my legs firmly together. I should have cut off
> my hands. (61–62)

This last statement echos gospel castigation for adultery which
states that "If your right hand causes you to sin, cut if off and throw
it away; it is better that you lose one of your members than that your
whole body go into hell."[81] Coincidentally, the biblical verse that
precedes the one just quoted refers to blindness: "If your eye causes
you to sin, pluck it out and throw it away."[82] Francisca's fear of blinding, transcribed here at length to illustrate her obsession, is another
form of punishment notably connected with sexuality:[83] "I was about
to be blinded in my right eye by a great spike which at the last moment swerved and thrust up between my legs," "besieged by the
man . . . who at this very moment will be waiting with a splinter of
glass to gouge out my eye," "I . . . realised that I would lose an eye,
that sooner or later it would be mercilessly gouged out with that
spike and I would lose it," "The man is outside walking meticulously
from side to side, a bird eager to launch itself at me. It is bound to
blind me," "There's a man waiting for me outside in the street to

put out my eye. In his hands he is hiding a nail to put out my right
eye," "a million workers could not protect me when the splinter
shafts my eye," "the black bird stole one of my eyes."[84]

In the context of this erotically charged chapter, Francisca's obsessive fear of losing such a precious human faculty as her eyesight suggests not only guilt but an analogy for the loss of her virginity, a very
valuable commodity for females in highly patriarchal societies. Labanyi observes that, "As a bleeding wound, blinding is related to the
novel's central motif of menstruation."[85] It certainly points to the
female body, but I would take it further and say that the violent nature of the blindness, often perpetrated by a man, implies rape, a
possibility that every woman lives with, but more so someone like
Francisca who is sexually active and in so being has waived the implicit protection and respect that Latin American culture, meaning
the Latin American man, customarily grants the "decent" unmarried female, the virgin.

Phallic symbols such as the "spike," "nail," "splinter," "beak"
that "thrusts," "shafts," "gouges," or "pecks" reinforce what Francisca resents and fears in heterosexual relations. Eltit's predominantly symbolic, rather than explicit, representation of sexual
intercourse demonstrates her expressed disinterest in writing an
"erotic" novel per se, "that mere label" she says "scares me."[86] This
does not mean, however, that Eltit's writing is not erotically-charged,
because it is sometimes very—unorthodoxically—so, as discussed in
the chapters on *E. Luminata*, [*For the Homeland*], and *The Fourth
World*.

Referring to *Sacred Cow*, Eltit has commented that the image of
birds constantly floated in her head while writing the novel,[87] an
image that connotes the penis in the Chilean symbolic order.[88] Notably, Francisca reiterates this euphemism throughout chapter 7 in an
introspective reflection that articulates the source of her oppression.
The accumulation of the bird symbol in the chapter creates the following textual weave: "a deaf and blind bird moves only to the
rhythms of its desires. That flattering, lying bird. You are holding
the bird in your hand, its wings in my bed. . . . I dry myself on the
sheet and the bird flies over to me"; "expressionless bird,"
"wretched, heartless bird"; "assassin bird"; "His saliva soothed me,
helped me to bear the birds' beaks"; "Little bird," "a bird always
pecks"; "The bird pecks on monotonously—boom, boom"; "self-
absorbed bird," "I climb a deafeningly dangerous man, a bird throt-
tled in its tree"; "a flock of demented birds," "conceited bird"; "a
bird eager to launch itself at me"; "The bird flew up to pin me to
the bed," "the bird rose up, ineffably proud"; "you moaning bird

who keeps throwing back in my face the fact that you support me. You stingy bird"; "cheating bird"; "A bird departed without warning, leaving me in a state of intense irritation."[89]

Out of context, perhaps the preceding transcription too proves irritating, but it is meant to convey the overwhelming male presence that looms over Francisca's life—literally every page of the chapter contains a reference to "bird" (it ends with Francisca dreaming that she dies from a great fall and even dead, her corpse is attacked by a bird). However, as Labanyi observes, "Birds in the novel function both as the image of a repressive order, and as an image of ecstatic release."[90]

Eltit manipulates this phallic symbol to inscribe an unebbing erotic charge that portrays a Francisca sexually dependent on and exploited by men in a culture where women internalize that they are nothing without a male partner. Based on more than a mind-set, in practical terms Francisca the worker does not earn a living wage that would allow her independence. "Soon I shall be twenty-two and I'll look for work. I shall be just one more employee," remarks Francisca (51), and later adds, "They have taken me on as a worker and I have to battle for my livelihood, arguing over each clause of my contract" (55).

Both bedroom and workplace are spaces for exploitation. "Shopkeepers, craftsmen, bricklayers, carpenters"—workers and lovers?— "all jostle in my memory" says Francisca, "like a bird splattered against a window. The world of work marches past before my eyes. The workers are walking in a straight line and their noses are bleeding. I want to bleed, to file past with my fist in the air, yelling for the restitution of our rights. . . ." (62–63). Ultimately, Francisca embodies the blood, sweat and tears—bodily fluids inscribed throughout *Sacred Cow*—not only of the Chilean working poor, but of women in general, the politically persecuted, and AIDS victims, all marginal and appropriate contributors to Eltit's proposal for an aesthetic of blood, a postmodern, socially conscious art rooted in Chilean reality.

6

The Controlling Gaze in *Los vigilantes*

By NOW READERS HAVE NOTED THAT ELTIT'S RECURRENT INTELLECTUAL concerns revolve around women's issues, the art of writing, and Chilean political circumstance within and beyond national borders. As mentioned in the introduction, Southern Cone women who wrote and published fiction in the aftermath of the region's military coups generally shifted their focus from domestic patriarchal oppression to dictatorial repression.

Today in Chile—as in other Latin American countries that are still dealing with post-dictatorship traumas—women, who by necessity suspended their gender-related struggles, find that patriarchy, like the phoenix, emerged alive and well from the embers of General Pinochet's reign. In fact, the state terrorized people by manipulating the cults of machismo and marianismo, so rooted in Hispanic culture.[1] Although the return to democratic rule made an enormous difference in the way Chileans conduct their civic affairs, for the majority of women little has changed to improve their status. Writers like Eltit realize that despite the years of struggle for a better homeland, for most Chileans the home remains a man's castle and women's prison or, at best, a gilded cage.

Los vigilantes/ [*Vigilant*] (1994) presents a protagonist who, unlike the male-reliant Francisca of *Sacred Cow*, has chosen a life independent of her husband but at the cost of living in poverty. Although the reader does not know the circumstance of the separation, the text suggests that this woman has traded the comforts afforded by marriage for a sense of freedom in a ghetto-like existence. But freedom is elusive in the novel, for surveillance—as alluded to by the title—is a key function in oppression and war. Spying or keeping watch over others aims to control by interfering with the subject's freedom to act. Loss of power to rule one's life naturally engenders fear, a theme that proliferates in literatures of subjugated peoples. Women by far compose the largest group of people for whom fear and lack of power is a way of life. Also, throughout their lives women

176

will experience more scrutiny than men, a reality Eltit's novel illustrates well.

In [*Vigilant*] the character of the tyrannical husband takes on multilayered meanings, which this study proposes to explore. Eltit's readers have come to expect a text rich in interpretative possibilities. However, this novel marks a turning point in her production. Eltit sheds the radical aspects of an avant-garde style that earned her the reputation for not making sense; a label she resented and yet nurtured because being at the margins of the conservative Chilean literary tradition is a distinguishing niche, after all.

The careful reader of Eltit's novels can discern that over the years the disjointed prose of the early works, discussed in respective chapters of this study, has attenuated—culminating in [*Vigilant*]. Does the linear narration of this novel constitute a return of the prodigal daughter to the canon's flock? Did the obstacles of nonconformity become too burdensome? In answering, Eltit points to the challenges this multilayered novel poses. Yet, the complexity she signals to does not compare to the disregard for syntax, the neologisms and genre anomalies of her earlier novels. In my view, with the publication of [*Vigilant*], and subsequently *Trabajadores de la muerte* [*Workers of Death*] (1998), the author may finally rid herself of the haunting "unreadability" label.

"[*Vigilant*]" may mark the beginning of a linear narrative approach for Eltit, but marginality remains the core theme of her literary production. The novel incorporates a spectrum of topics (the oppression of women, homelessness, political struggle, and mental disorder) already cultivated in earlier works. Among Eltit's creative precedents, we have discussed the narrating fetus of *The Fourth World*. In the initial nine-page section of [*Vigilant*], the retarded child's perspective, reminiscent of Juan Rulfo's "Macario,"[2] establishes his marginal status.

The epistolary mode introduced in the novel and associated with women's writing befits the housebound woman who writes letters to her estranged husband regarding their son. Both the linear narrative style and the traditional female role assumed by the protagonist seem to comply with conventional expectation throughout the novel until its concluding section where the focus once again turns to the son's point of view. Apparent conformity aside, an analysis of the plot reveals that Eltit weaves much more subversiveness into the text than is first evident.

The novel's title discloses scrutiny as a key element in the text. The term "vigilante" refers to "watchman, guard, a member of a volunteer committee organized to suppress and punish crime summarily."[3] Notably, the gaze is an important mechanism throughout Eltit's production. Let us recall that in *E. Luminata* a commercial sign intermittently illuminates the protagonist as she flaunts herself under the gaze of the homeless men who occupy the public plaza at nightfall. The parents' gaze is voyeuristic with respect to the sibling mating of *The Fourth World*. And as [*My Father*] suggests, homelessness produces a street dweller, a public figure that invites the other's glance. [*Soul's Infarct*] also directs our gaze. Photographs by Paz Errázuriz of the inhabitants of an insane asylum illustrate Eltit's narrative portrayal of life in confinement. In this case the images override the written text, turning readers into viewers. From a number of interpretive angles, [*Vigilant*] points to the other's critical—and ultimately controlling—gaze. But who is that "other?" Exploring the possible identities—the multiple layers of meaning—will facilitate an understanding of the novel beyond its conventional surface design.

The readily identifiable "other" is the protagonist's manipulative husband. But [*Vigilant*] also invites interpretation on a symbolic level. In varying degrees, there are three interpretive spheres simultaneously operating in the novel, which can be loosely labeled personal, political, and cultural. In relationship to these categories the female protagonist of [*Vigilant*] is respectively a mother, a citizen, and a writer. Consequently, within these prescribed roles, the "other" exercises power over the protagonist as husband, government, and literary canon.

Significantly, the authoritative husband serves as metonymic representation of patriarchal dominance in both the political and literary realms. Thus, an examination of issues of power on the interpersonal level will reveal significant power imbalances at a sociopolitical and cultural level as well.[4]

THE PERSONAL: MOTHER VS. PATRIARCH

In [*Vigilant*] the personal domain discloses a broken, dysfunctional family composed of a retarded son, a wife harassed by the child's father (who is also her estranged husband), and a meddling mother-in-law. The story is narrated in three sections: "BAAAM," "Amanece," and "BRRRR" [BAAAM, It Dawns, and BRRRR]. In the first and last sections the son reveals his own physical and mental conditions through stream of consciousness. "Mi cuerpo laxo habla, mi lengua no tiene musculatura. No habla. . . . Mi lengua es tan difícil que no impide que se me caiga la baba" (13) [My lax body talks,

my tongue has no muscles. It doesn't talk. . . . My tongue is so difficult that it doesn't prevent my drooling], he says of his bodily limitations. This is coupled, however, with behavior that suggests mental
deficiency as well. "Babeando lanzo una estruendosa risa. Ay, como
me río. Caigo al suelo y en el suelo me arrastro. Es bonito, duro,
dulce. Golpeo mi cabeza de tonto, PAC PAC PAC PAC suena duro mi
cabeza de tonto, de tonto. TON TON TON To" (14) [Drooling I
release a thunderous laugh. Oh boy! how I laugh. I fall to the floor
and on the floor I drag myself. It's pretty, hard, sweet. I pound my
idiot's head, PAC PAC PAC PAC it resonates hard this head of an
idiot, ID ID, ID Iot].

This first section discloses the son's identity and introduces the
mother/son relationship, which will be threatened by patriarchal
rule during the course of the second section. The prominence
placed on the son as the introductory figure in the novel alludes to
his importance within the narrative scheme and development. In essence, the second section that comprises the major part of the book
revolves around the primogenitor and the spousal conflict that
arises over his custody. Although the son's participation in the novel
is negligible, the concluding section featuring his perspective creates a cyclical structure that once more emphasizes the character's
significance.

The novel portrays the female protagonist as a single parent struggling to feed herself and her child. Scarcity of food, lack of heating,
and the pawning of items indicates that the household falls among
the statistics of those living under the poverty level.[5] A probable assumption here is that the absence from the home of the male spouse
has resulted in the neediness of mother and child. Downward mobility among women as a result of separation, divorce, abandonment,
or widowhood is a gender issue that transcends national borders and
cultures.[6] Social scientists commonly refer to "the feminization of
poverty" when addressing problems that affect women.[7]

In *Justice, Gender, and the Family*, Susan Moller Okin points to the
internal gender inequalities of the family.[8] "Women are made vulnerable both economically and socially," notes Okin, "by the inter-
connected traditions of female responsibility for rearing children
and female subordination and dependence, of which both the history and the contemporary practices of marriage form a significant
part."[9] Simply said, training for traditional female roles leaves
women ill prepared to sustain a household.[10]

In [*Vigilant*], the protagonist's story of hardship is revealed
through letters she writes to the estranged spouse. Her attempt to
rear her son without interference meets with grave resistance from

the boy's father who attempts to restore patriarchal rule in the home. Trapped in the institution of marriage, the protagonist remains nameless until the very last line of her account. In her next novel, *Los trabajadores de la muerte* [*Workers of Death*] (1998), Eltit returns to the vicissitudes of marriage and similarly universalizes women's lack of autonomy by emphasizing oppressive circumstances rather than the identity of an individual woman.

Much like the technique Mexican journalist and novelist Elena Poniatowska uses in *Querido Diego, te abraza Quiela* (1978)/*Dear Diego* (1986), only the woman's writing is available for reading. Other similarities as well exist between these texts.[11] Both the Chilean and Mexican stories involve women in some way dependent on an estranged spouse, sons who act as a link in the parental relationship, the (impending) loss of that son, and the participation of the male partner in the female's economic, social, and emotional ruin. However, unlike Poniatowska's protagonist who continues to write letters to her lover—Mexican muralist Diego Rivera—without ever receiving an answer, Eltit's text suggests that the wife does maintain a reciprocal correspondence with the spouse. The letters, which much like the husband, supposedly exist but are absent from the text, convey the patriarch's status in the household. Symbolically, Eltit grants him the voice men traditionally have had in life's affairs, yet she deprives him of readership.

In [*Vigilant*] the son's expulsion from school triggers the letter writing and the power struggle that ensues between the parents. The first letter sets the scene for the writing and alludes to a traditional division of labor that most likely has resulted in the difference in economic status of husband and wife. There is no evidence in the novel that the protagonist works outside the home, and, except for the hostile mother-in-law, there is no extended family to care for the child were the wife to secure employment. Moreover, the extremely cold apartment that mother and child inhabit underscores the economic disparity between the parents. "Ah, pero no es posible que lo entiendas porque tú, que no te encuentras expuesto a esta miserable temperatura, jamás podrías comprender esta penetrante sensación que me invade" (25) [Oh, it's impossible for you to understand it because you, who are not exposed to this miserable temperature, could never understand this penetrating sensation that invades me], points out the wife. Female and child impoverishment noted in the text and the wide gap between the economic well-being of the male head of the household and his dependents point to a social reality that extends beyond Chilean and Latin American borders.[12]

Despite inequality, the female protagonist in [*Vigilant*] does not express subordination. On the contrary, her stance regarding the son's expulsion from school demonstrates boldness and even a veiled threat, as depicted in the opening line of her second letter: "Pero, ¿cómo te atreviste a escribirme unas palabras semejantes?" (27) [But, how dare you write me such words?]. And she concludes: "Ahora exijo que retires tus palabras. . . . Limítate a escribir, con la sensatez que espero, una solución para esta tragedia que me resulta interminable" (28) [Now I demand that you retract your words. . . . Limit your writing, with good sense I hope, to resolving this tragedy that I find endless]. In essence, the wife demands a stop to the husband's criticisms, which have not produced a viable solution to the problem. Her language suggests assertiveness, an attribute far from the submissive behavior one would expect in situations of inequality. The mothers' stance in the early correspondence proves important because, as the spousal dispute flares, her posture will change under coercion.

Conflict in the novel helps underscore how much a part of Latin American female existence involves expending energy to resist patriarchal dictates. Urgings from her husband that she live with her parents or his mother are intolerable to the protagonist who rejects outside control of her life. In North American, and more so in Latin American, society, a woman's decision to live alone, to parent alone, and lead a self-governing life with attachments only to others of her choosing is an alternate lifestyle that society interprets as rebellious because it circumvents patriarchal values and structures.[13] Latin American culture directs women to live with parents, relatives, or a husband. Living alone or with individuals that are not blood kin still constitutes transgressive behavior for females in many parts of Latin America today.

One brief comment by the protagonist suggests that she had walked out of the marriage: "Deja ya la idea de ese jucio, no pretendas que vuelva a representar ante los jueces al animal escapado de su madriguera" (55) [Give up the idea of that trial, don't think that I will once more appear before the judges as that animal who has escaped from your lair]. Since divorce is nonexistent in Chile, the protagonist's resistance to patriarchal mandates warrants the threat of legal action by the husband. Economic vulnerability and the stamp of deviancy will be detrimental to the wife in the patriarch's campaign to regain control over her and their child. As the reader later learns, the protagonist does end up in court again, this time on account of the child. "Sé que aunque el resultado de este juicio me condene, no voy a morir en realidad" (111) [I know that even if the result of this trial condemns me, I won't really die], she

writes, as if trying to reassure herself that her life does not depend
on winning custody of her son. Whether repression exists in the
home or the homeland, those who have power "know it to be
ephemeral and costly"; in the novel the husband's behavior exemplifies that "constant effort and vigilance are required to keep subordinates subordinate."[14]

The vigilance announced in the novel's title appears in the third
letter. From this point on, the protagonist complains of a neighbor's
spying. Moreover, she suspects being followed and also that rumors
circulate about her. And indeed eventually neighbors function
much like the panoptic mechanism described by Michel Foucault in
Discipline and Punish: The Birth of the Prison.

Similar to guards in a penitentiary, community members take
turns monitoring the protagonist's activities. According to Foucault,
panopticism proves most effective in a power relation when it is "visible and unverifiable."[15] In the novel, although the protagonist can
look out her window or door and see the neighbors' apartments as
the locus of the spying, it is difficult to determine exactly when she
turns into the object of their gaze. Watched, stalked, and talked
about, she has become a target of surveillance.

Fear and surveillance are inextricably linked to the experience of
life under dictatorship. In [*Vigilant*], Eltit underscores the oppressive atmosphere characteristic of an authoritarian regime where citizens are urged to denounce any transgressive activity by their
neighbors. Although technically no such political rule is explicitly
manifested in the novel, the protagonist does allude to a general
obscure crisis. "La vigilancia ahora se extiende y cerca la ciudad"
[The viligance now spreads and hems in the city], the wife comments in a letter. "Esta vigilancia que auspician los vecinos para im-
plantar las leyes, que aseguran, pondrán freno a la decadencia que
se advierte" (32) [This vigilance endorsed by the neighbors in order
to introduce laws that, they assure, will curb the noticeable deca-
dence]. The neighbors' vigilance literally portrays the workings of
patriarchal society since the law that they, as a community, propose
to enforce is, in the words of Jacques Lacan, the Law of the Father.[16]

In Latin America, a woman, especially one without male tutelage,
readily becomes an object of public scrutiny. The novel depicts a
community acting on behalf of the absent patriarch. Since knowledge means power and the husband is not around, he depends on
others to spy and provide him with information necessary to exercise
power over the wife. The other's gaze, then, becomes the source of
the husband's ammunition and the protagonist's torment.

In [*Vigilant*] the mother-in-law plays a major part in upholding patriarchal culture. Literally, her interventions aim to insure the execution of her son's will. In Latin America, where there is less population mobility and children generally stay home until they marry, widowed mothers commonly look to an adult son to enforce the Law of the Father as patriarch. Responsibility still lies with the mother to safeguard patriarchal dictates that require policing other members of the family, especially unmarried females.

In rigid patriarchal societies common to Latin America, "female autonomy" constitutes a contradiction in terms. Thus, although the novel's protagonist has married, borne a child, separated from her spouse, and lives independently, the husband's dominion still looms over her. His mother, as emissary, conducts periodic and unexpected visits to monitor the daughter-in-law's conduct. "Pero dime, ¿era necesario hacernos pasar por una humillación de tal naturaleza?" (43) [But tell me, was it necessary to put us through such humiliation?] exhorts the protagonist about such intrusive behavior. But not solely a family affair, gossip from neighbors also contributes to the husband's suspicion. "Llegas a afirmar que es mi propia conducta la que te inspira desconfianza, pues ya más de un vecino te ha descrito mis curiosos movimientos" (33) [You come to affirm that it is my own conduct that arouses your distrust, since more than one neighbor already has described my odd comings and goings], complains the wife. In Latin America, where machismo remains deeply rooted in the culture, the gaze of the community, especially to curtail female freedom, abounds in literature written by women.

The societal inhibitor "What will people say?"—by no means exclusive to Hispanic culture—often serves as the catchall phrase for restricting female autonomy. Generations of women know the curbing effects of hearsay. "Dices que un vecino te ha informado que han desaparecido algunos objetos de mi casa" [You say a neighbor has informed you that some things have disappeared from my house], notes the protagonist, and then confirms, "Sí, es verdad que he vendido algunas de mis pertenencias, pero sabes que cuento con el privilegio, si así lo estimo conveniente, de deshacerme de mis propios bienes" (35) [Yes, it's true that I have sold some of my belongings, but you know that I'm entitled, if I think it fit, to rid myself of my personal property]. Her words stress independence (mi casa, mis pertenencias, mis propios bienes [my house, my belongings, my personal property]) and assert her right to it (cuento con el privilegio, si así lo estimo conveniente [I'm entitled, if I think it fit]). Yet she must fight to exercise that right since her mothering capacity is under scrutiny.

Given patriarchy's control of the female body, gender scrutiny often means censoring a woman's sexuality. Marriage and mother-hood do not exempt women from restrictions. While men can ex-pect lifelong autonomy despite their marital, economic, and social status, most women remain subordinates regardless of their life situ-ation. The protagonist's marital separation has not freed her from male control. Alluding to impropriety, the husband threatens to drag her to court because of certain "malos hábitos" (54) [bad hab-its]. Eventually, however, the accusation spells out sexual promiscu-ity: "Aseguras que mi comportamiento genital origina los más vergonzosos comentarios que traerán graves consecuencias para el futuro de tu hijo" (73) [You assert that my genital behavior gener-ates the most shameful remarks that will cause serious consequences in your son's future]. A male perspective insinuates incongruity be-tween motherhood and womanhood. Moreover, it suggests that an unmarried mother's sexual activity morally perverts her child. This type of conviction, were it applicable to a single/separated father, reveals Eltit's penetrating look at cultural beliefs that perpetuate gender inequality.

Commonly, a first step for women fighting gender discrimination requires resisting harassment within the family. The protagonist's indictment against the meddling mother-in-law rings clear in a let-ter: "Es preciso que le comuniques que no toleraré otra irrupción semejante. . . . Te anuncio que desde este instante le cerraré todas las puertas de la casa" (44) [It's essential that you make her aware that I will not tolerate another such intrusion. . . . I'm giving you notice that from this moment on I will close off to her all the doors to my house]. Paradoxically, here the space that traditionally has confined women turns into a battleground for waging autonomy.

At the core of barring the mother-in-law from the house lies the protagonist's attempt to eradicate the surveillance imposed upon women and children throughout the history of patriarchy. The hos-tility expressed in her next letter leaves readers to imagine the hus-band's unwillingness to loosen his constraints. "Te mataré" [I'll kill you], she writes back, "Sí. Te mataré algún día por lo que me obligas a hacer y me impides realizar. . . . Te mataré algún día para arreba-tarte este poder que no te mereces y que has ido incrementando, de manera despiadada . . ." (45) [Yes, I'll kill you someday for what you force me to do and prevent me from doing. . . . I'll kill you someday to wrest from you this power that you do not deserve and that you have continued to intensify in a heartless way].

Nowhere in the novel is the core issue of spousal conflict more lucidly depicted than in the wife's aggressive reaction to her power-lessness ("Te mataré algún día para arrebatarte este poder que no te mereces" [I'll kill you someday to wrest from you this power that you do not deserve). Literally out of control because she feels absolutely controlled by the male other, the protagonist manifests intense anger by explicitly reiterating the desire to kill her husband. And she ends the letter: "Sólo pienso ahora . . . en qué muerte será digna de tu cuerpo y cuál de todas las heridas estará al alcance de mi mano" (47) [Now I only ponder . . . the fitting death for your body and which type of wound my hand will inflict]. Feelings of victimization run deep in this woman who accuses the "tyrannical" patriarch of forcing her (me obligas) to do his will and of preventing her (me impides) from exercising her own.

Close analysis of the letter reveals that the protagonist of [*Vigilant*] retaliates against subordination comparable to slavery. "Has adoptado conmigo los antiguos hábitos que ya habían caído en desgracia y que fueran repudiados incluso por la poderosa historia de la dominación que los hubo de eliminar por inhumanos, relegándolos a la historia de las barbaries" (46), she points out [You have adopted with me the old customs that had fallen into disgrace and that were repudiated even by the powerful history of domination that eliminated them for being inhumane and relegated them to the history of barbarity]. Marriage appraised historically and from a feminist perspective may indeed fare worse than slavery because women are bound to a master for life without rights over their own bodies, offspring, or property, and without the possibility granted slaves of buying their freedom. From the protagonist's standpoint, the crime she announces befits the nature of the grievance.

Due to a long history of women's profound dissatisfaction with marriage, Latin American women writers, encouraged by feminist views proliferating in the 1980s, began inscribing repressed anger in female existence as theme in their fiction. Many of the female maladies—from depression to madness—festered in silence and were represented as such in the literature. A decade later, Eltit's protagonist expresses anger in more forthright terms, yet the woman is still defeated by patriarchal oppression.

Misiá señora/[Madam Missus] (1982) by Colombian Albalucía Angel is a feminist novel that portrays a woman's quest for autonomy. The stream of consciousness Angel employs to present the perspective of Mariana, the disturbed protagonist, poses narrative complexity contributing to the book's lack of critical and public acclaim. In this regard, Angel and Eltit have paid a price for not appealing to popular readership. Through other literary techniques such as unidentified interior monologues, intergenerational voices, and retrospective family memories, Angel portrays four generations of women within one Colombian family. Ultimately the novel depicts how women's roles have changed little in Colombia. Routine inequities between brother and sister provoke adolescent Mariana into angry confrontations at home. Yet failing to elude prescribed cultural roles, the mature Mariana reluctantly complies with patriarchal dictates but sinks into psyche alienation as a way of escape.

Puerto Rican writer Rosario Ferré's short story "La bella durmiente" ["Sleeping Beauty"][17] also depicts the psychological and physical harm that women have suffered in their quest for autonomy. Like Angel's novel, Ferré reveals her protagonist's feelings through interior monologue, thus, symbolically inscribing female voicelessness in Latin American society. In this story María de los Angeles orchestrates her own homicide at the hands of her husband in a last gesture to gain control over her life. The desperate act frees her from patriarchal oppression while condemning her husband to criminal charges.

The various forms of female self-annihilation depicted in women's literature conform to the manner in which men and women generally respond to inner conflict. During socialization males are encouraged to express feelings of aggression while females are urged to repress them. Harriet Lerner has studied the powerful prohibitions that result in the taboo against female anger and notes that expressions of anger, when thwarted, frequently turn into self-destructive symptoms.[18] This observation is certainly applicable to both Ferré's and Angel's protagonists. As illustrated by Eltit's protagonist in [Vigilant], women who show anger often incite more severe repression. For example, when outraged by the mother-in-law's intrusions, the protagonist threatens to kill her husband. This war cry prompts him to put his previous threat into action and file a legal injunction against her.

Intimidated, the protagonist eventually concedes to her mother-in-law's every wish, including the clothing her son should wear, the foods he should eat, the hours he should keep, and even the amount of lighting in her apartment. Like prison inmates or slaves, mother and child must tolerate that others control virtually every aspect of their daily life. In this regard the mother-in-law's role, as a woman exerting power over another female, can be compared to that of the slave overseer who, acting on behalf of the master, mistreated people of his own race. The mother-in-law is herself a pawn of the powerful patriarch (in this case her son), enslaved to his dictates and trained to perpetuate them.

"Unwritten law in totalitarian regimes," notes Marilyn French, "concerns itself with what citizens say and read and write, with whom they talk, what they wear, their hair styles, manners, and sexual habits."[19] Restrictions adopted as public policy by governments reflect those long enforced within patriarchy's private sphere. The distinction between these forms of power is that while totalitarian rule aims to control all social institutions and restrict the behavior of all citizens, patriarchal mandates mainly exert power over the lives of women and children.

The observation made by French proves most relevant in regard to the protagonist's association with a group of homeless people, for it is after sheltering them on an icy night that her husband bares his power. Immediately, he threatens to drag her to court, alleging that the presence of such pariahs in the home could endanger his son. "Dar por algunas horas un pedazo de techo no puede ser el delito que motive el inicio del juicio con el que una y otra vez me conminas" [Providing a roof for some hours cannot be such a crime that it prompts you to initiate the trial with which you constantly threaten me], the wife argues. "Si cometí una falta tan imperdonable, pues descuida que jamás volverás a escuchar una noticia similar" (75) [If I committed so unpardonable a mistake, don't worry because you will never again hear another criticism of the sort]. But promising to never repeat the episode proves unacceptable to the patriarch who continues to hold his threat like a noose over her head.

In the quote cited, the term "juicio" means trial or "judgment," that is "a formal utterance or pronouncing of an authoritative opinion after judging," or "a formal decision or determination given in a cause by a court or law or other tribunal."[20] But given the narrative context, it also alludes to the "judgment" passed against the protagonist. In the novel, the husband's law makes him into a judge who casts restrictions upon the wife. Perhaps "Judgment" with a capital letter, associated with "a divine sentence or decision" best describes the godlike power this patriarch exerts over his family.[21]

In [*Vigilant*], readers become witnesses to a process of subjugation that reduces an outspoken, enterprising, and assertive woman to one who concedes to paternalistic treatment by her husband. As the threat of losing her child becomes imminent, the protagonist abandons her initial combative attitude, capitulates to her mother-in-law's demands, adopts an apologetic tone towards her husband, and eventually kneels to him. Willingness to abide by the patriarchal order of things certifies her defeat. Psychologically tortured into compliance, the protagonist surrenders the managing of her own home as well as the right to control her fate and that of her son. Symbolically, she is as homeless and as much at the mercy of others as the group of frostbitten street dwellers she sheltered one night.

In a society where females are socialized to cater to the needs of others, paradoxically, helping the indigent ultimately causes the protagonist's downfall. The severity of the consequences levied for harboring some of the city's homeless exemplifies the patriarch's control of a woman's private space. In fact, she literally has no room of her own. But in a broader sense the incident with the homeless remains an issue throughout the narrative because it stands as a metaphor for social prohibitions against all those considered deviants. The protagonist's extreme precariousness at the end of the novel, as narrated by the son, demonstrates that she too has plummeted to the rank of pariah. Those who do not conform to mainstream society will become outcasts and jeopardize their well-being; this reflects reality within Chile's, now historical, totalitarian regime and its enduring patriarchal society of today.

THE POLITICAL: CITIZEN VS. GOVERNMENT

[*Vigilant*] is a novel about power, one in which spousal conflict serves as archetype for political and, as we shall explore later, cultural power struggles. Jean Lipman-Blumen maintains that gender roles "provide the blueprint for *all* other power relationships."[22] Until feminists began to study power, the topic was primarily analyzed in terms of the "powerful," in other words, men. However, in *Powers of the Weak*, Elizabeth Janeway explores the workings of power from the situation of the ruled instead of the rulers. According to Janeway, women make ideal representatives of the governed since they are "the oldest, largest, and most central group of human creatures in the wide category of the weak and ruled."[23] Women, be they of different ethnicities, nationalities, faiths, economic status, and educational levels, when compared to men in their group, have far less power and thus less control over their lives.

An inquiry into the nature of power reveals its inherently relational characteristic. For example, a nation's president, a business tycoon, or a religious leader would not be powerful if stranded alone on a desert island. Power comes into existence when relating with others. This holds true whether interaction falls within the private domain or the public sphere. Usually soon after taking over a government, an authoritarian leader suspends the rights and freedoms of the majority in order to create an imbalance in power. In this way a dictator and his governing cohorts make clear their intention to impose their will upon the citizenry. Once declared, power is main-tained by offering to reward collaboration and threatening to punish opposition.[24]

Under circumstances of powerlessness, citizens find ways to recuperate some sense of power, which, as Hilary Lips defines it, involves "the capacity to make things happen as one wants them to, to have an impact on one's world."[25] Generalized spying as a means of feeling in control thus becomes a way of life under authoritarian and totalitarian regimes.[26] "La vigilancia ahora se extiende y cerca la ciudad" (32) [The vigilance now spreads and closes in the city], observes Eltit's protagonist. As the novel progresses so does the extent of surveillance, which spreads as if the inhabitants were laying siege to the city. "Los vecinos se acusan los unos a los otros de todo" [The neighbors accuse one another of everything], describes the protagonist. "Viven para vigilar y vigilarse . . ." (73–74) [They live to keep watch and watch each other . . .]. Strife here clearly extends beyond the nuclear family, its dysfunction reflecting Chile's national circumstance under General Pinochet's rule.

During the years of dictatorship in Chile, neighbors literally persecuted other neighbors as diligently as the military. Lieutenant Colonel Olagier Benavente recalls how immediately after the coup d'état in 1973, right-wing civilians would show up at army regiments to incriminate left-wing supporters and pressure officers to make arrests. "On one occasion," says Benavente, "a cousin of ex-President Alessandri arrived with a list of people who should be detained. I asked him what crimes he was denouncing. He answered: this one is a communist, this one is a socialist, this one is a radical. . . . I pointed out that no code of law stipulated political partisanship as a crime. He left in a fury."[27]

The theme of spying and persecution recurs in Eltit's narrative and is common in work by Southern Cone women writers of her generation as well as others familiar with repressive regimes.[28] Exiled Argentine writers Marta Traba and Luisa Valenzuela were among the first to focus explicitly on the vestiges of state persecution in the homeland. In Traba's *Conversación al sur* (1981) / *Mothers and Shadows* (1986), the dread of being reported to police permeates society. For those not partisan to the military government, fear overshadows such mundane activities as conversation with friends, a ride on public transportation, or a festive get-together. Those who dare manifest their discontent take great risks when participating in street protests.

The representation of female subversion grew strong in the literature of Latin American women after the feminist awakening of the 1970s. Writers recurrently inscribed the inequities females endured

in their patriarchal culture and the transgressions women committed in their quest for autonomy. Through fiction, writers addressed
circumstances of female powerlessness, voicelessness, subjugation,
and all sorts of abuse while also depicting rebellious characters that
adopted an array of strategies of resistance. With the onset of political upheaval in the Southern Cone region in the 1970s the body became politicized and the insubordination women had practiced in
the privacy of the home turned into dissidence and outright insur-
rection in the public sphere. Women writers moved to representing
females who used their ingenuity and power tactics in response to
political circumstance.

Traba's *Mothers and Shadows* portrays women who deploy various
strategies in dealing with their political reality. Written and published in exile, the novel, which spans the capitals of the countries
of "El Cono Sur" (Uruguay, Argentina, Chile), appeared in 1981
while Argentina's military dictatorship (1976–83) was still in
power.[29] The actual conversation announced in the title takes place
between two old acquaintances (Dolores and Irene) in a beach
house in Montevideo, although the encounter could as well take
place anywhere political oppression stifles existence.

As noted earlier, women as a group have held unequal power with
men in virtually all spheres of life. But exclusion from positions of
authority does not mean total powerlessness. As with any disadvantaged group, the weak eventually develop strategies to influence the
powerful. Lacking authority themselves does not render women in
Mothers and Shadows powerless for they accomplish their particular
"political" goals by employing strategies to gain compliance from
those who do hold authority.[30]

Luisa, a free-spirited poet and somewhat of an eccentric, has no
official clout and would be risking imprisonment by letting Dolores's group of friends meet in her apartment, but bedding a high
commissioner exempts her from danger. Clearly, Luisa deploys her
body for a specific objective—securing safety for her friends. Despite
not having decision-making authority herself, Luisa does have the
power to affect others. A female's use of her body as bargaining tool
has long been stereotyped, but has nevertheless persisted because,
as Lips points out, frequently "sexuality is the major or only power
resource at hand" for women.[31]

Both *Mothers and Shadows* and [*Vigilant*] address the theme of
women and power in a politically dictatorial and culturally patriarchal Latin American society. Among the three sources of power
(personality, property, organization) identified by John Kenneth
Galbraith, personality—"the quality of physique, mind, speech,

moral certainty, or other personal traits"—best explains how Traba's character, Irene, succeeds in avoiding severe consequences during her brief arrest. One definition for "personality" is "a person of importance, prominence, renown, or notoriety."[32] Given that Irene is an actress, a public "personality," her professional achievements endow her with power in that her "image" is validated by a wide audience and officially disseminated by the media. However, detained at the police station, a place exclusively ruled by male hierarchy, Irene literally becomes a nobody. Irene's eventual deportment to Argentina under police custody, though not unconditional freedom, does indicate that her public image and influential contacts have affected the officer's decision to expedite her release.

Unlike Irene, Eltit's protagonist does not have any powerful contacts or personal clout of her own with which to intimidate her husband into dropping the charges against her. Also unlike [*Vigilant*], where the protagonist is isolated from the community and faces her crisis alone, in *Mothers and Shadows* women organize as a gendered group who suffer a common tragedy. Traba portrays the case of the Mothers of Plaza de Mayo in Argentina who gained international recognition for their struggle to locate disappeared family members. During the 1970s and 1980s women's groups sprung up in those Latin American countries where either dictatorship or outright war left women childless and widowed.[33]

In Chile, the "arpilleristas" were mothers who met under the auspices of the Catholic Church to hand stitch wall hangings, arpilleras,[34] which depicted and condemned police detentions during the Pinochet dictatorship. Women in such groups shared a common experience from which they drew moral—and often economic—support to alleviate the crisis that followed the loss of a family member. During the dictatorship poor women, although seemingly powerless and weak, organized communal kitchens to cope with the hunger that ensued in households left without a breadwinner.

In her study on power, Janeway sees the powers of the weak as falling into three stages. The first stage entails initiating the power that comes of mistrust, doubt, and dissent; the weak begin to question and doubt "what the powerful say when they define the world."[35] Once mistrust and doubt of the powerful take root, validation must be sought from others or else, in isolation, the doubt might be turned inward. During the second stage the weak find power through bonding; individual dissenters form a group in order to share their experiences.[36] In a third stage the group organizes joint action to fight the powerful. An important aspect of the dynamics of this last power stage is the expression of constancy through some act of ceremony and ritual that invokes and renews the shared bond.

As depicted in *Mothers and Shadows,* the mothers and grandmothers who rally every Thursday in the square across from the presidential "Casa Rosada" with white handkerchiefs tied around their necks and holding up pictures of the disappeared son or daughter are, in effect, engaging in ceremony and ritual as described by Janeway. Similarly, the fact that these women chant "¿dónde están?, ¿dónde están?" [where are they? where are they?] as one cohesive female mass consolidates the three powers of the weak basic to Janeway's theory: questioning, bonding, and joint action.

In [*Vigilant*] the protagonist does not get past the first "questioning" stage which includes mistrust, doubt, and open dissent because without sympathetic affiliations with whom to share her troubles and a support network of women with which to compare similar experiences, she cannot initiate the "bonding" of the second stage of power, let alone the third power stage that entails joint action against the powerful.[37] In essence, Eltit's protagonist is utterly alone in a city and neighborhood engulfed in a repressive atmosphere she cannot escape, despite attempts to turn her apartment into a sanctuary for herself and her child. The husband as personification of a dictator and the mother-in-law and neighbors as partisans to his reigning power eventually accomplish the protagonist's compliance.

Female resistance to patriarchal rule in the novel correlates with the defiance that dissidents manifest during authoritarian regimes. In fact, the protagonist's situation as presented by Eltit serves as a microcosm of Chilean society under Pinochet. The changes she undergoes, from outright rebelliousness to utter submission, resemble the resocialization ordeal political objectors typically underwent once authorities apprehended them. Also, in the novel the husband uses a series of strategies to control the wife that mirror those deployed by governments when curbing political subversion.

In Chile, during General Pinochet's regime, agents for the secret police or D.I.N.A. (Dirección de Inteligencia Nacional) penetrated all sectors of society. Agents could be present anywhere: on a factory assembly line, in a corporate office, in a condominium complex, in the school bazaar. The role of agents—or of those partisan to the military regime, to keep an eye out for any subversive behavior and report it back to a central power—corresponds to that of the mother-in-law and the neighbors in [*Vigilant*]. Widespread spying as depicted in the novel reflects just one mechanism for instilling fear in the population.

As Janeway points out, "state terror is a tool used to frighten people into policing themselves."[38] In the novel the arbitrariness of both the constant intrusions by the mother-in-law and the spying by neighbors leaves no doubt as to their agent-like role. "Mi vecina me vigila y vigila a tu hijo," complains the wife. "Ha dejado de lado a su propria familia y ahora se dedica únicamente a espiar todos mis movimientos" (29) [My neighbor spies on your son and me. She has set aside her own family and dedicates herself exclusively to spying my every move]. Apparently, for the neighbor repression has become an obsession and full-time endeavor which takes precedence over family obligations.

Another technique implemented to break dissidents involves the imposition of stigma. Marking a certain group undesirable because of race, ethnicity, gender, religious affiliation, or political partisanship is meant to perpetuate inferiority among members of the outcast group. In the protagonist's case, the husband labels her a woman of ill repute. The wife, realizing his strategy, comments, "Y es la vida que me otorgas la que te motiva a amenazarme con un juicio que, según tú, hará público el conjunto de mis malos hábitos" (54) [And it's the life you accuse me of leading that motivates you to threaten me with a trial, that according to you, will make public all my bad habits]. Regardless of the truth, given the Hispanic cultural adherence to the cult of "marianismo," where mothers should strive to model the Virgin Mary, the image of a tarnished female will hurt the protagonist's chances of keeping custody of her son.

In the novel the wife must also contend with the stigma and consequences of associating with vagrants. By housing the homeless group, albeit temporarily, she becomes an accomplice to those who defy established civic and political systems. In this regard, the social insubordination of the homeless alludes to the subversiveness of political dissidents that the Pinochet regime in Chile, and others like it in Latin America, attempted to eradicate. Anyone collaborating with dissident elements became a target for punishment by authorities. The husband, as the Law incarnate in [*Vigilant*], intends to reproach the wife in the manner most painful to a mother, separation from her child.

Manipulation of motherhood and women's bodies became a recurrent theme in Southern Cone literature of the 1980s, especially among women writers who had experienced dictatorship.[39] The number of organizations formed by mothers during the decades of the 1970s and 1980s attested to the effect repression was having on women's lives. In Argentina, since forceful removal of the Mothers of Plaza de Mayo from the city's central square would have called into question the government's denial of wrongdoing, authorities declared the mothers madwomen. Thus public stigma attached to those associated in any way with detainees acted as a deterrent for further mobilization against human rights violations.

Among the techniques that Janeway points to as employed by repressive states to maintain power, humiliation became an effective means for mistreating female dissidents since both persecutor and persecuted shared the cultural tenets of "marianismo," which weighs heavily with restrictions on the female body. In [*Vigilant*] the husband charges the wife with promiscuity not only to humiliate her but also to use it against her in court. Whereas spousal conflict in this post-Pinochet novel focuses on the private domain of the nuclear family, gender animosity in literature written about the dictatorial state focused on the political realm where men had power over women.

Southern Cone literature written by women depicts the use of humiliation to degrade women in a variety of ways. In Traba's *Mothers and Shadows,* years after the incident of arrest Irene still recalls feeling humiliated over a comment hurled at her at the police precinct: " 'Usted es una vieja . . . debería darle vergüenza andar enseñando así los muslos' " (52) [You ought to be ashamed of yourself. . . . An old woman like you going around showing your thighs like that].[40] Seemingly trivial, the comment about Irene's demeanor and dress reflects patriarchal dictates, which under military rule turn into absolute control.[41] Other female protagonists in Traba's novel do not fare as well as Irene. In Dolores's case the interrogation turns violent, inducing a miscarriage of the fetus she is carrying.

Argentine writer Luisa Valenzuela exemplifies the tactic of gender-specific humiliation in the title story of *Cambio de armas* (1982)/ *Other Weapons* (1985) where a military official keeps a political activist turned prisoner housed as his concubine in order to arbitrarily rape her. "Open your eyes, you bitch!. . . . move slut. Tell me you're a bitch, a whore. Tell me how the others fuck you. Do they fuck you like this?" he demands during coitus.[42]

Indirectly, the husband in [*Vigilant*] too labels the wife "puta" [whore] when he accuses her of promiscuous behavior and threatens to drag her through family court. For Eltit's protagonist, court represents as fearful a disciplinary state institution as the police, secret agents, and paramilitary officers that populate the stories by Traba and Valenzuela. These writers portray protagonists that are at odds with patriarchal institutions capable of inflicting great harm.

The consequences of political repression cut across national borders and manifest themselves in similar ways in Chilean and Argentine literatures. For instance, domestic confinement characterizes the situation of both Eltit's protagonist and the nameless woman in Valenzuela's *Other Weapons*. Both live in fear of arbitrary visits by people capable of causing punishment (the mother-in-law in Eltit's novel and the military officer in Valenzuela's short story). In both cases a patriarchal figure (husband and officer) systematically practices psychological torture on the female he controls.

Given the severity of repression, each woman has internalized immobilization, that is, both regard resistance as impossible. This assumption translates into the incapacity for risk-taking,[43] which for Valenzuela's protagonist means not attempting escape even though the key to the front door sits on the mantel. For the wife in [*Vigilant*], lack of risk-taking action means acquiescing to spousal domination. In both cases, once-assertive women have been subdued into absolute obedience. Clearly the patriarch's systematic application of psychological terrorism has successfully destroyed their morale and spirit of resistance. Paralysis as the outcome compared to the initial subversiveness of these women symbolizes the general despair of the population of the Southern Cone region where military regimes launched campaigns of psychological warfare against dissenting factions.

By extending the national allegory outside particular borders—as in our discussion of the sudaca element in *The Fourth World*—the women's ultimate obedience in the narratives parallels Chile's and other Latin American countries' predicament in relation to the United States. In fact, as reflected in Latin American fiction—and politics—survival often means cooperating with the oppressor. Like the wife in [*Vigilant*], Latin America has a long record of attempts at exercising free will and control of its own affairs. However, the United States—much like the powerful patriarch in the novel—has historically used pressure, coercion, and punitive legal action to achieve control over the other—usually a country weaker militarily, economically, and technologically. Thus, similar to the wife under spousal scrutiny in the novel, Latin American countries exist under the constant watch of the United States.

Historically, any activity in Latin America not in keeping with North American interests has been subject to political interference or even military intervention.[44] In relation to Latin American territories, U.S. policy makers in Washington represent, in essence, "los vigilantes" of the novel. If scrutiny by the mother-in-law and the neighbors can be interpreted as symbolic of the stifling surveillance of the Chilean secret police (D.I.N.A.), so too they point to the North American spy network which infiltrates Latin American nations in order to safeguard the political and business interests of the United States.[45]

Volodia Teitelboim points to U.S. participation in bringing about Chile's military coup (which ousted President Salvador Allende in 1973) and in supporting military dictatorships in Brazil, Argentina, and Uruguay.[46] Allende's Unidad Popular, with its program for peaceful revolution and government reform, made a commitment to alleviate the plight of the impoverished sectors in Chile. From Washington's perspective this agenda smelled of communism and thus posed a threat to the region and the United States.[47]

Let us recall that in [*Vigilant*] the wife's concern for the homeless, manifested in her sheltering them briefly, resulted in grave threats from the husband that aimed to thwart her struggle to achieve both personal autonomy and permanent custody of her son. Thus the manipulated wife can be read as a metaphor for Chile—and Latin America by extension. Both wife and the country are literally in the grip of a patriarchal/imperialistic power bent not only on controlling its neighbor's private (national) affairs but also on taking possession of the treasured "son." This son can be interpreted as Chile's national patrimony, that is the country's natural resources, but also its legally constituted government. In the novel the son is not the perfect child; he manifests defects in many aspects, yet although by no means perfect he is a legitimate son. Likewise Allende's government was by far not ideal, yet the Chilean people had legitimately elected it.

Teitelboim maintains that Allende's party, Unidad Popular, stood for a popular, nationalist, and revolutionary government, three characteristics unacceptable to the United States. "Revolutionary" was a term that the Pentagon interpreted as literally a declaration of war.[48] Allende (much like the wife's attempts at autonomous governance) faced interference from the manipulative schemes of a power infiltrating the *home*land. The brief self-rule demonstrated by both the wife in [*Vigilant*] and Allende in Chile was doomed to fail under the influence of a patriarchal/imperialistic power intent on destabilizing their domestic situation.[49]

Documents relating to that period of Chilean history reveal the "spoiling" strategies carried out by the U.S. government in Chile against Allende's coalition.[50] Once elected, covert tactics continued to deteriorate the country's infrastructure. Creating severe shortages of basic commodities provided a foolproof way of planting widespread discontent for Allende's government. This strategy encompassed such measures as the sabotage of production in industry, keeping farm products from getting to markets, and preventing distribution of those items that did make it to store shelves. Generally, living conditions indeed worsened, for the poor and bourgeoisie alike.

In [*Vigilant*] the household crisis portrays the wife pawning the few valuables she owns in order secure bare necessities. The husband adopts a passive-aggressive stance, standing by but not contributing economically to the obviously ailing household. The strategy clearly aims to weaken the wife into compliance. Similarly, the United States presented an image of nonintervention in Chile, while behind the scenes it collaborated in the economic collapse that plunged Chile into a deep crisis.

Metaphorically, the wife's process of deterioration and eventual defeat reflects Allende's frustrated government. Initially the wife in the novel stood up to the husband and was adamant in keeping the meddling mother-in-law out of her home and her affairs. Her approach was forceful and defiant of patriarchal dictates. However, her attempt to raise her son according to her own agenda was not acceptable to the husband, who feared losing control. In this regard, the wife's situation, read as a national allegory, suggests parallels with Allende's attempt to rule according to his own (socialist) agenda. In both cases defiance of patriarchal/imperialistic prerogatives results in a doomed quest for autonomy.

THE CULTURAL: WRITER VS. CANON

In [*Vigilant*] the wife's conflict with her husband as well as the difficulties she must endure and surmount in daily living compare to the struggles female writers face within the literary establishment. The protagonist, who must juggle parenting and writing, writes while her son is asleep because during the day his activities and bizarre laughter disturb her concentration. Accommodating her writing around the child's schedule and depriving herself of sleep accentuate the predicament of a single parent tackling two demanding careers.

Symbolically, the child's guffaws suggest the lunacy of her endeavor. After all, the woman in the novel sits down to write despite contending with preoccupations such as caring for an abnormal child, securing heat for the apartment, food for the pantry, and negotiating with a husband over the custody of their son. Undoubtedly the seriousness of each concern saps her stamina. In this respect the woman Eltit portrays represents generations of women writers. Yet the protagonist of [*Vigilant*] forges on in the letter-writing enterprise which turns into the book we read.

The very first line of the novel inscribes the child's awareness of his mother's writing and thus suggests the thematic importance of her task: "Mamá escribe. Mamá es la única que escribe" (13) [Mother writes. Mother is the only one who writes]. The first line also links the child directly to writing itself, for he will later disclose his textuality: "Existo sólo en un conjunto de papeles" (16) [I exist only in a collection of papers]. This revelation sheds light on an earlier allusion: "Mi cuerpo habla, mi boca está adormilada" [My body speaks, my mouth is drowsy], he says, and shortly thereafter emphasizes the point, "Mi cuerpo laxo habla, mi lengua no tiene musculatura. No habla" (13) [My lax body speaks, my tongue has no muscles. It doesn't speak]. As a textual entity he is incapable of oral speech, yet possesses a written communicative body. Thus, it is through the child that [*Vigilant*] discloses itself as a self-reflexive text.

In the first part of the novel, references to his dribbling, crawling, eating earth, and soiling his surroundings—incorporated into the disjointed story he narrates—mark the rudimentary stage of writing. Textual construction also distinguishes the son's narrative with a particular style, one that relies on repeating the last word of a sentence. Although the son will not demonstrate refinement in his expression until the concluding part of the novel, he does reveal some understanding of the difficulties that come with writing: "Mamá no está tranquila. . . . Tiene muchos pedacitos de piel desordenados. Desordenados. Los dedos que tengo están enojados con su desorden" (13) [Mother is not at peace. . . . She has a lot of tiny pieces of skin in disarray. In disarray. My fingers are angry with their disarray]. If the word "piel" [skin] is substituted for "papel" [paper], the link between mother and child in regard to writing surfaces as an adumbration in the first page of the novel.

As biological product of female conception, the son stands as a metaphor for the protagonist's literary production. In this respect, the child's "abnormality" represents Eltit's nonmainstream writing, which has "disturbed" readers and critics alike. Are the child's gleeful convulsions Eltit's laugh at the baffled reader/critics who toil at the exegesis of her texts? Is his (textual) guffaw a way of saying, "I may be strange and nontraditional but I've gotten you to pay critical attention to me"? Both the son's babble (which requires deciphering) and his constant playing around remind readers of the fragmented syntax, neologisms, and hermetic prose which made for arduous reading of earlier books already discussed. Particularly

E. Luminata and [*For the Homeland*] convey the impression that Eltit trifles with the unsuspecting reader. The son in [*Vigilant*] thus embodies the enigma and the aberration of Eltit's experimental texts that earned her the reputation for not being understood.

Throughout the first chapter the reader becomes aware that both child and writing constitute the focus of this woman's existence. "Ahora mamá está inclinada, escribiendo" [Now mother is hunched over, writing], points out the son, "Inclinada, mamá se empieza a fundir con la página" (16) [Hunched over, mother begins to fuse with the page]. This line reveals an important aspect of the mother's identity. She is a writer. Text and self are inextricable. The protagonist's struggle with her task is reflected in the challenge that language poses for her child: "Me meto los dedos en la boca para sacar la palabra que cavila entre los pocos dientes que tengo" (16) [I put my fingers in my mouth to pull out the word that muses between the few teeth that I have], points out the son. His fishing for words parallels the mother's effort in writing, an activity that absorbs her to the extent that she seems to "fuse with the page."

Intimacy characterizes her relationship with the biological son and the written page. She literally engenders both. And both compete for her attention. While the son alludes to a strong mother/child bond—"Yo le leo los pensamientos a mamá" (20) [I read mother's thoughts]—he nevertheless resents her writing. "Mamá me da la espalda para meterse en esas páginas de mentira" [Mother turns her back on me in order to dive into those make believe pages], he complains. "Mamá tiene la espalda torcida por sus páginas. Por sus páginas. Las palabras que escribe la tuercen y la mortifican. Yo quiero ser la única letra de mamá" (17) [Mother has a strained back because of her pages. Because of her pages. The words she writes strain and torment her. I want to be mother's only writing]. Both fiction writing [make-believe words] and son are physically taxing and demanding of the protagonist's time.

The nature of the mother's writing is suggestive of Eltit's own focus on social marginality in her fiction. Observations made by the son indicate that the poverty the mother witnesses in the city deeply affects her state of mind: "Mamá queda con el estado malo cuando ve cómo el hambre inunda las calles. Esa hambre la prende con una fuerza verdaderamente devastadora y a su cabeza entran las más peligrosas decisiones. Decisiones. Entra a la casa y deja en sus páginas la vergüenza que le provoca la salida" (21) [Mother is left in a bad state when she sees the hunger that floods the streets. That hunger seizes her with a remarkably devastating power and her head is filled with dangerous decisions. Decisions. She comes in and puts down on her pages the shame that the walk arouses]. Writing about social inequities would indeed constitute a "dangerous decision" for a writer living in a dictatorial state. As we know, this was the situation for Eltit when she published her first two novels during the Pinochet regime. To elude state censorship she masked her politically compromising writing with a hermetic style. However, that likewise involved a "dangerous decision" because if readers at the censor's office did not understand her novels, neither did the public at large.

In [*Vigilant*] the son—as text—voices a writer's commitment to her craft. As he remarks, during his mother's extraordinary absorption in writing he as well as the outside world that normally concern her seem to disappear. "Caigo buscando a mamá que ya no ve, que me vuelve la espalda, inclinada ante el desafío de su incierta página" [I fall looking for mother who can no longer see, who turns her back on me, hunched over the challenge of her uncertain page], comments the son. "Mamá que permanece ajena a la hambruna de la gente de las calles porque ahora mismo yace perdida. Yace perdida y solitaria y única entre las borrascosas palabras que la acercan al escaso cielo . . ." (22) [Mother remains completely detached from people's hunger out in the streets because right now she's lost to the world. She's lost to the world and solitary and alone among the tumultuous words that draw her near to the scarce heaven . . .]. The son's metatext runs through to the last line of his narration in part one of the novel: "Ahora mamá escribe. Me vuelve la espalda. La espalda. Escribe:" (22) [Now mother writes. She turns her back on me. Her back. She writes:].

The colon with which the son ends the first chapter (Escribe:) acts as a link to the second chapter where the focus turns to the content of the mother's writing. "Amanece mientras te escribo" (25) [It dawns while I write to you], begins the first letter to her husband. While the epistolary mode alludes to a female writing tradition, paradoxically, the correspondence reveals that this woman is waging a battle against tradition.[51]

The protagonist's desire to break with tradition is apparent in her reluctance to return to live with her family. In fact, when the husband suggests the idea, at first she points out that her parents are dead. There is no home to go back to. Later she admits that indeed they are alive, yet living with them remains out of the question. Symbolically, the break with the family of origin reflects the writer's separation from the established canon. The protagonist makes it clear that conforming to the dictates of the nuclear—and by extension the literary—family is not an option she contemplates. She seeks an alternate lifestyle and, metaphorically, an alternate writing style.

Eltit is a Latin American version of Nancy A. Walker's "disobedient writer," a (female) writer who borrows, revises, and recontextualizes a literary tradition of which she is not a part.[52]

The dysfunctional family in [*Vigilant*] acts as a palimpsest that inscribes women writers' vicarious position within the traditional literary canon. Notably, the novel revolves around "custody" of the son. Both parents claim the right to raise, educate, and mold their progeny as they see fit. Given that the son can serve as metaphor for literary production, whoever "controls" the son shapes the canon. As noted earlier, his "abnormal" babbling appropriately equates to Eltit's nonmainstream writing. Not surprisingly, as offspring of a "disobedient writer," this peculiar son has been expelled from a traditional (literary) school. Therefore, both mother (writer) and son (text) become objects of societal exclusion, much like women writers' experience within the literary establishment. The lesson becomes, if you cannot conform you cannot belong.

Exclusion from writing circles and publishing opportunities is a common complaint among Chilean women writers. When asked about their status, Eltit and other writers in Santiago—including Pía Barros, Alejandra Basualto, Sonia González, and Guadalupe Santa Cruz—agree that gender stacks against them, and more so in cases where writing is perceived as deviating from mainstream literary construction. As these writers attest, it is not uncommon that editors, acting as patriarchal gatekeepers of the canon, reprove "difference" with exclusion. Moreover, the obstacles multiply for those who live and write outside of Chile but want to publish in their country.[53]

Suggestive of editors' negative attitudes toward unconventional texts and books written by women, let us recall that in Eltit's novel the father refuses to accept the son's "abnormality" and demands his immediate return to a "traditional" school, which means integration into mainstream education and, by extension, molding the son in his own image. By contrast, the mother of this unique (literary?) progeny struggles to raise him outside the patriarchal tradition that will judge his difference as defective, unpolished, and odd. This "different" son, as symbol of female literary production, exemplifies Walker's point that "women writers have frequently revealed in their work an awareness of working against instead of inside cultural heritage."[54]

Despite the challenge and complications an abnormal son/text presents, the protagonist has faith in the intimacy of the bond between them: "Miro a tu hijo y me convenzo que nada podría separarnos, pues fuimos construyendo nuestra libertad cuando nos alejamos de tus órdenes y burlamos tu hiriente crueldad" (112), she writes to her husband. [I look at your son and I'm convinced that nothing could separate us because we began constructing our freedom when we distanced ourselves from your orders and evaded your hurtful cruelty]. Here the writer's voice rings with the uniqueness she has achieved by defying and scoffing at literary tradition. But the liberties she has taken in her writing do not go unpunished. Rejection of patriarchal heritage levies a high cost for the protagonist of [*Vigilant*]. She loses the court case and consequently her husband secures control of the son. Symbolically, the writer too has been on trial, and judgment favors the canon. The protagonist recognizes that she has been sentenced to the margins: "He sido expulsada hacia la falla de la orilla" (115) [I have been expelled towards failure at the margin]. Nevertheless, she concludes her narration by claiming—albeit timidly—the son/text as her own: "Sí, esta criatura me pertenece"(117) [Yes, this child belongs to me].

In the third and last part of the novel the son resumes self-reflexivity introduced in the first part. However, by now, as a developed textual entity, he becomes separate from his producer and attains a voice of his own. The son suggests that there comes a point in the process of writing where the text itself takes over as subject and the writer, in turn, becomes the object or means through which written expression is achieved. "Mamá está cansada y quiere dormir. Dormir. Mamá sólo piensa en dormir ahora que estoy por arrebatarle la página que la hacía impresionante, Impresionante" (122) [Mother is tired and wants to sleep. Sleep. Mother only thinks of sleeping now that I'm about to snatch from her the page that made her amazing. Amazing], he says of his mother/writer. Later, the inversion of mother/child roles confirms that the son has taken control of the writer's task: "Ahora yo escribo" [Now I write], he states. "Escribo con mamá agarrada de mi costado. . . . Ahora yo domino esta historia. Llevo a mamá por mi propio camino" (126) [I write with mother clutching my side. . . . Now I control the story. I take mother on my own path]. Here writing directs the writer. Yet both— writer and text—remain marginal figures within mainstream society. In fact, in this concluding part of the novel the son narrates the hardships of their (cultural) homelessness.

Textual construction in this part relies heavily on references to nightfall, darkness, vagrancy, obscurity, fear, hate, and defeat—with an occasional sprinkle of stars in the distant heavens—in its portrayal of a writer's laborious pursuit to succeed. A distinguishable goal of mother and son during the symbolic nocturnal journey is to reach the "bonfires." Given their homelessness, the bonfires may be their only chance for survival out in the streets. This aspect of the novel calls to mind the vagrants of the first novel, who also homeless start a fire in the plaza. In *E. Luminata* the protagonist uses the flames to burn the hand that seeks sexual pleasure whereas in [*Vigilant*] the hand seeks pleasure in the text it writes.

The stress given "the bonfires" in the last section of [*Vigilant*] signals their significance in the novel. "Llegaremos esta noche hasta las hogueras. Las hogueras. CRRRR, crepitan. Llegaremos y los hombres del fuego recibirán a mamá con desconfianza. La recibirán con indiferencia y desconfianza" (122), declares the son [We will reach the bonfires tonight. The bonfires. CRRR, Crackle. We will reach them and the keepers of the fire will receive mother with distrust. They will receive her with indifference and distrust]. While "bonfires" can provide life-sustaining warmth for survival, they can also cause destruction. From a writer's perspective, publishers, similarly to "the keepers of the fire," have the power to assign either fate.

The term "hogueras" connotes book burnings as well as witch burnings, both traditional practices under repressive rule. Historically men have sanctioned such actions. Men control the bonfires, as they do the presses, hence the son's reference to "los hombres del fuego." Besides the mental and physical energies expended by a writer in the creative stage, the search for the manuscript's publisher can be experienced as an odyssey. "Pero aún continuamos en este viaje oscuro y secreto para llegar hasta donde CRRRR, crepitan las hogueras que iluminan las orillas" [But we continue to forge on this dark and secretive trip to reach the CRRR crackling bonfires that illuminate the margins], comments the son. "AAAAY, mamá ha perdido gran parte de sus pensamientos en este terrible y cautelosa caminata" (123) [OOOOH, mother has lost a good portion of her thoughts on this terrible and cautious trek].

As suggested in the novel, a writer's vocation may entail enduring psychological distress before and after publication. "A mamá la enferma su letra" (121–22) [Mother's writing makes her ill], states the son. Also, getting a manuscript published does not necessarily mean survival. For once published, the writer may experience a critic's comments literally as an assault—"alguno *golpea* la letra de mamá"[55] (121) [someone pounds on mother's writing]. This is difficult to bear given that in [*Vigilant*] the mother/writer alludes to the years she has spent cultivating her craft, one that has become a personal pilgrimage. "Ya hace mucho que caminamos errantes actuando un nomadismo pobre. Y el hambre. El hambre que arrastramos por todas partes durante este largo, incontable tiempo" (117), refers to her relationship with her son/text, that is, the hardships of the craft [For a long time now we have been wandering around acting out a poor nomadism. And the hunger. The hunger that we drag everywhere during this long, countless time]. Here the writer suggests that her need for recognition compares to hunger gone unsatisfied for too long. Writing itself motivates and sustains the mother/writer; she cannot stop writing. "Tenemos hambre. Hambre. El hambre de mamá no se sacia con los alimentos" [We're hungry. Hungry. Mother's hunger is not satisfied with food], explains the son. "A mamá sólo la complacía su letra. Esa letra que ya no puede concluir" (123) [Only her writing gratified mother. That writing that she can no longer stop]. Despite all her dedication and sacrifice, the son observes his mother's dissatisfaction with her vocation.

In the concluding part of the novel, Eltit inscribes the public's disapproval as if anticipating a negative response to [*Vigilant*]. She ventures to take the lead at criticism aimed at both the reading public at large and literary critics. From the outset of part 3, the son comments about people's negative reception to his mother's writing:

> La gente de la calle apenas oculta su malestar. El malestar de la gente está en todas partes. SSSSSSS, se extiende el malestar. SSSSSSS. Alguno quisiera destruir a mamá. Lo sé. Destruir y acallar mamá. La gente que vigila las calles abomina de la presencia de mamá. De mamá. AAAAY, los odios me azotan. (121)

> [The people out on the street do not hide their displeasure. The people's displeasure is everywhere. SSSSSSS, spreads the displeasure. SSSSSSS. Someone would like to destroy mother. I know it. Destroy and silence mother. The people who watch over the streets detest mother's presence. Mother's presence. OOOOH, the loathing thrashes me].

Clearly, the reading public's—and critic's—verdict ranges from displeasure to outright loathing. Sentiments about destruction and silencing point to the animosity and misunderstanding nonmainstream writers have traditionally endured.

Without compromising her unique style, Eltit symbolically engenders a text that voices its own angst: "Pero el fracaso de mamá nos volvió nocturnos, despreciados, encogidos. Ah, sí, prófugos, odiados, nocturnos y despreciados. SHHHIIIT. AAAAY, el odio" (122) [But mother's failure made us nocturnal, despised, shrunken. Oh, yes, fugitives, loathed, nocturnal and despised. SHHHIIIT. OOOOH, the loathing]. However, the text also suggests the need for the mother/writer to overcome such crippling rejection: "Deseo que mamá sobrepase el odio y la indiferencia. El odio y la indiferencia a su letra" (123) [I wish for mother to surmount the loathing and indifference. The loathing and indifference to her writing].

Of the three readings—personal, political, cultural—discussed in this study, the third—a palimpsest of a writer's indictment of the canon—comes to light at the novel's conclusion when the son symbolically incarnates both the writer's production and her superego. Although similar to the first part where his narration abounds with references to writing, this part also includes self-criticism—characteristic of the superego. Remarks such as: "la oscuridad de su letra," "su palabra árida e inútil,' (121) [the obscurity of her writing, her dull, useless word] and "Ah, esas palabras que no pudo esclarecer" (123) [Oh, those words that she was not able to make clear] remind us of Eltit's hermetic writing. Perhaps experience with readers' opinion—as acknowledged by the son: "Tengo que. . . . llevar a mamá lejos de la irritación y de la burla y de la indiferencia que provoca su letra" (122) [I have to. . . . take mother far from the irritation, the mocking and the indifference that her writing provokes]—has prompted Eltit to reconsider her style.

Given the emphasis on "darkness" associated with writing in the novel, does the title "Amance" of the second part of the novel announce the dawn of a new writing for Eltit? "Amance mientras te escribo" (25) [It dawns while I write to you], begins the protagonist's first letter to her husband. And on the last page of her narration we read: "Amanece mientras escribo" (117) [It dawns while I write]. The absence of the pronoun "te" suggests that she no longer writes for an exclusive recipient. Textual construction reflects that her personal letter-writing enterprise has shifted to accommodate the possibility of a wider readership.

In a novel that already manifests a distinct change in Eltit's style, it is only in this concluding part that she insinuates a reason for pursuing a more conventional form. Besides the bitterness harbored towards a literary establishment whose exclusionary practices have made it extremely difficult for her to gain recognition, the writer simply finds herself exhausted by the earlier hermetic style: "Mamá tiene un intenso inescrupuloso resentimiento porque su antigua letra le extenuó el pensamiento" (125) [Mother has an intense unscrupulous resentment because her former writing exhausted her mind]. There is no naivete here; ever since her first novel Eltit has admitted awareness of the risks of unconventional writing. In this regard the son comments: "Mi cabeza de Ton Ton Ton To siempre adivinó que mamá iba a ser derrotada por la aridez de la página" (123) [My Id Id Id iot's head always guessed that mother was going to be defeated by the dullness of her page].

The text also hints that at the beginning of her writing career, Eltit consciously chose marginality over belonging to the mainstream establishment because it would have entailed compromising her style. In the following statement by the son, the "center" alludes to both the dictatorship—in effect at the time when Eltit first began to write—as well as the traditional Chilean literary canon: "Cierto ojo vigilante nos sigue con toda clase de miradas. Nos vigilan esas peligrosas miradas desde el centro, y la letra de mamá necesita oscurecerse más, más para defendernos" (124) [A certain vigilant eye follows us with all sorts of looks. Those dangerous glances watch us from the center, and mother's writing needs to become more obscure, the more to defend us]. Patriarchy, dictatorship, and the canon administer a controlling gaze with the power to discipline those who do not conform to the order of things. For Eltit, whose unorthodox writing has acted as both self-defense mechanism and distinguishable feature, moving away from an obscure style may prove difficult.

In the novel, writing ultimately saves the writer. This is exemplified by the inversion of roles that takes place in the concluding part. The son—as literary production—achieves independence while the mother—her work done—turns into a dumb-mute. Symbolically, the text becomes a source of sustenance for the writer: "Extraigo las últimas, las últimas, las últimas gotas de leche del pecho de mamá y pongo mi boca en su boca. En su boca. Mamá siente su leche en la boca y quiere escupirla, pero yo le cierro la boca con todas las fuerzas que tengo," remarks the son (127). [I extract the last, the last drops of milk from mother's breast and place my mouth on her mouth. On her mouth. Mother feels her milk in her mouth and wants to spit it out, but I shut her mouth with all my strength]. The son—or the book—saves the mother—or the writer—from perishing altogether by nourishing her. And as he comments, "Gracias a mí, la letra oscura de mamá no ha fracasado por completo" (122) [Thanks to me, mother's obscure writing has not failed completely]. As Eltit's own work proves, despite a writer's many frustrations, the written text as cultural artifact contributes to the national patrimony even if not recognized as such at the time of production.

Characteristic of Eltit's novels, [*Vigilant*] is a multilayered text that addresses social, political, and cultural concerns. This aspect of her writing has not changed. However, the text's readability and content indicate a move towards a "different" writing. The novel is suggestive of a variety of issues on gender inequities, political oppression, and writing itself. [*Vigilant*] is indeed a metatext, one that uses its self-reflexivity to look beyond its Chilean borders and speak to oppressed women, victims of state repression, and struggling writers alike.

Epilogue: *Los trabajadores de la muerte*

LOS TRABAJADORES DE LA MUERTE [*WORKERS OF DEATH*] (1998), PUBLISHED near century's end, occupies the distinctive position of bridging what Eltit has written thus far and the next generation of books that eventually will come from a more seasoned writer. Here I only propose to situate [*Workers of Death*] within Eltit's writing continuum and hope that the collection of essays presented here serves as an invitation for following this continuum into the new millennium.

The absence of a political theme, which makes [*Workers of Death*] unique from all the novels discussed here, suggests that Eltit has begun to put closure to the Pinochet era as the underlining core in her writing. Indicative of Chile's return to its democratic system, the novel literally ends with the hint of a political race underway. However, the mention of video cameras which scan the streets remind us that the state of "vigilance" and the traumas associated with a repressive regime linger well after free elections are reinstated. The novel's very title may well call to mind this morbid period in national history.[1]

Remarkably, [*Workers of Death*], released in the fall of 1998, coincided with Pinochet's October trip to London where, during his sojourn for medical treatment, he was arrested at the request of a court judge in Spain for extradition on the charge of crimes against humanity. Unable to muster political clout abroad as customary at home, the former dictator was denied diplomatic immunity by English ruling and powerless to return to Chile. Pinochet's health continued to deteriorate in London where, a year later, he remained detained while waiting a possible trial in Spain.[2] Symbolically, then, Eltit's extirpation of the dictator's presence in [*Workers of Death*] registers Pinochet's political and physical demise as a closing chapter in Chile's modern history, which also happens to coincide with the end of the millennium.

While the absence of a political theme in the novel reflects the very important change in national circumstance, Eltit's systematic focus on gender relations as well as on the theme of writing registers two ongoing concerns for the author. After all, political leaders and their governments may come and go, but Eltit will remain a woman and probably a writer for a lifetime. Intimate experiences related to femaleness and to the craft of writing can be gleaned throughout the fiction discussed here, but it is from *The Fourth World* on that the recording of bodily functions, connected with maternity and menstruation, for example, becomes more overt.

On the topic of gender, [*Vigilant*] and [*Workers of Death*] are quite similar in their portrayal of women in crisis. Both novels entail impoverished mothers struggling to raise children while trapped in a bad marriage. Also, both protagonists must endure a husband's mistreatment. The severity of the situation, however, is more acute in [*Workers of Death*] since the husband lives under the same roof and his physical as well as verbal abuse targets an exhausted mother of newborns. In [*Workers of Death*] there is no trace of the initially defiant mother of [*Vigilant*]. Mistreated and endlessly humiliated, the powerless wife and mother in [*Workers of Death*] waits for vengeance and achieves it, but at another's hand and only after the death of the abusive patriarch. Symbolically, this echoes reality for many Chileans, who unable to seek justice directly against Pinochet at home, hoped and waited for Spain to bring him to trial for his crimes.[3]

As if picking up on the motif of the defeated woman depicted at the conclusion of [*Vigilant*], this next novel presents a lamentably downtrodden counterpart. The lack of recourse against a husband's adultery, bigamy, and eventual abandonment makes the wife in [*Workers of Death*] the weakest of Eltit's female protagonists. The realism with which Eltit depicts aspects of maternity, including labor, breastfeeding, caretaking, fatigue, and bodily deterioration, reinforces the believable nature of her female protagonist in [*Workers of Death*]. Hence, by comparison to previous novels, the domestic situations in [*Vigilant*] and [*Workers of Death*] also point to a shift toward more lifelike characters.

Much like in [*Vigilant*], the theme of writing must be unearthed in [*Workers of Death*]. The opening page of the novel presents a girl with a mutilated arm who the narrator refers to as someone demanding that her "conditions be understood," touting an "intransigent attitude," keen on establishing "exclusionary rules" and attaining a "questionable renown" (20, 21)—all phrases applicable to Eltit as nonmainstream writer within, what seems to her, a stiflingly provincial literary establishment.

References to an "enigma," to "mirrors" that "deform objects" and to photographs of aviation accidents showing "fragmented bodies" further suggest the linguistic distortions associated with Eltit's early writing (17, 23). In the same vein, the text's coded references suggest writing as "night," and hence, that which is obscure. "The night lies," declares the protagonist-son in the novel. "I know it lies because I have caught its infinite contradictions . . . I love lies because I revere contradictions" (69). Significantly, this son identifies closely with the night and, as in [*Vigilant*], the text suggests equating him with writing itself.

In a dream he refers to himself as "the last surviving volume" in the great fire consuming the Library at Alexandria (72), and he continues this textual self-identification by using such terms as his "pages" (80), his "bookshelf" (81), and refers to a "rival, anguished reader" (81). For this nocturnal son, embodiment of hermetic writing, conventional language with its set of rules has little bearing on him. "The wise night has taught me much more than any grammar book," he declares (68). And as if anticipating a reader's complaint, he counters by saying that: "[The night's] complex wisdom requires *a constant exercise in decipherment* [and] an alert mind" (68).[4]

Given the abundance and type of allusions to writing, I read in [*Workers of Death*], even more so than in other books discussed in this study, signs of textual reflexivity that verge on a writer's manifesto. Voicing her perspective through the narrator, Eltit seems to acknowledge, as well as justify, her style of writing. "Es verdad que las palabras pueden ser usadas en un sentido absolutamente contrario a lo que indican" (78) [It is true that words can be used in a sense contradictory to their meaning], states the narrator at one point. And again, as if trying to shift some responsibility to the reader, he goes on to say: "pero la atención programada del que escucha lo lleva a descifrar lo que realmente yace detrás del imperceptible temblor de una expresión" (78) [but the careful attention of the listener permits him/her to decipher what truly lies behind the imperceptible tremor of an expression].

The analogy of writing as battleground emerges with frequent mention of "rivals." Despite the competition, however, the narrator hints of attaining success. "[F]ueron . . . mis rivales los que me adiestraron en el arte de conjeturar. Para enfrentarlos, cada movimiento, gesto o palabra debía estar cuidadosamente programado. . . . De esa manera, sin que esperara ser admirado ni menos reconocido, conseguí convertirme en un perfecto estratega" (72) [My rivals were the ones who trained me in the art of conjecture. In order to face them, every movement, gesture or word had to be carefully programmed. . . . In that way, without expecting to be admired and less so recognized, I managed to become a perfect strategist]. Proud of his perseverance, he later states: "Mis victorias, lo sé, se deben en gran parte a mi inmenso poder de convicción" (73) [I know that my successes, to a great extent, are due to the immense power of my conviction]. These words likewise ring true of Eltit the writer.

Interpreting the night as non-mainstream writing leads to correlating the day with clear, traditionally linear narratives, those bestsellers produced for mass consumption. In this context it makes sense that the narrator associates the day with constant "mediocrity," noting that the day is "nourished" by the "propaganda of its followers." Here resentment surfaces toward a literary establishment that supports and promotes the consumer's taste for the easy read at the expense of alternative literature. A writer's refusal to produce for the marketplace and thus develop a "following" courted by publishers comes at the price of being labeled a misfit: "Mi inevitable disidencia con las normas del día, me trajo el costo de innumerables enemigos" (84) [My inevitable dissidence toward the norms of the day cost me countless enemies]. Again, I read the "day" as representing conventional writing, popular literature, or the best-seller.

Standing out as "different" also takes a toll with respect to other writers who chide the renegade among their ranks. "La libertad de la que gozo," comments the narrator, "provoca una envidia indiscernible entre los que me rodean, quienes reconocen en mí una superioridad a la cual ellos renunciaron para sumergirse obedientes en una desdicha que a cada momento los disminuye y los irrita" (119) [The liberty that I enjoy provokes imperceptible envy among those who surround me and recognize in me a superiority that they gave up in order to submerge themselves in an obedient misfortune that belittles and irritates them with every passing moment]. The narrator goes on to blame others' envy for his solitude, a state he willingly bears as the fine levied for rejecting membership in the status quo. "[N]o me plegaré a ordenanzas cuyo destino es una mediocridad semejante al extenso silencio que antecede a la muerte" (119) [I will not give in to regulations whose fate means a similar mediocrity to the silence that precedes death], he declares. Ultimately the narrator conveys that each writer chooses which type of literature to produce, and every choice brings benefits as well as consequences.

[*Workers of Death*] includes other telltale signs that it is part of Eltit's established writing continuum. Appearing only in the introductory and concluding sections of the novel, the nameless girl, who loiters the city streets with two invalids in search of an enigma, most immediately reminds us of Eltit's own disfigurement as recorded in *E. Luminata*'s "Dress Rehearsal." The character's vagrancy with disabled buddies conjures E. Luminata's homeless cohorts in a city plaza as well as the real-life situation of the mentally disturbed man depicted in [*My Father*]. As bar patrons, these characters in [*Workers of Death*] also parallel the shanty dwellers in [*For the Homeland*]. Moreover, the physical challenge of the girl's companions recalls the handicapped son in [*Vigilant*], a son who can be read as embodiment of an "abnormal" and thus a "challenging" text. As previously noted, in [*Workers of Death*] the son's stated reverence for lying reinforces the literary difficulty and furthermore reminds us of the narrator/protagonist's similar taste in *Sacred Cow*, whose first line begins: "I sleep, I dream, I lie a lot" (1). From another perspective, in [*Workers of Death*] the "invalids" themselves, who the girl with the mutilated arms mothers and protects, also suggest Eltit's very writing, her books "invalidated" by some readers and labeled enigmatic.

The theme of incest, significant in [*For the Homeland*] and further developed in *The Fourth World*, becomes a key element in [*Workers of Death*] since its plot is based on a distortion of the Oedipus legend. Discussion of the role that this myth plays in the novel falls outside the realm of this epilogue. However, I will point out that this is not the first time where the father surfaces as an important figure in Eltit's writing. Let us recall that in *E. Luminata* the giant godlike neon light baptizing the protagonist's body with its intermittent words acts as a symbolic source of the Logos. Its combination of words and light recall the Creation story ("God said, 'Let there be light' "),[5] as well as the Gospel according to John ("When all things began, the Word already was. The Word dwelt with God").[6] [*For the Homeland*] presents a more flesh and blood father, one whose marginality is rooted in indigenous ancestry and crucial to the daughter's search for identity. Eltit continues the search for origins in [*Workers of Death*]. However, in this novel the search involves a son's journey. He must fulfill a mother's orders to visit the town of Concepción—literally conception—where his father settled, remarried, and fathered a daughter after abandoning his first family. Let us recall that the father figure in [*Vigilant*] embodies the many faces of the controlling patriarch—husband, dictator, literary canon—which until now have made up the crux of Eltit's writing continuum. But as noted above, in [*Workers of Death*] the dictator's presence and political circumstance has been eradicated from the narrative. This may mark the one theme in the author's writing continuum that will not cross the bridge into the new twenty-first century. Then again, we know that the death of the author's biological father greatly affected her writing at the time.

Pinochet may yet constitute an unwitting source of literary inspiration for Eltit. In any case, [*Workers of Death*] upholds the author's preoccupation with issues of gender and writing. As a Latin American, a woman, and an obscure writer, Eltit continues to filter these themes through the lens of marginality.

Conclusion

THIS STUDY HAS PRESENTED INTERPRETIVE POSSIBILITIES FOR READING the first fifteen years of Eltit's literary production. Despite the publication of six novels and two nonfiction texts, her work remains relatively unknown outside of Chile. The author's rejection of linear narrative, conventional plot, and standard syntax as well as the mixing of genres and language registers, as those found in *E. Luminata* and [*For the Homeland*], exemplify the type of challenge readers encounter in Eltit's earliest novels. The textual obscurity or, borrowing Robert Neustadt's phrase, the "narrative pandemonium" of those first two books set the stage for a reputation of unreadability which has followed the author ever since.[1] While Eltit abhors the "unintelligible" label, she recognizes that it describes some readers' experience with her books. By way of justifying her writing style, over the years the author has adopted a defense posture detectable in several of the texts commented on in this book's essays.

After publishing [*For the Homeland*], Eltit's writing changed, as evidenced by the linear prose and the attempt at a plot in *The Fourth World*, a book the author has said she consciously set out to write "like a lady." Eltit tried to sustain the semblance of narrative conformity in her next novel, too, but *Sacred Cow* turned out to be a complex postmodern text comparable to the "hypertext" of modern technology. Narratively speaking, the writing of [*Vigilant*] and [*Workers of Death*] continues where *The Fourth World* left off. In her last two novels of the twentieth century, Eltit radically attenuates the postmodern qualities found in *Sacred Cow* and her earliest books. In [*Vigilant*] and [*Workers of Death*] she returns to family-centered stories with apparent plots and straightforward prose that, from my critical perspective, pose fewer difficulties for readers.

I am not, however, implying that Eltit's writing has evolved into a family romance type of fiction for mass consumption. Even when her texts show signs of conventional literary artifice, the highly symbolic writing calls readers to critically venture beyond the surface design. As noted in the introduction, Roland Barthes' notion of a "scriptible" text applies well to Eltit's production since her books

213

demand that we actively create meaning from an array of ambiguous signifiers. While the author curtailed intricate narrative devices in *The Fourth World*, [*Vigilant*], and [*Workers of Death*], her texts remain replete with symbolic complexities.

By way of example, the dysfunctional family that appears often in Eltit's books connotes deeper meaning than what meets the (uncritical) eye. In conflict-ridden relationships wives and mothers must fend for their children by themselves, either by choice, as depicted in [*Vigilant*], or because of a partner's abandonment, as is the case in [*Workers of Death*]. In [*For the Homeland*] the fatherless Chilean "huacho," conceived by an absent patriarch, reverts back to the Spanish Conquest of Latin America, as do also the women whose children were the fruit of abusive relationships or rape portrayed in [*Workers of Death*] and *The Fourth World*. The hardships and uncertain futures that families face in Eltit's novels symbolically point to a Latin American family of nations likewise stricken with serious problems, not the least of which entails contending with Uncle Sam, historically a superpower as oppressive as Mother Spain, the European colonizer.

Likewise, in [*For the Homeland*], *The Fourth World*, and [*Workers of Death*], incestuous relationships, at face value, suggest troubled families. In each novel a character's search for identity leads to some questioning regarding biological conception, family origin, or ethnic roots. On another symbolic level, Eltit aims at linguistic incest, that is, perverting cultured language and conventional literature which, as part of her writing agenda, undermines the mainstream "literary" family. Typically, in Eltit's novels "language" deserves analysis as a character in itself.

My scrutiny of language in [*For the Homeland*] reveals indicators of Chile's virtually ignored indigenous ancestry. Linguistic cues in the novel change the context in which incest should be read, since native people's kinship systems admit relationships considered deviant by Judeo-Christian standards. And traditional standards are precisely what Eltit rejects. Anomalies—whether vis-à-vis family affiliations, textual construction, language, or characters—compose the "marginalities" of Eltit's writing, one whose symbolic nature demands a "different" reading.

Among society's marginals, those who are homeless, mentally ill, incarcerated, sexually deviant, politically persecuted, indigenous peoples, and women find representation in the books discussed in this study. Eltit has made known in interviews that her concern for Latin America's oppressed is a driving force in her writing. That is why critics like Juan Carlos Lértora observe that Eltit's entire production "is rooted in a profound and genuine solidarity with the helpless and voiceless of humanity in Latin America."[2]

Of the underprivileged, the author most often positions women as central figures. In fact, except for the nonfiction books [*My Father*] and [*Soul's Infarct*], all of Eltit's protagonists are females. This focus translates into an array of female-centered issues, including those associated with the body. The protagonists of *E. Luminata*, [*For the Homeland*], *The Fourth World*, and *Sacred Cow* exhibit sexual liberties at odds with tradition. In Eltit's novels it is common to find the depiction of physiological functions, especially the physical tribulations of birthing and those nonbiological struggles that come with motherhood. Continuing on the key theme of maternity in [*Vigilant*], [*Workers of Death*] poignantly renders the predicament of a physically exhausted mother of newborns who must endure her husband's mistreatment. In my reading, the centrality of gender throughout all of Eltit's novels manifests the author's preoccupation with the status of Latin American women, a group whose vast number of members live oppressed and at the margins of patriarchal society.

The inclusion of political repression is another recurring topic in the books discussed here. This is understandable given the dictatorial period in which Eltit struggled to support her family while writing and publishing under state censorship. Surely her zeal as an emerging writer helped her through the arduous time of making a mark in Santiago's literary establishment.

Not surprisingly, *E. Luminata*, [*For the Homeland*], *The Fourth World*, *Sacred Cow*, and [*Vigilant*] cannot be read without taking into account politics, gender, and writing. Only [*Workers of Death*]—a novel published practically a decade after the 1990 restoration of democratic rule in Chile—lacks appreciable references to Pinochet's reign. Hence, before [*Workers of Death*] all of Eltit's fiction weaves political elements into a female-centered, self-reflexive text. National politics, gender, and writing compose the thematic backbone of the author's postmodern novels.

In Eltit's books, the "gaze" appears as a recurring mechanism that connects issues of politics, gender, and writing. If by its very nature a dictatorial regime must keep an eye on the citizenry in order to extirpate dissent, patriarchy basically does the same with respect to women, as too the literary canon vis-à-vis nonmainstream writers. Symbolically, in Eltit's books the ever watchful "gaze" of these three repressive institutions serves to keep nonconformists in line.

Readers first encounter the "gaze" in *E. Luminata* in the form of a giant neon sign, which I read as the godlike eye of the biblical

Father. The novel's protagonist not only transgresses patriarchal dictates by exhibiting her sexuality in a public square, but she defies the state by being out during curfew and furthermore challenges the literary canon by writing publicly under the "gaze" of the male cohorts who also inhabit the plaza.

The dynamics between patriarchy, politics, and the writing establishment culminates in [*Vigilant*]. In this multilayered novel the mechanism of the "gaze" links the personal, political, and cultural aspects of the book's protagonist. As a mother this woman comes up against a punitive patriarch, as a citizen she contends with life under surveillance, and as a writer she struggles for recognition by the literary establishment.

As already noted, Eltit's characters are marginal, social "misfits" in a variety of ways. A less noticeable characteristic of her novels, however, is the correlation between the characters in her books and narrative construction. This association forms naturally in the case of [*My Father*] since the distorted syntax records the verbatim babbling of a disturbed mind. In fiction, *E. Luminata*'s writing reflects the unconventional and audacious manner of the protagonist whose sexual freedom parallels the text's narrative liberties. Likewise, in [*For the Homeland*] the disjointed narrative reproduces Coya's life circumstance as a member of a dysfunctional family within a segregated shanty community. The breakdown of syntax and structure compares with Coya's physical and psychological torments during a period of incarceration, a process that threatens to break her body and spirit. Furthermore, the mixing of genres and language registers, noted earlier, result in a hybrid text which suggests the halfbreed, the Latin American mestizo born of mixed blood which, like Eltit's books, mainstream society marginalizes. Similarly the female protagonists in *The Fourth World* and *Sacred Cow* demonstrate taboo behavior that thwarts social conventions. Hence, their defiance of the status quo is manifested in extraordinary story lines that deviate from traditional Chilean literature.

Ultimately, Eltit's writing is about power—those who wield it and those who struggle under its yoke. The "dictator" bears different faces in the books discussed here. Be it Pinochet, the United States, Imperial Spain, a family patriarch, the literary establishment, or mainstream Chilean society, the author calls attention to repressive systems. As a Latin American, a woman, and a writer Eltit has been touched by several of these forms of power. What little she has revealed about herself begins to explain her literary commitment with the oppressed. Eltit's books, as a collection of creative marginalities, serve to undermine traditional writing while voicing protest and a sense of brotherhood with Latin America's underclass. In my view, this fundamental connection with the margins will not change in future writings. On the other hand, I believe the hermetism of the early novels is now gone and readers will continue to see an aperture in the author's style. This modification in Diamela Eltit's writing will surely facilitate further critical study and the work of translation crucial in disseminating her books outside Chilean borders.

RITTER LIBRARY
BALDWIN-WALLACE COLLEGE

Notes

INTRODUCTION

In this study I quote from the published English translations *E. Luminata*, *The Fourth World*, and *Sacred Cow*. Translations that are mine of Eltit's other books, including titles, appear in brackets. Quotes incorporated into this text from interviews with Eltit are my translation unless otherwise noted. Also, in each chapter the page number in parentheses noted in the text after a quoted passage corresponds to the particular novel under discussion.

1. Piña, *Conversaciones*, 237.
2. Diamela Eltit, "El color," interview by Roberto García Bonilla, 6, 9.
3. Eagleton, *Literary Theory*, 137–38.
4. Diamela Eltit, "Diamela Eltit en rebeldía," interview by Faride Zerán, 5.
5. "Postmodernity" generally refers to a broad conceptual category, while the term "postmodern" denotes a more limited aesthetic and cultural realm as applied to various art forms.
6. Waugh, *Feminine Fictions*, 4–5. To trace the origins of the term "postmodernism," see Bertens in *Postmodern Reader*, 28, and Hassan, *Postmodern Turn*, 85–86.
7. McCaffery, *Postmodern Fiction*, xiv; Graff, *Literature Against Itself*, 32, 62; Yúdice, "Puede hablarse," 108.
8. Fiedler, "From Cross the Border," 32; Hassan, *Postmodern Turn*, 91–92.
9. Huyssen, *After the Great Divide*, 188–89.
10. Natoli and Hutcheon, *Postmodern Reader*, ix.
11. Lyotard, *The Postmodern Condition*, xxiii (my emphasis).
12. Richard, *Postmodern*, 3; Subercaseaux, "Nueva sensibilidad," 142; Gutiérrez Mouat, "Autoridad," 121.
13. Richard, *Postmodern*, 3–4.
14. Yúdice, "Puede hablarse," 105.
15. Neil Larsen, "Postmodernism and Imperialism," 280
16. Tompkins, "Intertextuality as Difference," 163.
17. Zermeño, "La postmodernidad," 64–65.
18. Neustadt, *(Con)Fusing*, xv.
19. Leitch, *Postmodernism*, 156.
20. Jameson, *Postmodernism, or the Cultural Logic of Late Capitalism*, 6.
21. My translation. Tafra, *Rito de pasaje*, 20.
22. Martín-Barbero, "Communication and Modernity," 23.
23. Sommer and Yúdice, "Latin American Literature," 189.
24. Ibid.
25. Passage found in *E. Luminata*, 77.
26. Sklodowska, *La parodia*, 157.
27. Higgins, "Spanish America's New Narrative," 90–91.

28. Ibid., 92.

29. Owens, "Discourse of Others," 61.

30. Fullbrook, "Whose Postmodernism," 73.

31. Franco, "From Romance to Refractory Aesthetic," 226.

32. Diamela Eltit, "L. Iluminada en sus ficciones," interview by Burgos and Fenwick, 359.

33. Franco, "From Romance to Refractory Aesthetic," 228.

34. Cornier Michael, *Feminism and the Postmodern Impulse*, 1.

35. Ibid., 24.

36. In Chile, María Luisa Bombal (*La amortajada* 1938/ *The Shrouded Woman* 1948), Marta Brunet ("Soledad de la sangre" 1967/"Solitude of Blood," in a collection edited by Marjorie Agosín), and Mercedes Valdivieso (*La brecha* 1961/ *Breakthrough* 1986) are considered precursors in feminist narrative. Other Latin American prose writers who inscribed an explicit feminist posture in the 1960s and 1970s with respect to women's situation vis-á-vis patriarchy include Rosario Castellanos (Mexico), Elena Poniatowska (Mexico), and Rosario Ferré (Puerto Rico).

37. Karl, *American Fictions*, 439.

38. Barthes, *Image, Music, Text*, 142–48.

39. Waugh, *Feminine Fictions*, 9.

40. Waugh, "From Modernism," 201.

41. Sherzer, "Postmodernism and Feminism," 168.

42. Leitch, *Postmodernism*, 133.

43. Ibid., 110.

44. Ibid.

45. I am thinking of Lewis's *Five Families* (1959) and *The Children of Sánchez* (1961).

46. Sherzer, "Postmodernism and Feminism," 156.

47. The original Spanish title, *Lumpérica*, suggests the conjunction of "lump," and "America." According to the *American Heritage Dictionary of the English Language* (3rd ed. 1992), "lumpenproletariat" was used originally in Marxist theory to describe those members of the proletariat, especially criminals, vagrants, and the unemployed, who lacked class consciousness; the word is rooted in the German "lumpen," plural of "lump," ragamuffin, a term which describes "the underclass of a human population." Also, Neustadt points out that the title contains the term "perica," Chilean slang for a prostitute (58).

48. Diamela Eltit, "Diamela Eltit en rebeldía," interview by Faride Zerán, 5.

49. Diamela Eltit, "L. Iluminada en sus ficciones," interview by Fernando Burgos and M. J. Fenwick, 358.

50. Piña, *Conversaciones*, 246, and see note 49 interview by Faride Zerán, 5.

51. Diamela Eltit, "Diamela Eltit en rebeldía," interview by Faride Zerán, 4.

52. Piña, *Conversaciones*, 227–28.

53. Ibid., 229.

54. Diamela Eltit, "L. Iluminada en sus ficciones," interview by Burgos and Fenwick, 343.

55. Diamela Eltit, "El cuerpo femenino," interview by Ana María Larraín, 1.

CHAPTER 1. *Lumpérica*

1. Here revised, this chapter first appeared as part of the dissertation project titled, *Four Latin American Writers Liberating Taboo: Albalucía Angel, Marta Traba, Sylvia Molloy, Diamela Eltit*. Washington University, 1991. DA9209181.

2. My translation. García-Corales, "La desconstrucción del poder en *Lumpérica*," 122.

3. Diamela Eltit, "Acoplamiento incestuoso," interview by Ana María Foxley, 41.

4. See Elzbieta Sklodowska's study of parody for a discussion of *E. Luminata* as postmodern text in dialogue with the aesthetics of modernism (156–57). For a focus on postmodern characteristics in Eltit's writing see chapter 5, "*Vaca sagrada*: A Feminist/Postmodern Novel," in this study.

5. Irigaray, "This Sex," 103.

6. Ibid.

7. Ibid.

8. Eltit, *E. Luminata*, 199. Hereafter page numbers will appear in parentheses in the text following quoted passages from *E. Luminata*.

9. Gen. 1:3, Revised English Bible.

10. Gen. 1:5.

11. Gligo, "*Lumpérica*: Un libro excepcional," 417.

12. John 1:1.

13. The notion of a red-light district—a delimited and marginal zone where business operations are typically nocturnal—may provide a plausible explanation of why the police look the other way and do not intervene in the plaza despite curfew. No matter what regime is in power, a patriarchal society presupposes the male prerogative of sexual gratification, and therefore will not dismantle the industry that provides for the sexual needs of its male population.

14. Bibliographic material on pornography is extensive, and within it lies the controversy of definition. For example, what constitutes soft, hard-core pornography, artistic erotic art? As Mariana Valverde points out in *Sex, Power and Pleasure*, "there are no litmus tests for what is or is not pornography" (124–25). I have chosen to use a broad yet basic definition of pornography since my intention is not to study the topic of pornography itself but rather to examine how Eltit reappropriates this patriarchal medium of representing women to address or re-present female sexuality, eroticism, and desire from a woman's perspective.

15. Christensen, *Pornography*, 38.

16. In Spanish, "Los desarrapados de Santiago, pálidos y malolientes" (7) can suggest an all-male group.

17. Agata Gligo has noted the importance of the gaze in *E. Luminata*: "Pareciera que una conciencia externa al personaje—sea la luz del letrero, la mirada del lumperío, el lente de la posible filmación—la completa, la ayuda a existir, o más exactamente, a ser. Miradas desembozadas u ocultas la buscan durante toda la novela y ella cuenta permanentemente con el hecho de ser mirada. Esta presencia de un ojo ajeno tiene la virtud de acrecentar su energía erótica" ("Lumpérica," 417) [It's as if a consciousness external to the character—be it the light from the sign, the lumpen's gaze, the lens from the possible filming—completes her, helps her to exist, or more precisely, to "be." Unmasked or hidden eyes look for her throughout the entire novel and she invariably counts on the fact that she is being watched. This presence of the other's eye has the power to increase her erotic charge]. Gligo evidently has made the connection between the gaze and eroticism. In her reading of *E. Luminata* Elzbieta Sklodowska also refers to the importance of the gaze in the text and notes Eltit's use of cinema and photography (*La parodia*, 156).

18. Mulvey, "Visual Pleasure," 11.

19. Ibid., 12.

20. Humm, "Is the Gaze Feminist?" 70.

21. Mulvey, "Visual Pleasure," 10.

22. Freud referred to scopophilia or "pleasure in looking" in his study of sexual perversions such as voyeurism (*Three Essays*, 23). However, he noted that scopophilia is discernible in children even before the erotogenic zones become sexualized. Since children are basically without shame they uninhibitedly expose their bodies. When socialized that such exposure, especially of the genitals, is forbidden, children become curious about other people's bodies and genitals and hence take "pleasure in looking" (Freud, *Three Essays*, 58).

23. De Lauretis, *Alice Doesn't*, 142.

24. For the significance hair plays in the definition of femininity see Susan Brownmiller, *Femininity*. In regard to its erotic value Brownmiller mentions how traditionally the Catholic nun and the orthodox Jewish wife were denied a natural head of hair in an attempt to desexualize them (*Femininity*, 61). For an interpretation of cropped hair as symbolic of castration see Tafra's reading of Eltit's writing as rite of passage (*El rito de pasaje*, 44).

25. Although focus on the actual hair-cutting scene and the dress appears in the last chapter, the protagonist bears this look early in the book: "The snipping of her hair was too regular . . . " (23); "[A] dress of thick gray wool covers her. On her, scarcely functional clothing, but nevertheless it particularizes her. Her practically razed head shines under the sign's lights . . . "(38).

26. The cincture or girdle symbolizes chastity. "Wrapping it about the alb the priest prays: 'Bind me, O Lord, with the cincture of purity and chastity.' " "As a cord, or often as a broad sash, it is included in almost every form of religious or ecclesiastical costume." (*The New Catholic Encyclopedia Dictionary*, Vatican edition, s.v. "girdle.")

27. Day, "Looking at Women," 85.

28. Sara Castro-Klarén similarly notes the masculine character of the sign in its frustrated attempt to possess the female's body: "El luminoso no puede hacer suyo ese cuerpo. Despacha su luz, pero no mira, proyecta sus letras pero no mira, no posee" (*Escritura*, 204). [The lighted sign cannot make that body its own. It gives off its light, but it does not look, it projects its letters but does not look, does not possess.]

29. Castro-Klarén, *Escritura*, 199.

30. Diamela Eltit, "El trabajo es la vida," interview by Ana María Larraín, 5.

31. In *My Secret Garden*, Nancy Friday compiles the sexual fantasies of women, a task undertaken to break the silence on this aspect of female sexuality. Applicable to Hispanic culture as well, Friday notes that "For men, talking about sex, writing . . . boasting about it in the locker room is usually thought to be very much the mark of a man's man. . . . But the same culture that gave men their freedom sternly barred it to women, leaving us sexually mistrustful of each other, forcing us . . . above all [into] silence" (*My Secret Garden*, 20).

32. Michelson, "Women and Pornorotica," 136.

33. As a note of interest, in "Fragment of an Analysis of a Case of Hysteria," Freud records his treatment of a young woman he calls Dora. In one of her dreams Freud interprets the same religious image as a manifestation of guilt: "[T]he notion of 'Madonna' is a favorite counter-idea in the mind of girls who feel themselves oppressed by imputations of sexual guilt . . ." ("Fragment," 104 n. 2).

34. Griffin, *Pornography and Silence*, 15.

35. I am thinking of Ezra Pound when applying this denomination to Eltit's work since his name appears among the literary patriarchs listed at the beginning of chapter 4: Lezama, James Joyce, Pablo Neruda, Juan Rulfo, E. Pound, Robbe-

Grillet. *E. Luminata* shares points of comparison with the works of all these authors, but I am here concerned with *The Cantos* of Ezra Pound for such characteristics as: obscurity, fragmentation, eroticism, marginality, incoherence, and moral transgression. Like *E. Luminata, The Cantos* do not adhere to any one subject. As Guy Davenport points out, Pound had "a reputation for innovation and obscurity" and "reading *The Cantos*" [like *E. Luminata*, I must add] "is from end to end, an imaginative act" (Davenport, *Cities on Hills*, 3, 5). However, I must also note that Sklodowska considers Joyce, Robbe-Grillet, Eliot and especially Neruda to have a more apparent link with Eltit's work than the other writers listed (*La parodia*, 158). As a brief example, Sklodowska notes the following in her intertextual reading of Neruda's poetry and *E. Luminata*: "[L]a óptica femenina de la novela y el enfoque en la sexualidad libre de la mujer sugieren una polémica con la imagen de la mujer forjada en la poesía erótica de Neruda: mujer-objeto, mujer-objeto sexual, mujer-en función del hombre" (*La parodia*, 160) [The novel's feminine perspective and its focus on women's liberated sexuality suggests a polemic with the female image forged in Neruda's erotic poetry: woman as object, woman as sexual object, woman in terms of man].

36. Susan Griffin begins *Pornography and Silence* by referring to the painter Franz Marc's animal motifs, especially horses, as a reflection of the artist's own bestiality in his erotic link to nature (8). She also discusses the association between women and animals in pornography (Griffin, 25–29). Specifically referring to *E. Luminata*, Agata Gligo also makes note of the chapter on the mare: "En el capítulo 3, la parte animal de la protagonista corre libre y suelta en fragmentos de gran belleza que subrayan y desarrollan su peculiar postura sexual" (*Lumpérica*, 418) [In chapter 3, the animal part of the protagonist runs free and easy in pieces of great beauty that underscore and develop her peculiar sexual posture].

37. Michelson, "Women and Pornorotica," 135.

38. In the Spanish version "would stop following orders" appears as "deso-becedería" (54), I suspect an intentional misspelling on Eltit's part as implied later in the text: "Se imprimirá con erratas conscientes" (93) / "It will be printed with conscious errors" (101).

39. On the subject of masturbation and the clitoris see: Anne Koedt, "The Myth of the Vaginal Orgasm"; Ethel Spector Person, "Sexuality as the Mainstay of Identity"; Shere Hite, *The Hite Report*, based on the answers given by women on a nationwide questionnaire; French feminists Luce Irigaray, "This Sex Which Is Not One," and Hélène Cixous, "The Laugh of the Medusa," relate the topic to women and writing.

40. Sklodowska, *La parodia*, 157.

41. Day, "Looking at Women," 84.

42. Castro-Klarén, *Escritura*, 103.

43. Given the political climate at the time the novel was written, I am not convinced by Silvia Tafra's ahistorical interpretation of violence. Tafra reads Eltit's writing as a rite of passage wherein violence is sacred, that is, a part of the mutilation or sacrifice found in all ritual and whose ultimate purpose is to attain peace (*Diamela Eltit: El rito de pasaje*, 26).

44. Castro-Klarén has noted the mutuality of pain and desire in the text though in regard to writing. Commenting on a passage which ends with: "Convulsions with fingernails across flesh: desire opens furrows" (*E. Luminata*, 17), Castro-Klarén writes: "Otra vez aparece el dolor en conjunción con el deseo. Las uñas rajan la piel, rasgan los surcos de la escritura como la pluma rasga el papel" (*Escritura*, 205) [Pain appears again in conjunction with desire. The fingernails cut into the skin, they rip into the furrows of writing like the pen scratching paper].

45. In her attempt to define postmodernism, Linda Hutcheon points out that, "In general terms it takes the form of self-conscious, self-contradictory, self-undermining statement. . . ." (*Politics*, 2). The effect of postmodernism according to Hutcheon is to "highlight" and at the same time to "subvert" or "de-naturalize." In this regard, Eltit's text shares a characteristic Hutcheon identifies with postmodernism in that it "highlights" a scene like the burning of the hand only to later "subvert" the effect by invalidating it altogether: "They have done the scene over and then she has not plunged her hand into the fire. . . . They knew always that the scene would be done over, nobody desires such sufferings for herself" (*E. Luminata*, 48). There are other examples in the book where the text constructs and later dismantles itself. In her study, Sklodowska discusses *E. Luminata* specifically in terms of postmodernism: "[N]o nos parece exagerado definir la poética de *Lumpérica* en términos de la estética postmoderna" (*La parodia*, 158) [It does not seem an exaggeration to define the poetics of *Lumpérica* in terms of a postmodern aesthetics].

46. I thank María Inés Lagos for bringing to my attention Nelly Richard's book, *Margins and Institutions: Art in Chile Since 1973*. Richard's writing on Eltit's use of the body as instrument for artistic, social, and political expression has confirmed the motifs of pornography and religion in my initial reading of *Lumpérica*.

47. I insert "would anoint her lips" as my own translation for the Spanish "le untaría los labios" (*Lumpérica*, 34) because the translation Ronald Christ uses ("even the most ragged of them, will join lips to hers") does not convey the religious allusion captured by the original term "untar" [anoint].

48. John 19:28–29.

49. Lagos, "Escritura y sujeto femenino en tres narraciones hispanoamericanas de los 80," paper read MLA, Chicago, 30 December 1990. Regarding reality and fiction, Eltit states in an interview with Ana María Larraín: "I look for the connection between life and literature: I find it difficult to believe that someone can write without taking experience into account. . . . For me the novel is just that, a space of liberty. Now . . . only experience can corroborate or amplify certain conceptions in a way that the reelaboration of reality is imaginative and creative, but . . . 'real' " ("El trabajo es la vida," 5).

50. Neustadt, *(Con)fusing Signs*, 47–54.

51. The dedication to Zurita is left out altogether from the translation, *E. Luminata*. Eltit is very guarded about her personal life. She was married to the poet and in an interview with Graciela Romero she refers in passing to her years as Mrs. Zurita ("En la sexualidad," 63).

52. Richard, *Margins*, 66.

53. As Neustadt documents, the author is also reticent about discussing the video, *Maipu*, which shows her displaying her burnt and slashed arms while reading from the book's manuscript in a brothel located on Maipu Street in Santiago (*(Con)fusing Signs*, 54, 58, 73). For the various subversive bodily acts committed by Zurita see Richard, *Margins*. Richard's book contains several pictures of Eltit. Among them is the one on the book cover, which is actually the projection of her face on a wall opposite the brothel where she read her work. Another is a different version of the picture displaying her cut arms which appears in *Lumpérica*. There is also one of Eltit washing the entrance to the brothel, and another of her reading a part of her book inside the brothel.

54. See note 3 in Richard, *Margins*, 73.

55. Lippard, *From the Center*, 121.

56. Ibid., 126.

57. Ibid., 135.
58. Ibid.
59. Bushnell, *Moscow Graffiti*, 4–7.
60. Ibid., 9.
61. *The New Catholic Encyclopedia*, s.v. "Quo Vadis."
62. *Quo Vadis?* (1896) by Polish Nobel laureate Henryk Sienkiewicz is also the title of a historically accurate novel portraying Rome during the time of Nero. Seemingly nothing to do with Poland, the book works as "an allegory, a mirror held up to the Polish people at the end of the last century" (*Quo Vadis?* vii). The book's patriotic allegory coupled with Sienkiewicz's lifelong concern for Poland point to common ground with *E. Luminata* and Eltit the author.

63. See Craig Castleman, *Getting Up: Subway Graffiti in New York,* for a study of the world of the inner-city youths for whom graffiti provides a status symbol as well as a form of artistic expression. In *Moscow Graffiti: Language and Subculture,* John Bushnell examines graffiti-writing groups such as soccer and rock and roll fans, hippies, pacifists, and punks.

64. In terms of parody, Sklodowska has also pointed out this chapter. Let us note her interpretation: "La proliferación de definiciones de la escritura en la parte sexta de la novela . . . irremediablemente conduce a una autoparodia. El sentido autoparódico del texto queda realzado por las muestras de la escritura que siguen a cada una de las definiciones/aproximaciones y aparecen en forma de una nota al pie de página . . . " (*La parodia,* 161) [The proliferation of definitions of writing in the sixth part of the novel . . . inevitably leads to self-parody. The text's sense of self-parody is accomplished by the writing samples that follow each of the definitions/approximations and appear as footnotes on the page].

65. The only mention in the text of a family structure is presented in a negative light. The mother is denounced not only for early weaning, but for an abandonment which literally signifies handing over the child to an incestuous father: "[T]hey wean her early, mother more ungodly her madonna master for leaving her on the concrete in the square. . . . [H]er wicked matermadona . . . snatches the teat from him, that ample milky part robs him and her hungry muzzle sucks from the father his product which he gives her in order to perpetuate her" (92). Some form of the word incest recurs throughout section 4.5: "Thincest works painlessly. . . . Thincestress recognizes her breed. . . . The surname incestser. . . . Thincest of the theft of her alias . . . " (91–93). The topic of incest recurs in [*For the Homeland*] and is further developed in *The Fourth World.*

66. Unlike the translator, here I interpret the Spanish indirect object pronoun "(le) presté mi cuerpo" as referring to a female since there is an indication that E. Luminata directs her words to a woman, as in the phrase "párteme con las ramas madona, enardéceme con las hojas."

67. This is my translation of the original "me ensucia ese desarrapado madona, me mancha" (115) instead of Ronald Christ's version "she besmirches me this madonna in rags, stains me" (125).

68. The topic of literary censorship appearing in other parts of the section points to political repression which has affected not only the national literature, but Latin American literature in general: "Marginalized from all production, delusively we separate ourselves in order to indict the foundations. . . . It's been told to us that on these foundations there were conquerors and conquered. I say that's a half truth: there were conquered and corpses. Nothing else" (*E. Luminata,* 132–33).

69. Diamela Eltit, "Entrevistas," interview by Sandra Garabano and Guillermo García-Corales, 67.

CHAPTER 2. *EL PADRE MÍO* AND *EL INFARTO DEL ALMA*

Reference to the book, [*My Father*], will appear in brackets and italicized. The homeless man, My Father, is identified as a proper name in capitals. The name will appear in quotes—"My Father"—when it identifies a powerful government official.

1. Piña, *Conversaciones*, 237–38.

2. The Spanish title is capitalized because Eltit exclusively refers to the protagonist as "el Padre Mío," hence the denomination acts as his proper name.

3. This particular book reminds us of the work of the late American photographer Diane Arbus, whose posthumously published *Untitled* (New York: Aperture, 1995) exclusively features anonymous residents of institutions for the mentally retarded. In fact, akin to Eltit's appeal for people on the margins of society, during her career Arbus showed special interest in photographing such subjects as transvestites, dwarfs, giants, nudists, derelicts, and carnival freaks (*.diane arbus.* Millerton, New York: Aperture, 1972).

4. Bouchard, *Michel Foucault*, 209.

5. Dorfman, "Where Anonymous Was a Woman," 17.

6. Iser, "The Reading Process," 55.

7. Piña, *Conversaciones*, 246–47. My translation.

8. Kadir, *The Other Writing*, 183.

9. Piña, *Conversaciones*, 238.

10. Diamela Eltit, "Experiencia literaria," 25.

11. Ibid.

12. See Roberto González Echevarría's chapter study of Sarduy's *Cobra* in his volume *Celestina's Brood: Continuities of the Baroque in Spanish and Latin American Literature* (Durham: Duke University Press, 1993).

13. Ibid., 197.

14. For a study of the neo-baroque in Eltit's second novel, [*For the Homeland*], see Gail Bulman, "Neo-Baroque Reflections on the Extra-Textual and Intra-Textual Constructions of Violent Space in Three Women Writers from the Southern Cone" (Ph.D. diss., Syracuse University, 1995), 129–70.

15. Kadir, *The Other Writing*, 183–84.

16. Piña, *Conversaciones*, 237.

17. Kadir, *The Other Writing*, 188.

18. Calabrese, *Neo-Baroque: A Sign of the Times*, 163.

19. Ibid., 193.

20. Ibid.

21. Here periphery does not depict the outskirts of the city as the exclusive area of marginality. Poverty-stricken sectors or neighborhoods do exist within the inner (geographic) boundaries of city lines.

22. Piña, *Conversaciones*, 233.

23. Ibid.

24. Ibid.

25. In fact, one of the protagonist's dreams manifests repressed fear as well as feelings of resistance to the government takeover of the city: "Soñé que el médico de la tortura organizaba el tráfico de la ciudad. Salgamos a recorrerla, Octavio. Hagámosla nuestra, antes que él la conozca" (170) [I dreamed that the torture doctor organized traffic in the city. Let's tour it, Octavio. Let's make it ours, before he does].

26. Piña, *Conversaciones*, 238.

27. Calabrese, *Neo-Baroque: A Sign of the Times*, 187.

28. Gonzáles Echevarría, *Celestina's Brood*, 81, 104, 198.
29. Piña, *Conversaciones*, 239.
30. VanderStaay, *Street Lives*, 119.
31. Under page heading: "Juana la loca." [*Soul's Infarct*] does not include page numbers, a feature that reflects the difficulty in identifying the anonymous patients depicted in the book.
32. Laub, "An Event Without a Witness," 75.
33. Ibid., 76.
34. Ibid.
35. ribettes, *Loca verdad*, 155.
36. Consolli, "El relato del psicótico," 50.
37. Ibid., 51.
38. Greimas, "The Veridiction Contract," 653. Following Greimas, I am using "plausible" in connection with any discourse that reveals a "certain reality, or rather, a concept of reality" that is extraliterary and in keeping with a specific cultural, geographic, or historical context ("Veridiction," 651). This means that if My Father were a vagrant living in some lot in a U.S. city who was voicing accusations of government oppression involving such names as Allende, Pinochet, Frei, Alessandri, etc., then his story would be much less plausible because it lacks "cultural relativism."
39. Consolli, "El relato del psicótico," 53.
40. Ibid., 53–54.
41. [*Soul's Infarct*], see page heading: "Diario de viaje."
42. Eltit, [my Father], 17.
43. Jameson, "Third-World Literature," 69.
44. Lyotard, *The Differend*, 13.
45. Ibid.
46. Ibid.
47. Laub, "An Event Without a Witness," 79.
48. Munizaga and Ochsenius, "El discurso público de Pinochet," 77–78.
49. Chilean fiction such as *Cita capital* by Guadalupe Santa Cruz reflects mental illness at different levels. Throughout the book, Sandra, the protagonist, shows signs of a mental affliction difficult to diagnose by Octavio, the male protagonist and a psychiatrist. Also in the novel, a woman on the metro who carries on a conversation by herself (128–29) and the agitation of a disturbed man on the bus (132) portray clear manifestations of mental illness among the populace.
50. Laub, "An Event Without a Witness," 80–82.
51. See Montecino, *Madres y huachos*, 113, for other services dedicated to feeding the needy such as: Comedores Infantiles, Comprando Juntos, Comités de Abastecimiento, and Bolsas de Cesantes. [Children's Dining Halls, Cooperative Buying, Supplies Organizations, and Aide for the Unemployed].
52. A decade earlier Cuba's Casa de las Américas had instituted the testimonio as genre, thus endorsing an award for this category; see John Beverley, "The Margin at the Center," 93.
53. Ibid., 92–93.
54. Ibid., 94.
55. Ibid., 94–95.
56. Yúdice, "Puede hablarse," 17.
57. Beverley, "The Margin at the Center," 94.
58. Greimas, "Veridiction Contract," 654.
59. Sklodowska, "Spanish American Testimonio," 38.

60. Montejo, *The Autobiography of a Runaway Slave*, 8.

61. Ibid.

62. Larry Rohter, *New York Times*, International, 15 December 1998, section A, p. 1.

63. Ibid., section A, p. 10.

64. Beverley, "The Margin at the Center," 94.

65. Geisdorfer Feal, "Spanish American Ethnobiography and the Slave Narrative Tradition," 102.

66. On 27 October 1970, President Frei appointed General Prats commander in chief of the army to succeed Gen. René Schneider Chereau, who had fallen victim to an assassination attempt just days prior to the congressional vote of 24 October 1970 that proclaimed Salvador Allende as the next president of the republic. Like Schneider, Prats upheld the constitution and refused to involve the army in a coup d'etat to prevent Allende from assuming power, or later to oust him from the presidency. Pressure and plots from within the armed forces drove him to resign after a forty-year military career. On 30 September 1974 (coincidentally, ten days after completing the prologue to his memoirs) Prats and his wife were assassinated while exiled in Buenos Aires.

67. I am indebted to Elzbieta Sklodowksa for this insight.

68. Regarding the role and authority of the compiler in the production of "testimonios," see Beverley, "The Margin at the Center," 97–101.

69. Sklodowska, *Testimonio*, 73, 86.

70. Ibid., 72–73.

71. Hernán Valdés expresses his testimonial intent in *Tejas Verdes: Diario de un campo de concentración en Chile* [*Green Tiles: Diary of a Concentration Camp in Chile*] (1974) yet he also notes in the prologue that despite being a writer himself, in this case he aims for readability and not aesthetic recognition: "These pages are written in a hurry (while the memory is still warm). Because of this, do not look for any type of literary elaboration. The language is fundamentally functional and this has meant for me a new experience" (my trans., p. 6). Lack of "literariness" here does not disqualify [*Green Tiles*] as a powerful testimony against political persecution.

72. Sklodowska, *Testimonio*, 73.

73. Greimas, "The Veridiction Contract," 654.

74. Geisdorfer Feal, "Spanish American Ethnobiography," 101.

75. Laub, "An Event Without a Witness," 84.

76. Ibid., 79.

77. Eltit, "Nomadic," 42. This article was published in English and is not my translation.

78. Ibid., 43.

79. Ibid., 45.

80. Sklodowska, "Spanish American Testimonial Novel," 35.

81. Beverley, "The Margin at the Center," 103.

82. I borrow the phrase from Doris Sommer's essay " 'Not Just a Personal Story': Women's *Testimonios* and the Plural Self."

83. In arguing that Miguel Barnet's *The Autobiography of a Runaway Slave* is actually an "ethnography," Geisdorfer Feal points out that Esteban Montejo, the centenarian informant, represents the life of runaways like him, yet he admits to being pretty much a loner. Therefore, unlike Rigoberta Menchú's activism in community struggle, in Montejo's case representing a group does not necessarily mean maintaining close affiliation. Eltit's informant's solitary existence resembles that of the former runaway slave. Despite differences in urban and rural settings, both men,

for example, live exposed to the elements and sustain themselves on what they can scavenge. Both are survivors of cruel oppression and have escaped death.

84. For a discussion of "truth effect" see Beverley, "The Margin at the Center," 95; for "truthsaying," see Greimas, "The Veridiction Contract," and Sklodowska, "Spanish American Testimonial Novel," 35; for "authentic narrative," see Yúdice, "Testimonio and Postmodernism," 17.

85. VanderStaay, *Street Lives*, 119.

86. Ibid.

87. Sklodowska, *Testimonio*, 126–28.

88. Sklodowska, "Spanish American Testimonial Novel," 33.

89. Iser, "The Reading Process," 55.

90. Malverde Disselkoen, "Esquizofrenia y literatura: La obsesión discursiva en *El Padre Mío* de Diamela Eltit," 158–59.

91. Sklodowska, *Testimonio*, 126.

92. Laub, "An Event Without a Witness," 78.

93. Let's not forget that in the text "My Father" is also the alias of the government official responsible for the informant's persecution and demise.

94. My translation. Malverde Disselkoen, "Esquizofrenia y literatura," 156.

95. Felman, "Camus' The Plague, or a Monument to Witnessing," 114.

96. Ibid.

97. Curiously, 1989 marked the year when a national plebiscite was to determine whether Gen. Augusto Pinochet would continue in power until 1997. Thus a sixteen-year "lag" separated the bloody coup of 1973 from the kind of public manifestation where Chileans finally assumed the "consciousness" as a nation to vote and determine their political future.

98. Following Beverley, this is a term popularized during the Chinese Cultural Revolution ("The Margin at the Center," 94).

99. Felman, *Writing and Madness*, 80.

100. Ibid., 84.

101. Ibid., 36.

102. Early on during the first recording, the vagrant, aware of a camera, warns: "Pero usted me sacó una fotografía, puede perder la existencia de la vida porque yo soy un hombre poderoso al dar órdenes" (27) [But you have taken my picture, and this could mean your demise because I am a powerful man when I give orders].

103. Sommer, "Not Just a Personal Story," 118.

104. Felman, *Writing and Madness*, 66.

105. See various news stories in the "Panorama de Iberoamérica" section of *Diario las Américas*, May–July 1995, p. 2.

CHAPTER 3. CLAIMING INDIGENOUS ROOTS IN *POR LA PATRIA*

1. Eltit came upon this name in her readings on Inca culture (interview by Claudia Donoso, "Tenemos puesto el espejo," 47). In Andean world order, supreme authority rested in the "Inca" and his "Coya," as fashioned after the first Inca, Manco Capac, and his sister-wife, Mama Ocllahuaco (Muriel, *Las mujeres de hispanoamérica*, 203), also known as Mama Ocllo who, within a dual hierarchy of power as earthly representatives of the sun and moon respectively, ruled over the male and female populace (Hernández and Murguialday, *Mujeres indígenas ayer y hoy*, 22, 74). Josefina Muriel explains that political organization was such that the Inca became so by inheritance, lineage that was transmitted under so strict a system

that the elected queen was also the Inca's sister in the image of the first Coya (*Mujeres de hispanoamérica*, 205).

2. With varying degrees in clan size and cultural disintegration, the indigenous population of Chile is composed of the Aymaras and Atacameños in the extreme north of the country; the Diaguitas in the "norte chico" area; the Picunches of the central zone; the Mapuches, Huilliches and Pehuenches of the center-south zone; the Alacalufes, Tehuelches, Selk'Nam, and Yamanas in the extreme south; and the Rapa Nui of Easter Island (*Indigenous Chile*, 14).

3. Malú Sierra, *Donde todo es altar: Mapuche gente de la tierra*, 14.

4. Ibid., 16.

5. My translation. Ibid.

6. Isabel Allende, *Paula* (English translation, 1995), 14.

7. Ibid., 93.

8. Ana María del Río, *Tiempo que ladra*, 12.

9. Gligo, *Mi pobre tercer deseo*, 9, 90, 92.

10. Quezada, *Gabriela Mistral: Escritos políticos*, 10.

11. Rodríguez Valdés, *Invitación a Gabriela Mistral*, 7.

12. Eltit, "Experiencia literaria y palabra en duelo," 26.

13. An anthropologist by training and a fiction writer and poet by calling, Arguedas (1911–69) was a bicultural mestizo who used his understanding of the languages and cultures of the criollos and Quechua Indians to inscribe the ethos of indigenous life in "a hybrid literary language, constructed from Spanish speech and Quechua syntax" (Julio Ortega, "José María Arguedas," *Latin American Writers*, 1132).

14. Eltit, "Resistencia y sujeto femenino," interview by Julio Ortega, 232.

15. Ibid.

16. Eltit, "Experiencia literaria y palabra en duelo," 27.

17. Under a legitimately dubious 1980 constitution, Pinochet, who took power in 1973, was to govern as president of Chile and commander in chief of the armed forces until 1989, at which time a national plebiscite was to be held before the end of his term. Victory of the "yes" vote meant Pinochet would continue in power until 1997; but the "no" vote won and presidential elections held in 1989 declared Patricio Aylwin of the Christian Democratic Party as the next president (Carothers, *In the Name of Democracy: U.S. Policy Toward Latin America in the Reagan Years*, 152, 162).

18. Tierney-Tello, "Re-making the Margins: From Subalterity to Subjectivity in Diamela Eltit's *Por la patria*, 205.

19. Ibid., 206.

20. Brito, "El doble relato en la novela *Por la patria*, de Diamela Eltit," 247.

21. The Mapuche of Chile identify male deities with the term "fucha" or father, whereas female or maternal qualities are called "kuche," thus within the dual order of their supernatural world one finds the following examples: Huillifucha/kushe (god and goddess of the sea), antufucha/kushe (god and goddess of the sun), kuyenfucha/kushe (god and goddess of the moon); see Louis Faron, *Hawks of the Sun*, 51–53, and Sonia Montecino, *Mujeres*, 145.

22. Sierra, *Donde todo es altar*, 74.

23. Eltit, "Tenemos puesto el espejo," interview by Claudia Donoso, 47.

24. Yosuke Kuramochi and Juan Luis Nass, *Mitología mapuche*, 176.

25. For a focus on the mother in the novel see Gail Bulman's study, "Neo-Baroque Reflections," which includes the following sections: Mother/Patria, The Abject Mother, and Mother as Sight of Baroque Tension.

26. *Larousse Spanish Dictionary*, unabridged edition (Spanish/English) 1993, s.v. "rucio."

27. Quezada, *Gabriela Mistral: Escritos políticos*, 45.

28. Montecino, *Mujeres de la tierra*, 48.

29. Ibid.

30. Faron, *The Mapuche Indians of Chile*, 37; Muriel, *Las mujeres de hispanoamérica*, 205.

31. Eltit, "Tenemos puesto el espejo," interview by Claudia Donoso, 48.

32. My translation. Tafra, *Rito de pasaje*, 70.

33. Eltit, "Tenemos puesto el espejo," interview by Claudia Donoso, 47.

34. My translation. Sierra, *Donde todo es altar*, 228.

35. Montecino documents the urban migration of Mapuche women and instances of return to their rural family home (*Mujeres de la tierra*, 126–33).

36. Montecino, *Madres y huachos*, 43.

37. The word "huacho" comes from the Quechua term "huachuy"—to commit adultery—and identifies an illegitimate child as well as an orphan (Ibid., 43).

38. Ibid., 59.

39. Ibid., 50.

40. Hernández and Murguialday, *Mujeres indígenas ayer y hoy*, 22.

41. Ibid., 22–23.

42. My translation. Sierra, *Donde todo es altar*, 219.

43. Ibid.

44. My translation. Quezada, *Gabriela Mistral: Escritos políticos*, 47.

45. My translation. Patricio Manns, *Violeta Parra*, 108.

46. Robert Charles Padden points out that both Spanish troops and Mapuche warriors used similar war strategies, including brutal raids on civilian settlements ("Cultural Adaptation and Militant Autonomy among the Araucanians of Chile," 77).

47. Sierra, *Donde todo es altar*, 234.

48. The Chilean Left had a strong following among rural indigenous sectors because their peoples' sense of community easily identifies with communist ideology, which professes work towards a common good, and as victims of oppression themselves Indians also relate well with the working-class poor (Sierra, *Donde todo es altar*, 233). Eusebio Painemal, a Mapuche from Coihue, one of the many incarcerated during the dictatorship, recalls that in Boroa there was a hanging bridge for pedestrians to cross the Cautín River. After the coup all those listed as organizers of Mapuche agricultural cooperatives were rounded up and filed onto the bridge, where soldiers opened fire; as the bodies fell into the Cautín they were washed downstream (Sierra, *Donde todo es altar*, 239–40).

49. Ana Mariella Bacigalupo, "El poder de las mujeres machis en los valles centrales de la Araucania," 30; Louis Faron, *Hawks of the Sun*, 139; Malú Sierra, *Donde todo es altar*, 45.

50. Bacigalupo, "El poder de las mujeres machis," 25.

51. Ibid., 14.

52. Montecino, *Mujeres*, 24, 147.

53. Ibid., 146.

54. Sierra, *Donde todo es altar*, 44.

55. Faron, *Hawks of the Sun*, 139.

56. Mary Daly, *Gyn/Ecology: The Metaethics of Radical Feminism*, 182.

57. Ibid., 182–83.

58. Ibid., 183.

59. Ibid., 15.

60. Montecino, *Mujeres*, 65.

61. Ibid., 66–69.
62. Ibid., 69–75.
63. Ibid., 68–69.
64. Sierra, *Donde todo es altar*, 45.
65. My translation. Bacigalupo, "El poder de las mujeres machis," 23.
66. Ibid., 16–17, 22–23.
67. Harlow, *Resistance Literature*, 124–25.
68. Arrate P., "Los significados de la escritura y su relación con la identidad femenina latinoamericana en *Por la patria*, de Diamela Eltit," 142.
69. Eugenia Brito, "El doble relato en la novela *Por la patria*, de Diamela Eltit," 252; Mary-Beth Tierney-Tello, "Remaking the Margins," 212.
70. My translation. Arrate P., "Los significados de la escritura," 143.
71. Arrate P. suggests this in her study of the novel (Ibid., 146) and Sierra demonstrates it throughout *Mapuche gente de la tierra*.
72. Angel Rama, *The Lettered City*, 42.
73. Ibid., 37–38.
74. Ibid., 38.
75. Eltit, "Chile: Ni desprecio ni puro amor," interview by Patricio Ríos S., 30.
76. Ibid.
77. Sierra, *Donde todo es altar*, 67.
78. Raquel Olea, "Materiales críticos—Una épica de la marginalidad: *Por la patria*," 2.
79. Tierney-Tello, "Re-Making the Margins," 206.
80. Ibid.
81. Brito, "El doble relato en la novela *Por la patria*," 256.
82. See page 29 in the novel for an example of this.
83. *Mitología mapuche*, a series of Mapuche myths compiled by Yosuke Kuramochi and Juan Luis Nass, makes possible comparisons between Spanish and Mapudungun. For each mythical story the text includes the version in Mapudungun, its verbatim transcription into Spanish, a semi-ordered version in Spanish, and a final version that adheres to Spanish grammar and syntax.
84. Kadir, *The Other Writing*, 196.
85. In Chile, as elsewhere in Latin America, recuperation and preservation projects in connection with native peoples' culture has been undertaken more and more by their own political and cultural leaders, especially those who have undergone Western education. In 1990, Mapuche poet Leonel Lienlaf, for example, won the Municipal Literature Prize in Santiago for his book *Nepey Ni Güñún Piuke* [*The Bird in my Heart Has Awoken*], a text written in Mapudungun and translated into Spanish with Chilean poet Raúl Zurita (Sierra, *Donde todo es altar*, 7–8). The following year *Mitología mapuche* [*Mapuche Mythology*] was published by Yosuke Kuramochi and Juan Luis Nass, a book composed of transcriptions in Mapudungun of stories that have been handed down orally since the beginning of time.
86. Tierney-Tello, "Re-making the Margins," 209.
87. See pages 11 and 27 in the novel, 1986 edition.
88. Arrate P., "Los significados de la escritura," 146.
89. Ibid., 143.
90. Eltit, "Chile: Ni desprecio ni puro amor," interview by Patricio Ríos S., 30.
91. My translation. Tafra, *Rito de pasaje*, 53.
92. Watson, "James Joyce's 'Ulysses': Epic Novel," 202. Publications such as *Modern Epic: The World-System from Goethe to Garcías Márquez* (1996) by Franco Moretti and *Epic Grandeur: Toward a Comparative Poetics of the Epic* (1997) by Masaki Mori attest to the contemporaneity of this classic genre.

93. Murray, *Who's Who in Mythology: Classic Guide to the Ancient World*, 7.

94. Fox, *The Mythological Foundations of the Epic Genre: The Solar Voyage as the Hero's Journey*, 92.

95. Eliade, *Myth and Reality*, 1–2.

96. Ibid., 1.

97. Ibid., 5–6.

98. Murray, *Who's Who in Mythology*, 11.

99. Merchant, "Children of Homer: The Epic Strain in Modern Greek Literature," 95.

100. Winnifrith, "Postscript," in *Aspects of the Epic*, 116.

101. Gould, "Homeric Epic and the Tragic Moment," 34–35.

102. Ibid., 35.

103. Ibid., 37.

104. Ibid.

105. Pierrette Daly, *Heroic Tropes: Gender and Intertext*, 77.

106. Tafra, *Rito de pasaje*, 58.

107. Gould, "Homeric Epic and the Tragic Moment," 42.

108. Ibid.

109. Ibid., 36.

110. Dorfman, *Imaginación y Violencia en América*, 11.

111. Ibid., 21.

112. Ibid., 31.

113. Ibid., 238.

114. Murray, "Homer and the Bard," 2.

115. Ibid., 6.

116. Ibid.

117. Ibid.

118. Ibid., 9–10.

119. Murray, *Who's Who in Mythology*, 161.

120. Eliade, *Myth and Reality*, 120.

121. G. J. B. Watson, "James Joyce's 'Ulysses': Epic Novel," 201.

122. Eliade, *Myth and Reality*, 115, 119.

123. Ibid., 116.

124. Ibid., 121.

125. George de Forest Lord, *Trials of the Self: Heroic Ordeals in the Epic Tradition*, 10.

126. Ibid., 1.

127. Ibid., 6.

CHAPTER 4. *EL CUARTO MUNDO*

1. Tafra, *Rito de pasaje*, 33.

2. Other writers such as Pía Barros, Alejandra Basualto, Luisa Eguiluz, Sonia González, and Guadalupe Santa Cruz not only read and even critique each others' work, but most know each other personally.

3. Diamela Eltit, "Resistencia y sujeto femenino: entrevista con Diamela Eltit," interview by Julio Ortega, 236.

4. María Inés Lagos, "Reflexiones sobre la representación del sujeto en dos novelas de Diamela Eltit: *Lumpérica* y *El cuarto mundo*," 127–28.

5. Raquel Olea, "El cuerpo-mujer. Un recorte de lectura en la narrativa de Diamela Eltit," 84.

6. This chapter evolved from my article "Diálogo fraternal: *El cuarto mundo* de Diamela Eltit y *Cristóbal Nonato* de Carlos Fuentes," published in *Chasqui* 23 (1994): 74–85.

7. In a conversation with Eltit in April 1993 at the Montclair State University Annual Conference on Latin American Literature, she indicated not knowing of *Cristóbal Nonato* and expressed surprise at the similarities I observed between the novels.

8. Let us recall that the womb as creative and narrative space had already been introduced, albeit not developed, in [*For the Homeland*] when Coya suggests narration prior to her birth: "por qué la mamá no puja?. . . . abre las piernas pa que me quepa el hueso y nuestros pelos se enreden. . . . Ma ma ma me viro patas pa abajo y pido fuerzas pa la salida. . . . (11–12) [Why does mother not push?. . . . open your legs for my bone to fit and our hair becomes entangled in the untamed, sticky thicket. . . . Ma ma ma I turn feet first and ask for strength to exit. . . .].

9. Phrase on page 11.

10. See mother's description on pages 3–4.

11. Lacan, *Ecrits*, 65–68.

12. Fredric Jameson, "Imaginary and Symbolic in Lacan: Marxism, Psychoanalytic Criticism, and the Problem of the Subject," 384.

13. Lacan, *Ecrits*, 1–2.

14. Barbara Lee Loach, *Power and Women's Writing in Chile*, 154.

15. Lacan, *Ecrits*, 67.

16. Mexicans historically have been defined as "children of la Malinche," or children of an indigenous mother raped by the Spanish conquistador, Hernán Cortés. For an insight into rape as a key aspect of Mexican national identity see *La Malinche in Mexican Literature: From History to Myth* by Sandra Messinger Cypess, and *The Labyrinth of Solitude: Life and Thought in Mexico* by Nobel laureate Octavio Paz.

17. Baker Miller, *Toward a New Psychology of Women*, 10–11.

18. My emphasis added, page 9. The original Spanish reads: "Hastiado de su persecución, permití que se me acercara" (18). The term "harassment" better captures the sense of sexual persecution than Gerdes's use of "oppression."

19. Instead of "trembling" Gerdes uses "quivering," but the Spanish passage actually translates into tremor—"un temblor de tal magnitude" (18)—which conveys a stronger image of the female's physical experience than does the word "quiver."

20. In Eltit's prose the term "conocidos" ("Pudo ser al tercer o cuarto roce, cuando sentí uno de sus conocidos temblores," 18) suggests both the male's previous knowledge of the sister's tremors and the "routine" nature of such tremors, notions which are not translated in the English version: ". . . it might have been the third or fourth time we bumped into each other, or when I felt her quivering so hard that the turbulent waters hurled me against the surrounding walls" (10).

21. Robert Scholes, *Semiotics and Interpretation*, 134.

22. Whereas "machismo" relates to manifestations of virility, including sexual prowess, physical superiority, and a disdain for personal danger, "marianismo" refers to the attributes of the Virgin Mary. Hispanic culture socializes women to be morally and spiritually superior to men, sexually pure, self-sacrificing, submissive to fathers, husband, and sons, and forgiving of their sins. Devotion to the family through self-abnegation as wife and mother bestows women with respect and dignity.

23. The translation—"Not daring to move" (13)—conveys fear and not laziness or apathy as does Eltit's prose—"Yo no hice el menor esfuerzo" (22).

24. Henke, "Sexuality and Silence in Women's Literature," 46–47.

25. Houston, "The Matrix of War: Mother and Heroes," 134.

26. Elena Gianini Belotti has studied how the internalization of patriarchal attitudes, such as the preference for male babies and social validation of the women who bear them, affects mothers in their interaction with boys and girls during child rearing.

27. Let us take into account the difference in the market dissemination of the two novels compared here. The second printing of *Christopher Unborn* occurs within the same year of its publication, and a third printing runs the following year. In addition, although the book is over five hundred pages long, the English translation appears in 1989, two years after the Spanish original—which indicates that the English translation project got underway immediately after publication of the novel. Thus, translation of Fuentes's work is practically a given. This is not the case with Eltit's production. The translation of her much shorter novel appeared in 1995, and the first reprinting of *The Fourth World* ran in 1996, eight years after its original publication.

28. English translation by Ruth L. C. Simms appeared as *Recollections of Things to Come*.

29. Esquivel, *Like Water for Chocolate*, translated by Carol Christensen and Thomas Christensen appeared in 1992.

30. Critics have turned to psychology to explain this change in the male protagonist. María Inés Lagos considers the brother's new name as evidence of ambiguity inherent in his sexual identity ("Reflexciones," 130). Barbara Loach attributes the conversion to the boy's failure to reach a healthy psychological distance from his twin (*Power and Women's Writing in Chile*, 66). This study interprets the change as a subversive strategy to defy patriarchal convention.

31. Garber, *Vested Interests: Cross-Dressing and Cultural Anxiety*, 16.

32. Ibid.

33. Ibid., 11.

34. Richard, *Masculino/femenino*, 65.

35. Ibid.

36. Lagos, "Reflexiones," 135–36. As will be discussed in chapter 6, Eltit develops the "gaze" in *Los vigilantes*, a title suggestive of the novel's central theme.

37. *The American Heritage Dictionary of the English Language*, 3d ed., s.v. "fissure."

38. Julio Ortega reads the change from a male to female narrator in the second part of the novel as a way for the sister to manifest and expiate her guilt through a language of hysteria reflected in the hallucinations of incest ("Diamela Eltit y el imaginario de la virtualidad," 77–78). That interpretation is rejected here because it suggests a patriarchal perspective that traditionally has burdened women with guilt and has judged them as hysterics.

39. Lemaire, *Jacques Lacan*, 7.

40. Ibid., 83.

41. Ibid.

42. María Inés Lagos observes that this character's conventionally linear and logocentric narration identifies him as masculine, but his critical point of view regarding the parental relationship betrays his gender ambiguity ("Reflexiones," 130).

43. Eltit, "Palabra de mujer," 27.

44. Eltit, "Las aristas del congreso," 18–19.

45. Eltit, "Errante, errática," 24.

46. Ibid., 23–24.

47. Bassnett, "Coming Out of the Labyrinth: Women Writers in Contemporary Latin America," 249.

48. Ibid.

49. Ibid., 249–50.

50. Jameson, "Imaginary and Symbolic in Lacan," 384.

51. Eltit first incorporated her proper name in *E. Luminata*: "Her soul is not being called diamela eltit/ white sheets/ cadaver" (90).

52. Ortega, "Resistencia y sujeto femenino," 235, and Williams, "Truth Claims," 7.

53. Eltit, "Errante, errática," 24.

54. See *Christopher Unborn*, pages 82–87, 143–44.

55. A succinct differentiation would be that while colonialism "involves direct military, economic, and political control," imperialism describes "any relationship of dominance and subordination between nations, including the modern form of economic control" (Chaudhuri and Strobel, *Western Women and Imperialism: Complicity and Resistance*, 2).

56. My translation. Guzman, "La categoría blanco/no blanco," 61.

57. Ibid.

58. I consider "salvajemente" a key term in Eltit's text—"Estamos salvajemente preparados para la extinción" (101). In my view, Gerdes's translation—"We are fiercely prepared for extinction" (87)—does not trigger an association with "savage."

59. See pages 75, 85, 101 of the novel.

60. See page 75 of the novel.

61. See pages 72, 75, 94 of the novel.

62. Brito, "El doble relato en la novela *Por la patria*, 257.

63. García Corales, *Relaciones de poder y carnavalización en la novela chilena contemporánea*, 83–84.

64. Eltit's original text reads: "Todas mis voces me ordenan profundizar el descontento. *Este descontento sudaca, rojo y ávido de sangre*" (emphasis added, *El cuarto mundo*, 94). I have used my own translation to convey the second sentence instead of Gerdes's version which reads: "The voices inside me are telling me to sharpen our discontent, *make it the sudaca type, red and avaricious like blood*" (emphasis added, *The Fourth World*, 80).

65. For U.S. involvement in Chile see discussions by James F. Petras and Robert LaPorte, Jr. ("Chile: No"), Volodia Teitelboim (Chile, laboratorio de tres experimentos, 20 años) and U.S. Senate, *Hearings before the Select Committee to Study Governmental Operations with Respect to Intelligence Activities*.

66. Muñoz, "Chile: The Limits of 'Success,' " 161.

67. Petras and LaPorte, "Chile: No," 14.

68. Ibid., 12.

69. See also Petras and LaPorte for a similar case in Peru: "After the Velasco government nationalized the International Petroleum Company, U.S. aid dropped from $60 million to $9 million in 1969, causing the Peruvian President to accuse the Inter-American Development Bank 'of being used as a weapon of political pressure' " ("Chile: No," 18).

70. Ibid., 19.

71. Ibid., 22–23.

72. In the case of Chile, Petras and LaPorte document the pressures that were

put on Peru, Brazil, and Argentina by the United States in order to isolate the Allende government ("Chile: No," 13).

73. Williams, "Truth Claims," 7.

74. I have employed my own translation of Eltit's text: "Quiero hacer una obra sudaca terrible y molesta" (*El cuarto mundo*, 88) instead of Gerdes's version: "I want to create a creature that is terribly and scandalously sudaca" (*The Fourth World*, 74).

75. *The American Heritage Dictionary of the English Language*, 3d ed., s. v. "terrible."

76. For a discussion of the narrator/text relationship see Georgina García-Gutiérrez, "*Cristóbal Nonato*: profecía apocalíptica, experimentación lúdica, crítica certera;" Julio Ortega, "*Christopher Unborn*: Rage and Laughter;" Leticia Reyes-Tatinclaux, "*Cristóbal Nonato*, ¿descubrimiento o clausura del nuevo mundo?"

77. Charlotte Seymour-Smith, *Dictionary of Anthropology* (Boston: G. K. Hall, 1986), s. v. "Fourth World."

78. *The New Columbia Encyclopedia*, 4th ed., s. v. "Third World."

79. Bassnett, "Coming Out of the Labyrinth," 251.

80. Eltit, "Las aristas del congreso," 19.

CHAPTER 5. *Vaca sagrada*

1. Eltit, "El color de la infertilidad," interview by Roberto García Bonilla, 7.

2. Eltit, "Diamela Eltit en rebeldía," interview by Faride Zerán, 5.

3. Magali Cornier Michael, *Feminism and the Postmodern Impulse: Post–World War II Fiction*, 5.

4. For a history of the development of "hypertext" see Stuart Moulthrop, "You Say You Want a Revolution: Hypertext and the Laws of Media."

5. Deborah L. Madsen and Mark S. Madsen, "Hypertext and the Demise of Metanarrative," 143.

6. Moulthrop, "You Say You Want a Revolution," 72, 76.

7. Madsen and Madsen, "Hypertext and the Demise of Metanarrative," 143–44.

8. Graff, *Literature Against Itself: Literary Ideas in Modern Society*, 32.

9. Ibid., 33.

10. Hassan, *The Postmodern Turn: Essays in Postmodern Theory and Culture*, 168.

11. Thomas Docherty, "Postmodern Characterization: The Ethics of Alterity," 181.

12. Eltit, *Sacred Cow*, 30.

13. Emphasis mine, ibid., 47–48.

14. Ibid., 18, 41.

15. Docherty, "Postmodern Characterization," 173.

16. Ibid.

17. Graff, *Literature Against Itself*, 53.

18. See Eltit, *Sacred Cow*, pages 95 and 24 respectively.

19. Bertens, "The Postmodern 'Weltanschauung' and its Relation to Modernism: An Introductory Survey," 65.

20. Sarah Lauzen, "Notes on Metafiction: Every Essay Has a Title," 98–99.

21. My translation, Garabano, "Vaca sagrada de Diamela Eltit: del cuerpo femenino al cuerpo de la historia," 121.

22. According to *The New Shorter Oxford English Dictionary* (1993 ed.) "aporia"

comes from the Greek "aporos," meaning impassable; the expression of doubt; a perplexing difficulty.

23. At this point in the narrative the English translation may lead to an erroneous interpretation of more than one assailant. " 'How could *they* have left the door open?' " asks the narrator/protagonist to herself upon arriving at Francisca's place (emphasis mine, 12). The Spanish version clearly implies only one person: "Pero, como *pudo* dejar la puerta abierta? (emphasis mine, 35). Given the political indicators in the novel and the fact that the assault takes place at night, the English translation's third person plural could lead a reader to think that Francisca's beating was a result of a paramilitary raid.

24. Garabano, "Vaca sagrada de Diamela Eltit," 121, 124.

25. Hassan, *The Postmodern Turn*, 169.

26. Eltit, "Diamela Eltit en rebeldía," interview by Faride Zerán, 5.

27. Judith Butler, *Gender Trouble: Feminism and the Subversion of Identity*, 3.

28. Ibid., 1.

29. Brownmiller, *Femininity*, 194.

30. Grosz, *Volatile Bodies: Toward a Corporeal Feminism*, 203.

31. Piña, *Conversaciones*, 249–50.

32. Labanyi, "Topologies of Catastrophe: Horror and Abjection in Diamela Eltit's *Vaca sagrada*," 86.

33. Thomson, *Studies in Ancient Greek Society*, 205.

34. The word taboo may be rooted in the Polynesian term for menstruation: tupua. See Janice Delaney, Mary Jane Lupton, and Emily Toth, *The Curse: A Cultural History of Menstruation*, 3.

35. Labanyi, "Topologies of Catastrophe," 95.

36. Ibid., 96.

37. Eltit, "Las aristas del congreso," 19.

38. I have taken the liberty of writing "die by the hundreds" instead of the translator's phrase "die in their hundreds" (*Sacred Cow*, 22).

39. For further discussion of menstruating women's social exclusion see Thomas Buckley and Alma Gottlieb, *Blood Magic: The Anthropology of Menstruation*; Chris Knight, *Blood Relations: Menstruation and the Origins of Culture*; Janice Delaney, Mary Jane Lupton, and Emily Toth, *The Curse: A Cultural History of Menstruation*.

40. Munizaga and Ochsenius, "El discurso público de Pinochet (1973–1976)," 78.

41. Leviticus 15:19.

42. Delaney, Lupton, and Toth, " 'Not Tonight, Dear': Taboos of Sex," 23.

43. Leviticus, 18:19.

44. Ibid., 20:18.

45. Lipman-Blumen, *Gender Roles and Power*, 69.

46. Ibid., 86.

47. Vidal, "La Declaración de Principios de la Junta Militar Chilena como sistema literario: La lucha antifacista y el cuerpo humano," 44.

48. Ibid., 45.

49. Munizaga and Ochsenius observed that in General Pinochet's speeches women were described, among other things, as honest, diligent, defenders and transmitters of spiritual values, depositories of traditions, abnegated, sacrificing, the foundation of the family, and God-loving beings whose principal task is to "educate" in the home the "future of Chile" (Munizaga and Ochsenius, "El discurso público de Pinochet," 74).

50. Griffin, *Pornography and Silence*, 27.

51. Isabel Allende, *The House of the Spirits* (New York: Alfred A. Knopf, 1985), 274–75.

52. Literally translated as "The Rules of the Game," it is an appropriate and clever title considering the pun with "regla," in Spanish meaning rule and also menstrual period.

53. Grosz, *Volatile Bodies*, 196.

54. Ibid., 202.

55. Ibid., 205.

56. Eltit, *Sacred Cow*, 43.

57. Ibid., 44–45.

58. Valdés, *Tejas Verdes: Diario de un campo de concentración en Chile*, 10.

59. Sontag, *AIDS and Its Metaphors*, 38.

60. Eltit, "El cuerpo femenino es un territorio moral," interview by Ana María Larraín, 1.

61. Sontag, *AIDS and Its Metaphors*, 24–25.

62. Ibid., 25.

63. Graciela Biagini and María del Carmen Sánchez, *Actores Sociales y SIDA: Nuevos movimientos sociales? Nuevos agentes de salud?*, 46.

64. Eltit, "L. Iluminada en sus ficciones: Conversación con Diamela Eltit," interview by Fernando Burgos and M. J. Fenwick, 356–57.

65. A survey that focused on the means of AIDS virus transmission in the various geographic regions of Latin America, including the Andean area, the Southern Cone countries, Central America, the Caribbean, and Mexico, shows an increase of infection in the heterosexual population of all these areas and consequently the cases of HIV infected children is on the rise (Biagini and Sánchez, *Actores Sociales y SIDA*, 44).

66. Ibid., 36.

67. My translation from an excerpt of the testimony of "Ariel," patient at CEPSS (Centro de Educación y Prevención en Salud Social y SIDA) and reproduced in Christian Rodríguez, "El SIDA y sus políticas," interviewed by Revista de Crítica Cultura, 58.

68. Raquel Olea, "El cuerpo-mujer. Un recorte de lectura en la narrativa de Diamela Eltit," 94.

69. "Public Health or Church Morality," *The Economist*, 10 May 1997: 42, 44.

70. Joan M. Herold, María Solange Valenzuela, and Leo Morris, "Premarital Sexual Activity and Contraceptive Use in Santiago, Chile," 134–35.

71. Marcial Godoy, "El SIDA y sus políticas," 56.

72. For a brief report on the incident see "Public Health or Church Morality," *The Economist*, 10 May 1997: 42, 44. Details of the stages of the AIDS campaigns in Chile, which actually began in November 1991, and the full scope of the 1997 scandal, can be read via the electronic back files [http://www.copesa.cl/Casos/Sida/] of the news service COPESA (Consorcio Periodístico de Chile, S.A.) which provides summaries from three main Chilean newspapers.

73. See "Public Health or Church Morality," *The Economist*, 10 May 1997: 42. Also see "Premarital Sexual Activity and Contraceptive Use in Santiago, Chile" (*Studies in Family Planning*, March–April, 1992: 128–36) where Joan M. Herold, María Solange Valenzuela, and Leo Morris address a prior survey conducted among men and women aged 15–24 which concluded that in the capital "70 percent of first births were premaritally conceived, and more than one-third of these were born prior to union. The high rates of premarital and unintended pregnancy among young women and the low prevalence of effective contraceptive use indicate

a need for greater emphasis on sex education and family planning services directed at adolescents and unmarried young adults in Santiago" (page 128). Although as that study suggests, many couples marry as a result of an unplanned pregnancy, another source cites an even higher rate of children born out-of-wedlock. According to Guadalupe Santa Cruz, in 1990 it was estimated that 44.6 percent of children in Chile were born illegitimately. In other words, almost half of Chilean women initiate their maternity as single mothers ("Familia: Modelos y relaciones de poder," 120–21).

74. For the polemic surrounding the program see "Las Jocas que vienen" in the education section of *El Mercurio* (Santiago), Sunday, 27 July 1997: D12–13.

75. See Joan M. Herold, María Solange Valenzuela, and Leo Morris, "Premarital Sexual Activity and Contraceptive Use in Santiago, Chile," 128–36.

76. This is, for example, the case with divorce, which officially does not exist in Chile. However, everyone knows this is a farce since annulments are regularly granted to people married for years who have children. All a couple has to do is appear in court and state that one of them did not live in the district where the marriage license was originally registered (author's conversation with Eltit, July 1995).

77. Prior to the novel's publication this chapter appeared as the short-story "Diez noches de Francisca Lombardo" in the anthology *El muro y la intemperie: El nuevo cuento latinoamericano*, edited by Julio Ortega (Ediciones del Norte, 1989).

78. See Eltit, *Sacred Cow*, 51–52.

79. In her study of pornography, Susan Griffin remarks that in the pornographic mind "the bestiality of a man's nature is expressed in a woman's body," hence depictions of lust often feature women as beasts themselves or engaging in acts of perversion with animals (*Pornography and Silence*, 24–25).

80. See Eltit, *Sacred Cow*, 61.

81. Mathew 5:30.

82. Ibid., 5:29.

83. The biblical story of Samson and Delilah also involves heterosexual relations and the blinding of one of the partners—in this case the Philistines seize the head-shaven Samson and gouge out his eyes (Judges 16:21). Jo Labanyi also explores this motif of blindness from a psychoanalytic Freudian perspective and its connection to political terror in the novel ("Topologies of Catastrophe," 87, 94).

84. See Eltit, *Sacred Cow*, 49, 53, 55, 57, 61, 63. A more precise translation of "el pájaro negro me voló un ojo" (*Vaca sagrada*, 117) would be "the black bird blew out one of my eyes."

85. Labanyi, "Topologies of Catastrophe," 94.

86. Eltit, "L. Iluminada en sus ficciones," interview by Fernando Burgos and M. J. Fenwick, 356.

87. Piña, *Conversaciones*, 250.

88. This also holds true for the other Southern Cone countries, Argentina and Uruguay. Curiously, in the Spanish Caribbean "bird" in reference to men connotes homosexuality.

89. See Eltit, *Sacred Cow*, 47–53, 55, 57–59, 61.

90. Labanyi, "Topologies of Catastrophe," 100.

CHAPTER 6. THE CONTROLLING GAZE IN *LOS VIGILANTES*

1. See endnote 22 of chapter 4, *"El cuarto mundo:* A Dialogue in Gender Differences," for an explanation of "machismo" and "marianismo." In "Surviving Beyond

Fear: Women and Torture in Latin America," Ximena Bunster-Burotto discusses the many ways in which repressive states have drawn from cultural tenets to violate the sanctity of the home and women's conception of self. Raiding homes at night, enacting family torture, and physically violating women in front of family members or a statue of the Virgin have been common forms of punishment for those suspected of political subversion (304–12).

2. Besides similarities such as the interior monologue of a retarded male child and the themes of hunger and poverty, both protagonists make revelations about breast-feeding from a guardian figure. According to Macario's ponderings, "Felipa's milk is as sweet as hibiscus flowers. . . . Now it's been a long time since she has let me nurse the breasts that she has where we just have ribs, and where there comes outs, if you know how to get it, a better milk than the one Godmother gives us for lunch on Sundays" (Rulfo, *The Burning Plain, and Other Stories,* 4–5). From Eltit's protagonist the reader learns that "En extrañas oportunidades ella me da unas escasas gotas de leche. La leche de mamá es el contenido que ella esconde con sigilo. . . . Mamá conserva a través de los años un poquito de leche y la controla para que no se le acabe" (*Los vigilantes,* 20). [On rare opportunities she gives me some drops of milk. Mom's milk is the substance that she hides with discretion. . . . Over the years mom preserves a little milk and controls it in order not to run out].

3. *Webster's Ninth New Collegiate Dictionary,* s.v. "vigilante."

4. Thelma Jean Goodrich, *Women and Power: Perspective for Family Therapy,* 240.

5. In this regard the topic is consistent with Eltit's concern with social issues. The Instituto Interamericano del Niño (IIN) reported in 1995 that out of the more than 197 million children living in Latin America, 15 million lived in the streets, 6 million suffered malnutrition, and 30 million worked with no protection under the law. Moreover, of those living in homes, 60 percent lived in households with incomes under the poverty level (*Diario las Américas,* 29 June 1995).

6. In Latin America other factors besides marital conflict and divorce catapult women into head-of-the-household roles. Let us keep in mind that military regimes such as those of the Southern Cone in the 1970s and 1980s instituted disappearances and forced exile that mainly affected men. War in Nicaragua and El Salvador left many widows and orphans. Immigration has also claimed mostly male victims; we need only think of those who attempt to illegally cross the Mexican/U.S. border.

7. See M. E. Hawkesworth, *Beyond Oppression: Feminist Theory and Political Strategy,* 56; Paul W. Drake and Iván Jaksic, *The Struggle for Democracy in Chile, 1982–1990,* 168; Diane M. Schaffer, "The Feminization of Poverty: Prospects for an International Feminist Agenda," 223.

8. Okin, *Justice, Gender, and the Family,* 134.

9. Ibid., 139.

10. For an examination of how women across Latin America have empowered themselves despite economic adversity see: Elizabeth Jelin, ed., *Women and Social Change in Latin America* (London: Zed, 1990), and Alejandra Massolo, ed., *Mujeres y ciudades: Participación social, vivienda y vida cotidiana* (Mexico City: Colegio de México, 1992).

11. Poniatowska's book is based on the life of Russian émigré painter Angelina Beloff, who lived in Paris early in the twentieth century. There she met Mexican muralist Diego Rivera with whom she lived for ten years. They had a son, Dieguito, who died in infancy in 1917. In 1921, Rivera returned to Mexico and Beloff remained in Paris. The book is a compilation of the letters that Poniatowska imagined Beloff wrote to Rivera for years after his departure.

12. Lenore J. Weitzman, *The Divorce Revolution: The Unexpected Social and Economic Consequences for Women and Children in America,* 323.

13. Goodrich, *Women and Power*, 27.

14. Ibid., 9.

15. Foucault, *Discipline and Punish: The Birth of the Prison*, 201.

16. From Lacan, *Ecrits*, "On a Question Preliminary to any Possible Treatment of Psychosis."

17. Ferré, *Papeles de Pandora* [*Pandora's Papers*].

18. Lerner, "The Taboos Against Female Anger," 6.

19. French, *Beyond Power: On Women, Men, and Morals*, 348.

20. *Webster's Third New International Dictionary* (Springfield: Merriam, 1993).

21. Ibid. Jean Franco has also observed the male figure in the novel as "a more abstract entity—the name-of-the-father, or the divine" ("Afterword: From Romance to Refractory Aesthetic," 234).

22. Lipman-Blumen, *Gender Roles and Power*, 4–5.

23. Janeway, *Powers of the Weak*, 4.

24. Lipman-Blumen, *Gender Roles and Power*, 6.

25. Lips, *Women, Men, and Power*, 14.

26. Marilyn French clarifies that "Authoritarian regimes permit more 'freedom' than totalitarian states in two major areas: they give a free hand to business interests (which is why they are acceptable to the United States) and they allow emigration. But they lack even the semblance of concern for social justice and equality . . ." (*Beyond Power: On Women, Men, and Morals*, 345). Regarding the distinction, John Kenneth Galbraith notes that while authoritarian rule (like that of some South American, African, or Asian dictators) relies heavily on coercion for law enforcement, totalitarian regimes (such as in Communist countries) adopt a comprehensive use of coercion, compensatory, and conditioned power (*The Anatomy of Power*, 36–37). Coercion as an instrument of power uses persuasion with the implicit or explicit promise of punishment for nonconformity. Compensatory power relies on rewarding submission of one's will to another's. Conditioned power resembles indoctrination in that its exercise seems so natural that those involved may not always be aware that it is being exerted (Galbraith, *The Anatomy of Power*, 24). For example, in relationships between parents and children, husbands and wives, the church and its congregation, tradition dictated that one party wield authority while the other obey it.

27. My translation. Patricia Verdugo, *Caso Arellano: Los zarpazos del puma*, 41.

28. The topic of surveillance and the fear it spawned endured in the 1990s narratives of Chilean writers such as Pía Barros (*Astride*, 1992) and Guadalupe Santa Cruz (*Cita Capital*, 1992). Also, two Latina writers, Cuban-American Cristina García (*Dreaming in Cuban*, 1992) and Dominican-American Julia Alvarez (*In the Times of the Butterflies*, 1994) inscribe spying as a way of life in Cuba and the Dominican Republic under the Castro and Trujillo regimes, respectively. In fact, García's novel opens with a citizen on surveillance duty.

29. Gloria Bonder cites the eight years of military dictatorship and its devastating effects on Argentine society. However, this is not an isolated period in the country's history. Bonder also points out that from 1955 to 1983, Argentina had known only three constitutional governments, "all interrupted by military coups" ("Women's Organisations in Argentina's Transition to Democracy," 65).

30. Louise Lamphere, "Strategies, Cooperation, and Conflict Among Women in Domestic Groups," 99.

31. Lips, *Women, Men, and Power*, 115.

32. *Webster's Third New International Dictionary*, s.v. "personality."

33. In Mexico, ten years after the October 1968 clash between police and stu-

dent protestors at the Plaza de las Tres Culturas in Mexico City, mothers still organized to denounce the disappearance of student activists. The student massacre on the eve of the 1968 Olympics prompted Mexican journalist and writer Elena Poniatowska to record the bloodbath in *La noche de Tlatelolco: testimonios de historia oral* (1971)/*Massacre in Mexico* (1991). In 1980, Poniatowska published *Fuerte es el silencio* where she records how mothers organized around the issue of disappearance.

The organization—CO-MADRES—of El Salvador also began in the late 1970s as a small group of mothers searching for their imprisoned, disappeared, and assassinated relatives. (Lynn Stephen has translated and edited *Hear my Testimony: María Teresa Tula, Human Rights Activist of El Salvador* that portrays one member's life and her work in CO-MADRES.) Similarly to the international attention achieved by the Mothers of Plaza de Mayo, CO-MADRES activists, working to denounce human rights violations in wartorn El Salvador, transmitted their appeal in neighboring countries, the United States, and Europe.

34. Arpillera actually means burlap, the (only affordable) material onto which women stitched their personal stories of disappearance. See Marjorie Agosin, *Scraps of Life: Chilean arpilleras: Chilean Women and the Penschet Dictatorship.*

35. Janeway, *Powers of the Weak*, 161, 202.

36. Ibid., 169–74, 208.

37. Ibid., 217.

38. Ibid., 205.

39. Exploitation specifically directed at females by repressive states is also captured in novels not pertaining to the Southern Cone. Julia Alvarez's *In the Time of the Butterflies* (1994) fictionalizes the true story of four sisters who opposed the Trujillo family dictatorship of the 1930s–50s in her native Dominican Republic. In the novel, Alvarez depicts the ways in which sexual seduction and corporal torment were used to convince women to cooperate with the tyrant's wishes.

40. Traba, *Mothers and Shadows*, 48.

41. During Pinochet's regime in Chile, for example, police would stop women in the street who wore pants and cut their pant legs at the knee because proper ladies were not supposed to wear trousers in public.

42. Valenzuela, *Other Weapons*, 115–17.

43. Janeway, *Powers of the Weak*, 205.

44. In the second half of the twentieth century the United States carried out interventions in several Latin American countries—Guatemala (1954), Cuba (1961), the Dominican Republic (1965), Grenada (1983), Panama (1989), and Haiti (1994). Also, throughout the 1980s the United States was a presence in the Central American countries of El Salvador, Honduras, and Nicaragua (John D. Martz, *United States Policy in Latin America: A Decade of Crisis and Challenge*, 9–10, 84, 190, 193–201).

45. The published *Hearings Before the Select Committee to Study Governmental Operations With Respect to Intelligence Activities of the United States Senate* records the "involvement of the United States in covert activities in Chile from 1963 through 1973" (vol. 7, page 1). The committee's publication indicates that "covert action techniques that have been used by the U.S. Government since the end of World War II. . . . range from relatively passive actions, such as passing money to shape the outcome of elections, to the influencing of men's minds through propaganda and 'misinformation' placed in the media of other nations, to the more aggressive and belligerent techniques of organizing coup d'etat and engaging in paramilitary warfare" (*Hearings*, vol. 7, page 4).

46. Teitelboim, "Chile, laboratorio de tres experimentos (20 años)," 44. For

U.S. involvement see also IT & T records. Memos dating from 1970 indicate how U.S. corporations collaborated in the covert operation to keep Allende from the presidency: "Some business sectors are encouraging economic collapse, hoping this eventually will necessitate a military take-over. . . . Under cover efforts are being made to bring about the bankruptcy of one or two of the major savings and loan associations. This is expected to trigger a run on banks and the closure of some factories resulting in more unemployment. . . . [M]assive unemployment and unrest might produce enough violence to force the military to move" ("Subversion in Chile: The Complete Set of IT & T Memos," 3 [Under Heading: *Economic Pressures*]. (Distributed by: Non-Intervention in Chile [NICH], 731 State St., Madison, Wisconsin 53703).

From the standpoint of U.S. companies with heavy investments in Chile, the threat of Allende assuming power and nationalizing foreign businesses warranted pressuring the State Department to act on their behalf. In an interoffice memorandum one top IT & T official states: "I look for the silent pressure (?) which will call for a drying-up of aid and instructions to U.S. representatives in the international banks to vote against or abstain from voting on Chilean loans" ("Subversion in Chile: The Complete Set of IT & T Memos, memo dated 30 September 1970, from: J. D. Neal, to: Mr. W. R. Merriam).

47. Fear of communism stemmed from the fact that "Allende's platform included nationalization of the copper mines, accelerated agrarian reform, socialization of major sectors of the economy, wage increases, and improved relations with socialist and communist countries" (United States. Senate. *Hearings*, vol. 7, page 167). IT & T memos record the anxiety running through the foreign business community: "There is no doubt among trained professional observers with experience in the U.S., Europe and Latin America that if Allende and the UP take power, Chile will be transformed quickly into a harsh and tightly-controlled Communist state, like Cuba or Czechoslovakia today" ("Subversion in Chile: The Complete Set of IT & T Memos," page 4 of memo dated 17 September 1970 from: H. Hendrix/R. Berrellez, to: E. J. Gerrity).

In 1970 the likelihood that Allende would win presidential elections became alarming for the United States. That year "the 40 Committee* decided that the United States should not support any single candidate in the election but should instead wage 'spoiling' operations against the Popular Unity coalition which supported the Marxist candidate Salvador Allende" (*Hearings*, vol. 7, pages 166–67). Independent corporations like ITT, however—not bound to adhere to U.S. "official" policy—disbursed money to support non-Marxist candidates (*Hearings*, vol. 7, page 168).
    * "The 40 Committee is a sub-Cabinet level body of the Executive Branch whose mandate is to review proposed major covert actions" (*Hearings*, vol. 7, page 149).

48. Teitelboim, "Chile, laboratorio de tres experimentos (20 años)," 34.

49. Ibid., 36.

50. The United States Senate *Hearings* report on Chile documents the "scare campaign" launched by the U.S. government that "equated an Allende victory with violence and Stalinist repression" (vol. 7, page 168). This "spoiling" strategy was carried out as an "intensive propaganda campaign which made use of virtually all media within Chile and which placed and replayed items in the international press as well" (*Hearings*, vol. 7, page 168).

51. Among Latin American women writers, Venezuelan Teresa de la Parra exemplifies how women's writing often reinforced traditional female roles (*Ifigenia: diario de una señorita que escribió porque se fastidiaba*, 1924) and continued the practice

of an epistolary tradition (*Cartas*, 1951; *Epistolario íntimo*, 1953; *Cartas a Rafael Carías*, 1957).

52. Walker, *The Disobedient Writer: Women and Narrative Tradition*, 1–3.

53. This was the case for Patricia Vilches who recalls that editors, when rejecting her manuscript of *Karma desde el mar* (1992), commented that her style did not adhere to writing norms in Chile.

54. Walker, *The Disobedient Writer: Women and Narrative Tradition*, 6.

55. My emphasis.

EPILOGUE

1. There is much information being brought to light about the Pinochet era. During his administration President Clinton launched a project to declassify American records relating to abuses in Chile during those years. So far thousands of records have been released and are available on the Internet on the Freedom Of Information Act site (*http://foia.state.gov/*). For a capsulized account of the type of information contained in the government files see Diana Jean Schemo's article, "There's Still a Lot to Learn About the Pinochet Years" (*New York Times*, The World, 5 March 2000, 3).

2. Pinochet returned to Chile on 3 March 2000. After sixteen months of house arrest, Britain dropped extradition proceedings against him on the grounds that he was too ill to stand trial. (For public reaction see: Clifford Krauss, "Pinochet Receives Hero's Welcome on Return to Chile: But the Country Displays Its Lingering Divisions in Demonstrations on Santiago's Streets," *New York Times*, International, 4 March 2000, A3).

3. Some have not lost hope that justice will prevail despite the unfruitful attempt to try the former dictator abroad. Indeed, "Pinochet's immunity is under fire in Chile" (*Atlanta Journal-Constitution*, World, 7 March 2000, A4). Apparently while the former dictator was out of the country "a previously obscure appeals court judge in Santiago, Juan Guzmán Tapia . . . came up with an inventive legal interpretation that has jolted the military's impunity, opened the way for the arrests of 40 former military and police officers and forced the military to begin a dialogue with rights lawyers. . . . Judge Guzmán pushed ahead with the unthinkable: prosecuting General Pinochet himself" (Clifford Krauss, "Pinochet, at Home in Chile: a Real Nowhere Man, *New York Times*, International, 5 March 2000, 8). Consequently, on 8 August 2000, Chile's Supreme Court stripped General Pinochet of his senatorial immunity from prosecution, clearing the way for a possible arrest and trial ("Court in Chile Opens Door for Trial of Pinochet," *Atlanta Journal-Constitution*, 9 August 2000, A9).

4. My emphasis.

5. Genesis 1:3.

6. John 1:1.

CONCLUSION

1. Robert Neustadt, *(Con)Fusing Signs and Postmodern Positions: Spanish American Performance, Experimental Writing, and the Critique of Political Confusion*, 57.

2. My translation: Juan Carlos Lértora, *Una poética de literatura menor: La narrativa de Diamela Eltit*, 34.

Bibliography

Agosín, Marjorie, ed. *Landscapes of a New Land: Fiction by Latin American Women.* New York: White Pine Press, 1989.

———. *Scraps of Life: Chilean Arpilleras: Chilean Women and the Pinochet Dictatorship.* Translated by Cola Franzen. Trenton, NJ: Red Sea Press, 1987.

Allende, Isabel. *The House of the Spirits.* Translated by Magda Bogin. New York: Alfred A. Knopf, 1985. Originally published as *La casa de los espíritus* (Barcelona: Plaza & Janés, 1982).

———. *Paula.* Translated by Margaret Sayers Peden. New York: HarperCollins, 1995. Originally published as *Paula* (Madrid: Plaza & Janés, 1994).

Alvarez, Julia. *In the Time of the Butterflies.* Chapel Hill, N.C.: Algonquin, 1994.

Angel, Albalucía. *Misiá señora.* Barcelona: Argos Vergara, 1982.

———. *Las andariegas.* Barcelona: Argos Vergara, 1984.

Arce, Luz. *El infierno.* Santiago, Chile: Planeta, 1992.

Arrate P., Marina. "Los significados de la escritura y su relación con la identidad femenina latinoamericana en *Por la patria,* de Diamela Eltit." In *Una poética de literatura menor: La narrativa de Diamela Eltit.* Edited by Juan Carlos Lértora, 141–54. Santiago, Chile: Cuarto Propio, 1993.

Bacigalupo, Ana Mariella. "El poder de las mujeres machis en los valles centrales de la Araucania." In *Comprensión del pensamiento indígena a través de sus expresiones verbales: XIII Congreso Internacional de Ciencias Antropológicas y Etnológicas (Simposio, México).* Edited by Yosuke Kuramochi, 11–55. Quito, Ecuador: Ediciones ABYA-YALA, 1994.

Baker Miller, Jean. *Toward a New Psychology of Women.* 2d ed. Boston: Beacon, 1986.

Barros, Pía. *Astride/A horcajadas.* Santiago, Chile: Editorial Asterión, 1992.

Barthes, Roland. *Image, Music, Text.* New York: Hill and Wang, 1977.

Bassnett, Susan. "Coming Out of the Labyrinth: Women Writers in Contemporary Latin America." In *On Modern Latin American Fiction.* Edited by John King, 247–67. New York: Hill and Wang, 1987.

Bertens, Hans. "The Postmodern 'Weltanschauung' and its Relation to Modernism: An Introductory Survey." In *A Postmodern Reader.* Edited by Joseph Natoli and Linda Hutcheon, 25–70. Albany: State University of New York Press, 1993.

Beverley, John. "The Margin at the Center: On Testimonio (Testimonial Narrative)." In *De/Colonizing the Subject.* Edited by Sidonie Smith and Julia Watson, 91–114. Minneapolis: University of Minnesota Press, 1992.

Biagini, Graciela, and María del Carmen Sánchez. *Actores Sociales y SIDA: Nuevos movimientos sociales? Nuevos agentes de salud?* Buenos Aires: Espacio, 1995.

Biallas, Leonard J. *Myths: Gods, Heroes, and Saviors.* Mystic, Conn.: Twenty-Third Publications, 1989.

245

Bombal, María Luisa. *The Shrouded Woman.* New York: Farrar, Straus, 1948. Originally published as *La amortajada* (Buenos Aires: Sur, 1938).

Bonder, Gloria. "Women's Organisations in Argentina's Transition to Democracy." In *Women and Counter-Power.* Edited by Yolande Cohen, 65–85. Montreal: Black Rose, 1989.

Bouchard, Donald F., ed. *Michel Foucault: Language, Counter-Memory, Practice.* Translated by Donald F. Bouchard and Sherry Simon. Ithaca: Cornell University Press, 1977.

Brito, Eugenia. "El doble relato en la novela *Por la patria,* de Diamela Eltit." In *Escribir en los bordes: congreso internacional de literatura femenina latinoamericana 1987.* Edited by Carmen Berenguer, Eugenia Brito, Diamela Eltit, Raquel Olea, Eliana Ortega, and Nelly Richard, 243–58. Santiago, Chile: Cuarto Propio, 1990.

Brownmiller, Susan. *Femininity.* New York: Fawcett Columbine, 1984.

Buckley, Thomas, and Alma Gottlieb. *Blood Magic: The Anthropology of Menstruation.* Berkeley: University of California Press, 1988.

Bulman, Gail A. "Neo-Baroque Reflections on the Extra-Textual and Intra-Textual Constructions of Violent Space in Three Women Writers From the Southern Cone." Ph.D. diss., Syracuse University, 1995.

Bunster-Burotto, Ximena. "Surviving Beyond Fear: Women and Torture in Latin America." In *Women and Change in Latin America.* Edited by June Nash and Helen I. Safa, 297–325. Massachusetts: Bergin & Garvey, 1986.

Bushnell, John. *Moscow Graffiti: Language and Subculture.* Boston: Unwin Hyman, 1990.

Butler, Judith. *Gender Trouble: Feminism and the Subversion of Identity.* New York: Routledge, 1990.

Calabrese, Omar. *Neo-Baroque: A Sign of the Times.* Princeton: Princeton University Press, 1992.

Campos, Julieta. *The Fear of Losing Eurydice.* Translated by Leland H. Chambers. Normal, Ill.: Dalkey Archive, 1993. Originally published as *El miedo de perder a Euridice* (México, D.F.: Joaquin Mortiz, 1979).

Carothers, Thomas. *In the Name of Democracy: U.S. Policy Toward Latin America in the Reagan Years.* Berkeley: University of California Press, 1991.

Castellanos, Rosario. *The Nine Guardians.* Translated by Irene Nicholson. New York: Vanguard, 1960. Originally published as *Balún canán* (México, D.F.: Fondo de Cultura Económica, 1957).

Castleman, Craig. *Getting Up: Subway Graffiti in New York.* Cambridge, Mass.: The MIT Press, 1982.

Castro-Klarén, Sara. *Escritura, transgresión y sujeto en la literatura latinoamericana.* Puebla, México: Premiá, 1989.

———. "Escritura y cuerpo en *Lumpérica.*" In *Una poética de literatura menor: la narrativa de Diamela Eltit.* Edited by Juan Carlos Lértora, 97–110. Santiago, Chile: Cuarto Propio, 1993.

Chaudhuri, Nupur, and Margaret Strobel, eds. *Western Women and Imperialism: Complicity and Resistance.* Bloomington: Indiana University Press, 1992.

Christensen, F. M. *Pornography: The Other Side.* New York: Praeger, 1990.

Cixous, Hélène. "The Laugh of the Medusa." *Signs: Journal of Women in Culture and Society* 1, no. 4 (summer 1976): 875–93.

Consolli, Silla. "El relato del psicótico." In *Loca verdad: Verdad y verosimilitud del texto psicótico, seminario dirigido por Julia Kristeva,* edited by Jean Michel Ribettes. Translated by Martín Caparrós. 49–98. Madrid: Fundamentos, 1985. Originally published as *Folle verité: Verité et vraisemblence du texte psichotiquie* (Editions du Seuil, 1979).

Cornier Michael, Magali. *Feminism and the Postmodern Impulse: Post–World War II Fiction.* New York: State University of New York Press, 1996.

Cypess, Sandra Messinger. *La Malinche in Mexican Literature: From History to Myth.* Austin: University of Texas Press, 1991.

Daly, Mary. *Gyn/Ecology: The Metaethics of Radical Feminism.* Boston: Beacon, 1978.

Daly, Pierrette. *Heroic Tropes: Gender and Intertext.* Detroit: Wayne State University Press, 1993.

Davenport, Guy. *Cities on Hills: A Study of I–XXX of Ezra Pound's Cantos.* Ann Arbor: UMI Research Press, 1983.

Day, Gary. "Looking at Women: Notes Toward a Theory of Porn." In *Perspectives on Pornography: Sexuality in Film and Literature.* Edited by Gary Day and Clive Bloom, 83–100. New York: St. Martin's Press, 1988.

Delaney, Janice, Mary Jane Lupton, and Emily Toth. *The Curse: A Cultural History of Menstruation.* Urbana: University of Illinois Press, 1988.

Docherty, Thomas. "Postmodern Characterization: The Ethics of Alterity." In *Postmodernism and Contemporary Fiction.* Edited by Edmund J. Smyth, 169–88. London: B. T. Batsford, 1991.

Dorfman, Ariel. *Imaginación y Violencia en América.* Barcelona: Anagrama, 1972.

Dorfman, Elsa. "Where Anonymous Was a Woman." *The Women's Review of Books* (January 1996): 17.

Drake, Paul W., and Iván Jaksic, eds. *The Struggle for Democracy in Chile, 1982–1990.* Lincoln: University of Nebraska Press, 1991.

Eagleton, Terry. *Literary Theory: An Introduction.* Minneapolis: University of Minnesota Press, 1983.

Eliade, Mircea. *Myth and Reality.* Translated by Willard R. Trask. New York: Harper and Row, 1963. Translation of *Aspects du mythe* (Paris: Gallimard, 1963).

Eltit, Diamela. *E. Luminata.* Translated by Ronald Christ. Santa Fe, N.M.: Lumens, 1997. Originally published as *Lumpérica* (Santiago, Chile: Las Ediciones del Ornitorrinco, 1983).

———. "Acoplamiento incestuoso." Interviewed by Ana María Foxley. *Hoy,* no. 421 (12–18 August 1985): 41.

———. *Por la patria.* Santiago, Chile: Ornitorrinco, 1986.

———. "Tenemos puesto el espejo para el otro lado." Interview by Claudia Donoso. *APSI* (26 January–8 February 1987): 47–48.

———. "Palabra de mujer." *LAR: Revista de literatura.* Concepción, Chile: 11 (agosto 1987): 27–28.

———. *El Padre Mío.* Santiago: Francisco Zegers, 1989.

———. "El trabajo es la vida y mi vida." Interview by Ana María Larraín. *Revista de Libros de El Mercurio* (21 May 1989): 1, 4–5.

———. "Las aristas del congreso." In *Escribir en los bordes: Congreso Internacional de Literatura Femenina Latinoamericana.* Edited by Carmen Berenguer, et al., 17–19. Santiago, Chile: Cuarto Propio, 1990.

———. "Experiencia literaria y palabra en duelo." In *Duelo y creatividad.* Edited by Eleonora Casaula, Edmundo Covarrubias, and Diamela Eltit, 21–27. Santiago, Chile: Cuarto Propio, 1990.

———. "Resistencia y sujeto femenino: entrevista con Diamela Eltit." Interview by Julio Ortega. *La torre: revista general de la Universidad de Puerto Rico* 4, no. 14 (April–June 1990): 229–41.

———. "En la sexualidad la estamos errando." Interview by Graciela Romero. *Paula* 577 (July 1990): 62–63.

———. "El cuerpo femenino es un territorio moral." Interview by Ana María Larraín. *Revista de libros: El Mercurio*, Santiago, no. 140 (5 January 1992): 1, 4.

———. "Diamela Eltit en rebeldía." Interview by Faride Zerán. *La Epoca*, Supplement (3 May 1992): 4–5.

———. Interview by Sandra Garabano and Guillermo García Corales. *Hispamérica: Revista de literatura* 21, no. 62 (August 1992): 65–75.

———. "Errante, errática." In *Una poética de literatura menor: la narrativa de Diamela Eltit.* Edited by Juan Carlos Lértora, 17–25. Santiago, Chile: Cuarto Mundo, 1993.

———. "El color de la infertilidad." Interview by Roberto García Bonilla. *Los universitarios* 51 (September 1993): 6–9.

———. *Los vigilantes.* Santiago: Sudamericana, 1994.

———. *The Fourth World.* Translated by Dick Gerdes. Lincoln: University of Nebraska Press, 1995. Originally published as *El cuarto mundo* (Santiago, Chile: Planeta, 1988).

———. "L. Iluminada en sus ficciones: Conversación con Diamela Eltit." Interview with Fernando Burgos and M. J. Fenwick. *Inti: Revista de literatura hispánica* 40–41 (fall 1994–spring 1995): 335–66.

———. *Sacred Cow.* Translated by Amanda Hopkins. London: Serpent's Tail, 1995. Originally published as *Vaca sagrada* (Buenos Aires: Planeta, 1991).

———. "Nomadic Bodies." *Review: Latin American Literature and Arts*, no. 54 (spring 1997): 42–50.

———. *Los trabajadores de la muerte.* Santiago: Planeta, 1998.

Eltit, Diamela, and Paz Errázurriz. *El infarto del alma.* Santiago: Francisco Zegers, 1994.

Esquivel, Laura. *Like Water for Chocolate: A Novel in Monthly Installments, with Recipes, Romances, and Home Remedies.* Translated by Carol Christensen and Thomas Christensen. New York: Doubleday, 1992. Originally published as *Como agua para chocolate: Novela de entregas mensuales con recetas, amores y remedios caseros* (México, D.F.: Editorial Planeta, 1989).

Faron, Louis C. *Hawks of the Sun: Mapuche Morality and Its Ritual Attributes.* Pittsburgh: University of Pittsburgh Press, 1964.

———. *The Mapuche Indians of Chile.* New York: Holt, Rinehart and Winston, 1968.

Felman, Shoshana. *Writing and Madness: Literature/Philosophy/Psychanalysis.* Translated by Martha Noel Evans and the author with the assistance of Brian Massumi. Ithaca: Cornell University Press, 1985. Originally published as *La folie et la chose littéraire* (Paris: Seuil, 1978).

———. "Camus' The Plague, or a Monument to Witnessing." In *Testimony: Crisis of Witnessing in Literature, Psychoanalysis, and History*, 93–119. Shoshana Felman and Dori Laub, M.D. New York: Routledge, 1992.

Ferré, Rosario. *Papeles de Pandora.* México: Joaquín Mortiz, 1976.

Fiedler, Leslie. "From Cross the Border—Close the Gap." In *Posmodernism: A Reader.* Edited by Patricia Waugh, 31–48. London: Edward Arnold, 1992.

Forest Lord, George de. *Trials of the Self: Heroic Ordeals in the Epic Tradition.* Hamden, Conn.: Archon, 1983.

Foucault, Michel. *Discipline and Punish: The Birth of the Prison.* Translated by Alan Sheridan. New York: Pantheon, 1977. Originally published as *Surveiller et punir: Naissance de la prison* (Paris: Gallimard, 1975).

Fox, Hugh. *The Mythological Foundations of the Epic Genre: The Solar Voyage as the Hero's Journey.* Lewiston, N.Y.: The Edwin Mellen Press, 1989.

Franco, Jean. "Afterword: From Romance to Refractory Aesthetic." In *Latin American Women's Writing: Feminist Readings in Theory and Crisis.* Edited by Anny Brooksbank Jones and Catherine Davies, 226–37. New York: Oxford University Press, 1996.

Fraser, Nancy, and Linda Nicholson. "Social Criticism without Philosophy: An Encounter between Feminism and Postmodernism." In *Universal Abandon?: The Politics of Postmodernism.* Edited by Andrew Ross, 83–104. Minneapolis: University of Minnesota Press, 1988.

French, Marilyn. *Beyond Power: On Women, Men, and Morals.* New York: Summit, 1985.

Freud, Sigmund. "Fragment of an Analysis of a Case of Hysteria." In *The Standard Edition of the Complete Psychological Works of Sigmund Freud.* 1953. Edited and translated by James Strachey in collaboration with Anna Freud, 15–111. Vol. 7. London: Hogarth Press and the Institute of Psycho-Analysis, 1966.

———. *Three Essays on the Theory of Sexuality.* 1962. Edited and translated by James Strachey. New York: Basic Books, 1975. Originally published as *Drei Abhandlungen zur Sexualtheorie* (Leipzig: F. Deuticke, 1905).

Friday, Nancy. *My Secret Garden: Women's Sexual Fantasies.* New York: Trident Press, 1973.

Fuentes, Carlos. *Christopher Unborn.* Translated by Alfred MacAdam and the author. New York: Farrar, Straus and Giroux, 1989. Originally published as *Cristóbal Nonato* (Mexico: Fondo de Cultura Económica, 1987).

Fullbrook, Kate. "Whose Postmodernism?" In *Postmodern Subjects/Postmodern Texts.* Edited by Jane Dowson and Steven Earnshaw, 71–87. Atlanta, Ga.: Rodopi, 1995.

Galbraith, John Kenneth. *The Anatomy of Power.* Boston: Houghton Mifflin, 1983.

Garabano, Sandra. "Vaca sagrada de Diamela Eltit: del cuerpo femenino al cuerpo de la historia." *Hispamérica: Revista de literatura* 25, no. 73 (April 1996): 121–27.

Garber, Marjorie. *Vested Interests: Cross-Dressing and Cultural Anxiety.* New York: Routledge, 1992.

García, Cristina. *Dreaming in Cuban.* New York: Ballantine, 1992.

García Corales, Guillermo. "La desconstrucción del poder en *Lumpérica.*" In *Una poética de literatura menor: la narrativa de Diamela Eltit.* Edited by Juan Carlos Lértera, 111–25. Santiago, Chile: Cuarto Propio, 1993.

———. *Relaciones de poder y carnavalización en la novela chilena contemporánea.* Santiago, Chile: Asterion, 1995.

García-Gutiérrez, Georgina. "*Cristóbal Nonato:* profecía apocalíptica, experimentación lúdica, crítica certera." In *La obra de Carlos Fuentes: Una visión múltiple.* Edited by Ana María Hernández de López, 277–85. Madrid: Pliegos, 1988.

Garro, Elena. *Recollections of Things to Come.* Translated by Ruth L. C. Simms. Austin:

University of Texas Press, 1969. Originally published as *Los recuerdos del porvenir.* 1963. (México, D.F.: Joaquín Mortiz, 1963).

Geisdorfer Feal, Rosemary. "Spanish American Ethnobiography and the Slave Narrative Tradition: *Biografía de un cimarrón* and *Me llamo Rigoberta Menchú.*" *Modern Language Studies* 20, no. 1 (winter 1990): 100–111.

Gianini Belotti, Elena. *Little Girls: Social Conditioning and its Effects on the Stereotyped Role of Women During Infancy.* Translated by Lisa Appignanesi et al. London: Writers and Readers Publishing Cooperative, 1975. Originally published as *Dalla parte delle bambine* (Milano: Giangiacomo Feltrinelli, 1973).

Gligo, Agata. "*Lumpérica*: Un libro excepcional." *Mensaje* 34, no. 343 (October 1985) 417–18.

———. *Mi pobre tercer deseo.* Santiago, Chile: Planeta, 1990.

Godoy, Marcial. "El SIDA y sus políticas." *Revista de crítica cultural,* no. 12 (July 1996): 56.

González Echevarría, Roberto. *Celestina's Brood: Continuities of the Baroque in Spanish and Latin American Literature.* Durham: Duke University Press, 1993.

Goodrich, Thelma Jean. *Women and Power: Perspective for Family Therapy.* New York: W. W. Norton, 1991.

Gould, John. "Homeric Epic and the Tragic Moment." In *Aspects of the Epic.* Edited by Tom Winnifrith, Penelope Murray, and K. W. Gransden, 2–45. London: Mac-Millan, 1983.

Graff, Gerald. *Literature Against Itself: Literary Ideas in Modern Society.* Chicago: University of Chicago Press, 1979.

Greimas, Algirdas Julien. "The Veridiction Contract." *New Literary History: A Journal of Theory and Interpretation* 20, no. 3 (spring 1989): 651–60.

Griffin, Susan. *Pornography and Silence: Culture's Revenge Against Nature.* New York: Harper and Row, 1982.

Grosz, Elizabeth. *Volatile Bodies: Toward a Corporeal Feminism.* Bloomington: Indiana University Press, 1994.

Gutiérrez Mouat, Ricardo. "Autoridad moderna y posmoderna en la narrativa hispanoamericana." *Nuevo texto crítico* 3, no. 6 (1990): 121–34.

Guzmán, Jorge. "La categoría blanco/no blanco." *Debate feminista* 5 (March 1992): 60–67.

Harlow, Barbara. *Resistance Literature.* New York: Methuen, 1987.

Hassan, Ihab. *The Postmodern Turn: Essays in Postmodern Theory and Culture.* Ohio State University Press, 1987.

Hawkesworth, M. E. *Beyond Oppression: Feminist Theory and Political Strategy.* New York: Continuum, 1990.

Hearings Before the Select Committee to Study Governmental Operations With Respect to Intelligence Activities of the United States. 94th Congress, 1st session, vol 7. Senate Resolution 21. Covert Action, 4 and 5 December 1975. Washington: GPO, 1976.

Henke, Suzette A. "Sexuality and Silence in Women's Literature." In *Power, Gender, Values.* Edited by Judith Genova, 45–62. Edmonton, Canada: Academic Printing & Publishing, 1986.

Hernández, Teresita, and Clara Murguialday. *Mujeres indígenas ayer y hoy.* Managua, Nicaragua: Puntos de Encuentro, 1993.

Herold, Joan M., María Solange Valenzuela, and Leo Morris. "Premarital Sexual

Activity and Contraceptive Use in Santiago, Chile." *Studies in Family Planning* 23 (March–April 1992): 128–36.

Higgins, James. "Spanish America's New Narrative." In *Postmodernism and Contemporary Fiction*. Edited by Edmund J. Smyth, 90–102. London: B. T. Batsford, 1991.

Hite, Shere. *The Hite Report: A Nationwide Study of Female Sexuality*. New York: MacMillan, 1976.

Houston, Nancy. "The Matrix of War: Mothers and Heroes." In *The Female Body in Western Culture*. Edited by Susan Rubin Suleiman, 119–36. Cambridge, Mass.: Harvard University Press,1986.

Humm, Maggie. "Is the Gaze Feminist?: Pornography, Film and Feminism." In *Perspectives on Pornography: Sexuality in Film and Literature*. Edited by Gary Day and Clive Bloom, 69–82. St. Martin's Press, 1988.

Hutcheon, Linda. *The Politics of Postmodernism*. New York: Routledge, 1989.

Huyssen, Andreas. *After the Great Divide: Modernism, Mass Culture, Postmodernism*. Bloomington: Indiana University Press, 1986.

Indigenous Chile. Santiago: Santiago Archaeological Museum, Chile, 1991.

Irigaray, Luce. "This Sex Which Is Not One." In *New French Feminisms*. Edited by Elaine Marks and Isabelle de Courtivron, 99–106. Amherst: The University of Massachusetts Press, 1980.

Iser, Wolfgang. "The Reading Process: A Phenomenological Approach." In *Reader-Response Criticism: From Formalism to Post-Structuralism*. Edited by Jane P. Tompkins, 50–69. Baltimore: Johns Hopkins University Press, 1980.

"IT & T Memos." *Subversion in Chile: The Complete Set of IT & T Memos*. Madison, Wis.: Non-Intervention in Chile (NICH), 1970.

Jameson, Fredric. "Imaginary and Symbolic in Lacan: Marxism, Psychoanalytic Criticism, and the Problem of the Subject." *Yale French Studies*, no. 55/56 (1977): 338–95.

———. *Postmodernism, or the Cultural Logic of Late Capitalism*. Durham: Duke University Press, 1991.

———. "Third-World Literature in the Era of Multinational Capitalism." *Social Text* 15 (1986): 65–88.

Janeway, Elizabeth. *Powers of the Weak*. New York: Alfred A. Knopf, 1980.

Kadir, Djelal. *The Other Writing: Postcolonial Essays in Latin America's Writing Culture*. West Lafayette, Ind.: Purdue University Press, 1993.

Karl, Frederick R. *American Fictions: 1940–1980*. New York: Harper and Row, 1983.

Knight, Chris. *Blood Relations: Menstruation and the Origins of Culture*. New Haven: Yale University Press, 1991.

Koedt, Anne. "The Myth of the Vaginal Orgasm." In *Voices From Women's Liberation*. Edited by Leslie B. Tanner, 158–66. New York: Signet, 1970.

Kuramochi, Yosuke. *Me contó la gente de la tierra: Relatos orales de los mapuches del centro sur de Chile*. Santiago, Chile: Universidad Católica de Chile, 1992.

Kuramochi, Yosuke, and Juan Luis Nass. *Mitología mapuche*. Translated by Rosendo Huisca Melinao. Quito, Ecuador: Ediciones ABYA-YALA, 1991.

Labanyi, Jo. "Topologies of Catastrophe: Horror and Abjection in Diamela Eltit's *Vaca Sagrada*." In *Latin American Women's Writing: Feminist Readings in Theory and Crisis*. Edited by Anny Brooksbank Jones and Catherine Davies, 85–103. New York: Oxford University Press, 1996.

Lacan, Jacques. *Ecrits: A Selection*. Translated by Alan Sheridan. New York: W. W. Norton, 1977. Originally published as *Ecrits* (Paris: Editions du Seuil, 1966).

Lagos, María Inés. "Escritura y sujeto femenino en tres narraciones hispanoamericanas de los 80." Proceedings of the session by Feministas Unidas: In Search of a Liberated Female Character. MLA, Chicago. 30 December 1990, 1–6.

———. "Reflexiones sobre la representación del sujeto en dos novelas de Diamela Eltit: *Lumpérica* y *El cuarto mundo*. In *Una poética de literatura menor: La narrativa de Diamela Eltit*. Edited by Juan Carlos Lértora, 127–40. Santiago, Chile: Cuarto Propio, 1993.

Lamphere, Louise. "Strategies, Cooperation, and Conflict Among Women in Domestic Groups." In *Woman, Culture, and Society*. Edited by Michelle Zimbalist Rosaldo and Louise Lamphere, 97–112. Stanford: Stanford University Press, 1974.

Larsen, Neil. "Postmodernism and Imperialism: Theory and Politics in Latin America." In *Essays in Postmodern Culture*. Edited by Eyal Amiran and John Unsworth, 265–93. New York: Oxford University Press, 1993.

Laub, Dori. "An Event Without a Witness: Truth, Testimony and Survival." In *Testimony: Crisis of Witnessing in Literature, Psychoanalysis, and History*. 75–92. Shoshana Felman and Dori Laub, M.D. New York: Routledge, 1992.

Lauretis, Teresa de. *Alice Doesn't: Feminism, Semiotics, Cinema*. Bloomington: Indiana University Press, 1984.

Lauzen, Sarah E. "Notes on Metafiction: Every Essay has a Title." In *Postmodern Fiction: A Bio-Bibliographical Guide*. Edited by Larry McCaffery, 93–116. New York: Greenwood, 1986.

Leitch, Vincent B. *Postmodernism—Local Effects, Global Flows*. Albany: State University of New York Press, 1996.

Lemaire, Anika Rifflet. *Jacques Lacan*. Translated by David Macey. London: Routledge and Kegan Paul, 1977. Originally published as *Jacques Lacan* (Brussels: C. Dessart, 1970).

Lerner, Gerda. *The Creation of Patriarchy*. New York: Oxford University Press, 1986.

Lerner, Harriet. "The Taboos Against Female Anger." *Menninger Perspective* (winter 1977): 5–11.

Lértora, Juan Carlos, ed. *Una poética de literatura menor: La narrativa de Diamela Eltit*. Santiago, Chile: Cuarto Propio, 1993.

Lienlaf, Leonel. *Se ha despertado el ave de mi corazón*. Translated by Leonel Lienlaf and Raúl Zurita. Santiago, Chile: Editorial Universitaria, 1989. Translation of *Nepey Ni Güñún Piuke*.

Lipman-Blumen, Jean. *Gender Roles and Power*. Englewood Cliffs, N.J.: Prentice-Hall, 1984.

Lippard, Lucy R. *From The Center: Feminist Essays On Women's Art*. New York: Dutton, 1976.

Lips, Hilary M. *Women, Men, and Power*. Mountain View, Cal.: Mayfield, 1991.

Lipschutz, Alejandro. *El problema racial en la conquista de América y el mestizaje*. Santiago, Chile: Austral, 1963.

Lispector, Clarice. *Agua viva*. Translated by Haydee M. Jofre Barroso. Buenos Aires: Sudamericana, 1975. Originally published as *Agua viva* (Rio de Janeiro: Artenova, 1973).

Loach, Barbara Lee. *Power and Women's Writing in Chile*. Madrid: Pliegos, 1994.

Lyotard, Jean-François. *The Differend: Phrases in Dispute*. Translated by Georges Van

Den Abbeele. Minneapolis: University of Minnesota Press, 1988. Originally published as *Le Différend* (Les Editions de Minuit, 1983).

———. *The Postmodern Condition: A Report on Knowledge*. Translated by Geoff Bennington and Brian Massumi. Minneapolis: University of Minnesota Press, 1984. Originally published as *La condition postmoderne: Rapport sur le savoir* (Paris: Editions de Minuit, 1979).

Madsen, Deborah L., and Mark S. Madsen. "Hypertext and the Demise of Metanarrative." In *Postmodern Subjects/Postmodern Texts*. Edited by Jane Dowson and Steven Earnshaw, 143–57. Atlanta, Ga.: Rodopi, 1995.

Malverde Disselkoen, Ivette. "Esquizofrenia y literatura: La obsesión discursiva en *El Padre Mío* de Diamela Eltit." In *Una poética de literatura menor: la narrativa de Diamela Eltit*. Edited by Juan Carlos Lértora, 155–66. Santiago: Cuarto Propio, 1993.

Manns, Patricio, ed. *Violeta Parra*. Madrid: Júcar, 1977.

Martín-Barbero, Jesús. "Communication and Modernity in Latin America." In *The Postmodern in Latin and Latino American Cultural Narratives*, 15–27. New York: Garland, 1996.

Martz, John D. ed. *United States Policy in Latin America: A Decade of Crisis and Challenge*. Lincoln: University of Nebraska Press, 1995.

McCaffery, Larry, ed. *Postmodern Fiction: A Bio-Bibliographical Guide*. New York: Greenwood, 1986.

McGowan, John. *Postmodernism and Its Critics*. Ithaca: Cornell University Press, 1991.

Menchú, Rigoberta. *I, Rigoberta Menchú: An Indian Woman in Guatemala*. Edited and introduced by Elisabeth Burgos-Debray. Translated by Ann Wright. London: Verso, 1984.

Merchant, Paul. "Children of Homer: The Epic Strain in Modern Greek Literature." In *Aspects of the Epic*. Edited by Tom Winnifrith, Penelope Murray, and K. W. Gransden, 92–108. London: MacMillan, 1983.

Merino Vega, Marcia Alejandra. *Mi verdad: más allá del horror, yo acuso*. Santiago: [s.n.],, 1993.

Michelson, Peter. "Women and Pornorotica." *Another Chicago Magazine* 16 (1986) 130–76.

Mistral, Gabriela. "El pueblo araucano." In *Gabriela Mistral: Escritos políticos*. Edited by Jaime Quezada, 45–49. México, D.F.: Fondo de Cultura Económica, 1994.

Montecino, Sonia. *Mujeres de la tierra*. Santiago, Chile: CEM-PEMCI, 1984.

———. *Madres y huachos: Alegorías del mestizaje chileno*. 1991. Santiago, Chile: Cuarto Propio, 1993.

Montejo, Esteban. *The Autobiography of a Runaway Slave*. Edited by Miguel Barnet. Translated by Jocasta Innes. New York: Pantheon Books, 1968. Originally published as *Biografía de un cimarrón* (La Habana: Academia de Ciencias de Cuba, Instituto de Etnología y Folklore, 1966).

Moretti, Franco. *Modern Epic: The World-System from Goethe to García Márquez*. Translated by Quintin Hoare. London: Verso, 1996.

Mori, Masaki. *Epic Grandeur: Toward a Comparative Poetics of the Epic*. Albany: State University of New York Press, 1997.

Moulthrop, Stuart. "You Say You Want a Revolution: Hypertext and the Laws of Media." In *Essays in Postmodern Culture*. Edited by Eyal Amiran and John Unsworth, 69–97. New York: Oxford University Press, 1993.

Mulvey, Laura. "Visual Pleasure and Narrative Cinema." *Screen* 16 (1975): 6–18.

Munizaga, Giselle, and Carlos Ochsenius. "El discurso público de Pinochet (1973–1976)." In *The Discourse of Power: Culture, Hegemony and the Authoritarian State*. Edited by Neil Larsen, 67–112. Minneapolis: Institute for the Study of Ideologies and Literature, 1983.

Muñoz, Heraldo. "Chile: The Limits of 'Success.' " In *Exporting Democracy: The United States and Latin America*. Edited by Abraham F. Lowenthal, 161–74. Baltimore: Johns Hopkins University Press, 1991.

Muriel, Josefina. *Las mujeres de hispanoamérica: Epoca colonial*. Madrid: Editorial MAPFRE, 1992.

Murray, Alexander S. *Who's Who in Mythology: Classic Guide to the Ancient World*. New York: Crescent, 1988.

Murray, Penelope. "Homer and the Bard." In *Aspects of the Epic*. Edited by Tom Winnifrith, Penelope Murray, and K. W. Gransden, 1–15. London: MacMillan, 1983.

Natoli, Joseph, and Linda Hutcheon. *A Postmodern Reader*. Albany: State University of New York Press, 1993.

Neumann, Erich. *The Origins and History of Consciousness*. Translated by R. F. C. Hull. New York: Pantheon, 1954. Originally published as *Ursprungsgeschichte des Bewusstseins* (Zürich: Rascher, 1949).

Neustadt, Robert. *(Con)Fusing Signs and Postmodern Positions: Spanish American Performance, Experimental Writing, and the Critique of Political Confusion*. New York: Garland, 1999.

Okin, Susan Moller. *Justice, Gender, and the Family*. New York: Basic, 1989.

Olea, Raquel. "Materiales críticos—Una épica de la marginalidad: *Por la patria*." *LAR: Revista de literatura* 11 (August 1987): 2–6.

———. "El cuerpo-mujer. Un recorte de lectura en la narrativa de Diamela Eltit." In *Una poética de literatura menor: La narrativa de Diamela Eltit*. Edited by Juan Carlos Lértora, 83–95. Santiago, Chile: Cuarto Propio, 1993.

Ortega, Julio. "*Christopher Unborn*: Rage and Laughter." Translated by Carl Mentley. *The Review of Contemporary Fiction* 8, no. 2 (summer 1988): 285–91.

———. "José María Arguedas." In *Latin American Writers*. Edited by Carlos A. Solé, 1131–38. New York: Charles Scribner's Sons, 1989.

———. "Resistencia y sujeto femenino: entrevista con Diamela Eltit." *La torre: Revista general de la Universidad de Puerto Rico* 4 (June 1990): 229–41.

———. "Diamela Eltit y el imaginario de la virtualidad." In *Una poética de literatura menor: La narrativa de Diamela Eltit*. Edited by Juan Carlos Lértora, 53–81. Santiago, Chile: Cuarto Propio, 1993.

Owens, Craig. "The Discourse of Others: Feminists and Postmodernism." In *The Anti-Aesthetic: Essays on Postmodern Culture*. Edited by Hal Foster, 57–82. Seattle: Bay Press, 1983.

Padden, Robert Charles. "Cultural Adaptation and Militant Autonomy among the Araucanians of Chile." In *The Indian in Latin American History: Resistance, Resilience, and Acculturation*. Edited by John E. Kicza, 69–88. Wilmington, Del.: Jaguar Books, Scholarly Resources, 1993.

Parra, Teresa de la. *Iphigenia: The Diary of a Young Lady Who Wrote Because She Was Bored*. Translated by Bertie Acker. Austin: University of Texas Press, 1993. Originally published as *Ifigenia: diario de una señorita que escribió porque se fastidiaba* (Caracas: Editorial Las Novedades, 1924).

———. *Cartas.* Caracas: Cruz del sur, 1951.

———. *Epistolario íntimo.* Caracas: Línea Aeropostal Venezolano, 1953.

———. *Cartas a Rafael Carías.* Alcalá de Henares: Talleres Penitenciarios, 1957.

Partnoy, Alicia. *The Little School: Tales of Disappearance and Survival in Argentina.* Translated by Alicia Partnoy with Lois Athey and Sandra Braunstein. Pittsburg, PA: Cleis Press, 1986.

Paz, Octavio. *The Labyrinth of Solitude: Life and Thought in Mexico.* Translated by L. Kemp. New York: Grove Press, 1960. Originally published as *El laberinto de la soledad* (México: Cuadernos Americanos, 1947).

Person, Ethel Spector. "Sexuality as the Mainstay of Identity: Psychoanalytic Perspectives." In *Women: Sex and Sexuality.* Edited by Catherine R. Stimpson and Ethel Spector Person, 36–61. Chicago: University of Chicago Press, 1980.

Petras, James F., and Robert LaPorte, Jr. "Chile: No." In *Foreign Policy on Latin America, 1970–1980.* Edited by the staff of *Foreign Policy,* 10–23. Boulder: Westview Press and the Carnegie Endowment for International Peace, Washington D.C., 1983.

Piña, Juan Andrés. *Conversaciones con la narrativa chilena.* Chile: Los Andes, 1991.

Poniatowska, Elena. *Massacre in Mexico.* Translated by Helen R. Lane. Columbia: University of Missouri Press, 1991. Originally published as *La noche de Tlatelolco* (México: Ediciones Era, 1971).

———. *Dear Diego.* Translated by Katharine Silver. New York: Pantheon, 1986. Originally published as *Querido Diego, te abraza Quiela* (México: Ediciones Era, 1978).

———. *Gaby Brimmer.* Mexico City: Grijalbo, 1979.

———. *Fuerte es el silencio.* México: Ediciones Era, 1980.

Prats González, Carlos. *Memorias: Testimonio de un soldado.* Santiago: Pehuén, 1985.

Quezada, Jaime. *Gabriela Mistral: Escritos políticos.* México, D.F.: Fondo de Cultura Económica, 1994.

Rama, Angel. *The Lettered City.* Edited and translated by John Charles Chasteen. Durham: Duke University Press, 1996. Originally published as *La ciudad letrada* (Hanover, N.H.: Ediciones del Norte, 1984).

Reyes-Tatinclaux, Leticia. "*Cristóbal Nonato,* ¿descubrimiento o clausura del nuevo mundo?" *Revista de crítica literaria latinoamericana* 15, no. 30 (1989): 99–104.

Ribettes, Jean-Michel, ed. *Loca verdad: Verdad y verosimilitud del texto psicótico, seminario dirigido por Julia Kristeva.* Translated by Martín Caparrós. Madrid: Fundamentos, 1985. Originally published as *Folle vérité: Vérité et vraisemblance du texte psichotique* (Paris: Editions du Seuil, 1979).

Richard, Nelly. *Margins and Institutions: Art in Chile Since 1973.* Melbourne: Art and Text, 1986.

———. *Masculino/femenino: Prácticas de la diferencia y cultura democrática.* Santiago, Chile: Francisco Zegers, 1993.

———. "Cultural Alterity and Decentering." In *The Postmodern in Latin and Latino American Cultural Narrative.* Edited by Claudia Ferman, 3–13. New York: Garland, 1996.

Río, Ana María del. *Tiempo que ladra.* Santiago, Chile: Planeta, 1994.

Ríos S., Patricio. "Chile: Ni desprecio ni puro amor." *Cauce* 100 (23 March 1987): 30–31.

Rodríguez, Christian. "El SIDA y sus políticas." Interview by *Revista de crítica cultural*. *Revista de crítica cultural*, no. 12 (July 1996): 57–61.

Rodríguez Valdés, Gladys. *Invitación a Gabriela Mistral (1889–1989)*. México, D.F.: Fondo de Cultura Económica, 1990.

Rodríguez Villouta, Mili. *Ya nunca me verás como me vieras: Doce testimonios vivos del exilio*. Santiago: Ornitorrinco, 1990.

Rulfo, Juan. *The Burning Plain, and Other Stories*. Austin, University of Texas Press, 1967. Originally published as *El llano en llamas* (México, D.F.: Secretaría de Educación Pública, Cultura, 1953).

Santa Cruz, Guadalupe. *Cita capital*. Santiago, Chile: Cuarto Propio, 1992.

———. "Familia: Modelos y relaciones de poder." In *Un indecente deseo*. Edited by Victoria Hurtado, Guadalupe Santa Cruz, and Alejandra Valdés, 107–22. Santiago, Chile: Instituto de la Mujer, 1995.

Schaffer, Diane M. "The Feminization of Poverty: Prospects for an International Feminist Agenda." In *Women Power and Policy: Toward the Year 2000*. Edited by Ellen Boneparth and Emily Stoper, 223–46. New York: Pergamon, 1988.

Scholes, Robert. *Semiotics and Interpretation*. New Haven: Yale University Press, 1982.

Serrano, Marcela. *Antigua vida mía*. Santiago, Chile: Alfaguara, 1995.

Sherzer, Dina. "Postmodernism and Feminism." In *Postmodernism and Contemporary Fiction*. Edited by Edmund J. Smyth, 156–68. London: B. T. Batsford, 1991.

Sienkiewicz, Henryk. *Quo Vadis?* 1896. Translated by C. J. Hogarth. New York: Hippocrene, 1989. Originally published as *Quo Vadis?* (Warsaw: Naklad Gebethnera i Wolffa, 1900).

Sierra, Malú. *Donde todo es altar: Mapuche gente de la tierra*. Santiago, Chile: Persona, 1992.

Sklodowska, Elzbieta. *La parodia en la nueva novela hispanoamericana*. Purdue University Monographs in Romance Languages 34. Amsterdam: Benjamins, 1990.

———. *Testimonio hispanoamericano: Historia, teoría, poética*. New York: Peter Lang, 1992.

———. "Spanish American Testimonial Novel—Some Afterthoughts." *New Novel Review* 1, no. 2 (April 1994): 31–47.

Sommer, Doris, and George Yúdice. "Latin American Literature from the 'Boom.' " In *Postmodern Fiction: A Bio-Bibliographical Guide*. Edited by Larry McCaffery, 189–214. New York: Greenwood, 1986.

Sommer, Doris. " 'Not Just a Personal Story': Women's *Testimonios* and the Plural Self." In *Life/Lines: Theorizing Women's Autobiography*. Edited by Bella Brodzki and Celeste Schenck, 107–30. Ithaca: Cornell University Press, 1988.

Sontag, Susan. *AIDS and Its Metaphors*. New York: Farrar, Straus and Giroux, 1988.

Stephen, Lynn, ed. and trans. *Hear My Testimony: María Teresa Tula, Human Rights Activist of El Salvador*. Boston: South End Press, 1994.

Subercaseaux, Bernardo. "Nueva sensibilidad y horizonte 'post' en Chile." *Nuevo texto crítico* 3, no. 6 (1990): 135–45.

Tafra, Sylvia. *Diamela Eltit: El rito de pasaje como estrategia textual*. Santiago, Chile: RiL-Red Internacional del Libro, 1998.

Teitelboim, Volodia. "Chile, laboratorio de tres experimentos (20 años)." In *Chile:*

Más allá de la memoria. Edited by Cloromiro Almeyda, et al, 31–51. Mexico: Universidad Nacional Autónoma de México, 1986.

Thomson, George. *Studies in Ancient Greek Society.* London: Lawrence and Wishart, 1949.

Tierney-Tello, Mary-Beth. "Re-making the Margins: From Subalterity to Subjectivity in Diamela Eltit's *Por la patria.*" *Monographic Review: Revista Monográfica* 3 (1992): 205–22.

Tompkins, Cynthia M. "Intertextuality as Differance in Julieta Campos' *El miedo a perder a Eurídice:* A Symptomatic Case of Latin American Postmodernism." In *The Postmodern in Latin and Latino American Cultural Narrative: Collected Essays and Interviews.* Edited by Claudia Ferman, 153–80. New York: Garland, 1996.

Traba, Marta. *Mothers and Shadows.* Translated by Jo Labanyi. London: Readers International, 1986. Originally published as *Conversación al sur* (México, D.F.: Siglo Veintiuno, 1981).

Valdés, Hernán. *Tejas Verdes: Diario de un campo de concentración en Chile.* Barcelona: Editorial Ariel, 1974.

Valdivieso, Mercedes. *Breakthrough.* Translated by Graciela Daichman. Pittsburgh, Pa.: Latin American Literary Review, 1986. Originally published as *La brecha* (Santiago, Chile: Zig-Zag, 1961).

Valenzuela, Luisa. *El gato eficaz.* México, D.F.: Joaquin Mortiz, 1972.

———. *Other Weapons.* Translated by Deborah Bonner. Hanover, N.H.: Ediciones el Norte, 1985. Originally published as *Cambio de armas* (Hanover, NH: Ediciones del Norte, 1982).

Valverde, Mariana. *Sex, Power and Pleasure.* Toronto: The Women's Press, 1985.

VanderStaay, Steven. *Street Lives: An Oral History of Homeless Americans.* Philadelphia: New Society, 1992.

Verdugo, Patricia. *Caso Arellano: Los zarpazos del puma.* Santiago: Ediciones Chile-América, 1989.

Vidal, Hernán. "La Declaración de Principios de la Junta Militar Chilena como sistema literario: La lucha antifacista y el cuerpo humano." In *The Discourse of Power: Culture, Hegemony and the Authoritarian State.* Edited by Neil Larsen, 43–66. Minneapolis: Institute for the Study of Ideologies and Literature, 1983.

Vilches, Patricia. *Karma desde el mar.* Santiago, Chile: Documentas, 1992.

Walker, Nancy A. *The Disobedient Writer: Women and Narrative Tradition.* Austin: University of Texas Press, 1995.

Watson, G. J. B. "James Joyce's 'Ulysses': Epic Novel." In *The Epic: Developments in Criticism.* Edited by R. P. Draper, 197–204. London: MacMillan Education, 1990.

Waugh, Patricia. *Feminine Fictions: Revisiting the Postmodern.* London: Routledge, 1989.

———. "From Modernism, Postmodernism, Feminism: Gender and Autonomy Theory." In *Postmodernism: A Reader.* Edited by Patricia Waugh, 189–204. London: Edward Arnold, 1992.

Weitzman, Lenore J. *The Divorce Revolution: The Unexpected Social and Economic Consequences for Women and Children in America.* New York: Free Press, 1985.

Williams, Raymond L. "Truth Claims, Postmodernism, and the Latin American Novel." Modern Language Association's *Profession* (1992): 6–9.

Winnifrith, Tom. "Postscript." In *Aspects of the Epic.* Edited by Tom Winnifrith, Penelope Murray, and K. W. Gransden, 109–18. London: MacMillan, 1983.

Yúdice, George. "Puede hablarse de postmodernidad en America Latina?" *Revista de crítica literaria latinoamericana* 5, no. 29 (1989): 105–28.

———. "*Testimonio* and Postmodernism." *Voice of the Voiceless in Testimonial Literature*. Georg Gugelberger and Michael Kearney, eds. Special issue of *Latin American Perspectives* 18, no. 3 (1991): 15–31.

Zermeño, Sergio. "La posmodernidad: Una visión desde América Latina." *Revista mexicana de sociología* 5, no. 3 (July–September 1988): 61–70.

Index

259